HOW TO LOOK SEXY, SENSATIONAL AND SUCCESSFUL NO MATTER WHAT YOU WEIGH

By Babe Hope

New Horizon Press
Far Hills, New Jersey

Hope, Babe
Pretty Plus: How to Look Sexy, Sensational and Successful No Matter
What You Weigh
Cover design: Wendy Bass
Interior design: Susan M. Sanderson
Illustrations: April Dukes

Library of Congress Control Number: 2009927402

ISBN 13: 978-0-88282-317-1
New Horizon Press

Manufactured in the U.S.A.

2014   2013   2012   2011   2010   /   5   4   3   2   1

For my big sisters: Turn the pity party
into a pretty party and never look back.

AUTHOR'S NOTE

This book is based on the author's research and experience. The author's recommendations of brands, beauty treatments and clothing choices are completely her personal opinions. Some individuals' identities and names have been changed in order to protect privacy. Some characters are composites.

CONTENTS

Introduction 1

Chapter 1   Best Silhouette.. 11
             Diamond in the Rough

Chapter 2   Undergarments and Lingerie...........................21
             Beauty Comes from Within

Chapter 3   Activewear..37
             Tough to be a Sport

Chapter 4   Beachwear...43
             No Kidding!

Chapter 5   Petite Focus 47
             Tall Tales

Chapter 6   Coats 53
             Think Gift Wrap

Chapter 7   Shoes 65
             Find your Sole Mate!

Chapter 8   Accessories Rock! 79
             The Wear-with-All to Look Great

Chapter 9   Building a Pretty Party Wardrobe...................91
             Inventory Your Closet Ruthlessly

Chapter 10   Shop, Feed Yourself...107
Nurturance

Chapter 11   Shop, Edit, Alter 115
Manufacture Your Best Figure

Chapter 12   Babe's Dirty Dozen...127
Reality Check and How to Cope

Chapter 13   Bring Light to the Face....................................137
Spotlight You

Chapter 14   Create Your Best Feature.................................171
Only She Knows for Sure

Chapter 15   Yikes, My Closet's Naked! 179
Twenty-One Gun Salute

Chapter 16   Body Language 199
Got Twenty Seconds?

Afterword   Filing, Styling and Smiling............................207

Appendix A Sleek and Cheap 213

Appendix B Sample Go-To Clusters....................................217

Appendix C You'll Need 221

Appendix D Resources for Plus Size Clothing 223

Glossary...235

Bibliography..248

Acknowledgments..249

Introduction

"Clothes are never a frivolity: they always mean something."
~James Laver

The first of three epiphanies occurred about ten years ago when my husband, our five-year-old son and I were spending our winter vacation at a resort in Palm Beach, Florida. I had invited my friend, Terri, and her mom, with whom she was vacationing in a town nearby, to join me for lunch. We sat overlooking the azure blue ocean and chatting over our delicious lobster salads and tropical ice teas, served in the bent, blown green glasses that the restaurant is famous for—very chic! On the beach, my handsome husband, tan, tall, with silver hair, walked by holding the hand of our young son. Pointing, Terri said to her mom, "There are Babe's boys." Her mom glanced in their direction and then looked back at me, her hostess—a large, Rubenesque woman—and asked in a voice loud enough for other diners to hear, "How did a slob like you ever land *him*?" Shocked, wounded, but not down for the count, I took a deep breath, but said unconvincingly, "I don't think I'm a slob and obviously, *he* doesn't think so either." We finished our lunch rather quietly. I charged the one hundred dollar lunch tab to my hotel room, they thanked me for lunch and I thanked them for being my guests.

The event was painful. I didn't tell my husband or anyone else for a very long time. I was ashamed. Terri, in her mid-thirties, was still unmarried. Maybe her mom, jealous of me and my family and angry that Terri didn't have a husband of her own, just blurted out her feelings. Maybe she took pleasure in hurting me and maybe not. It didn't matter; she had. I felt confused and preoccupied with the scene for days. Then it dawned on me: I had given another person power over my security and I had to take the power back. Eleanor Roosevelt once said, "No one can make you feel inferior without your consent." The epiphany was, quite simply, that I would never give someone else the authority to make me question my appearance. I couldn't control what people thought or said because of the baggage they were carrying. But I could control how I presented myself. A diet was not the answer for me. I became driven to make fashion and its accoutrements, which I had loved from a distance, work for me. I took a hard look at myself and identified one area in particular that detracted from my overall appearance and then turned it into a star-quality signature, which I'll reveal to you in chapter 13. Over the last ten years I have become an expert at making plus size women as attractive and stylish as their diminutive counterparts.

An outsider might ask, "Why didn't you just go on a diet, lose weight and get this albatross off your back?" Honestly, if I could have, I would have years ago. But I've taken inspiration from the great UCLA Basketball Coach, John Wooden: "Do not let what you cannot do interfere with what you can do."

I weighed ten pounds six ounces when I was born. I was the second heaviest baby in the large hospital. One of my lungs didn't open, so the doctors put me in an incubator. The story goes that I was red, fat, bald and had my right arm in a sling. I took up every square inch of the life-saving cubicle, as they were usually reserved for tiny premature babies. Visitors stood outside the nursery, pointed at me and laughed. I heard this story for as long as I can remember. It was usually told in a jovial way, because I ended up healthy.

We lived in Brooklyn, New York, and it was the custom of the time for mothers and children to go upstate to the Catskill Mountains for the summer. So my mother, seven months pregnant, my nana (my maternal grandmother), my father's teenage sister, Abby, and I took a bungalow in the country. Things went terribly wrong for my naïve, young mom. She was sickly all summer and then lost forty pounds in a two-week period. Nana and Aunt Abby begged her to go to a doctor in the Catskills, but she refused. Finally, my mom became incoherent. Abby telephoned my dad to explain the gravity of the situation. My dad dispatched a hack (a taxi cab driver from the city, more than two hours away) to rescue her, but it was too late. By the time she and Abby were in the cab heading for the city, my mother was delirious—she kept insisting that Abby give her a drink of water from her pocketbook (this was before bottled water was commonplace).

At the hospital, the doctors confirmed my mother was a gestational diabetic. Within two hours of arriving, she slipped into a diabetic coma. Two days later she died at the age of twenty-two; I was a year and a half old. Years later, Abby explained to me that the reason my mother would not go to see a doctor in the country was that she was too ashamed of her body to get undressed in front of a doctor who was a stranger.

I don't remember my mother, but I am like her in many ways. There is a picture of my mom and dad on their honeymoon that reveals a bond between us that is hard to ignore. The couple is clad in bathing suits and, although their bodies are disguised by a huge heart of flowers, it is still apparent that she and I have the same figure. Further, not for the faint of heart, the story goes that my mom loved to eat lamb chop fat. I do, too. Most people are disgusted by it. She died when I was probably too young to have "learned" that behavior.

My dad was only twenty-two years old when my mother died and was struggling to cope, so for a while I lived with my maternal grandparents. They were older, so it was hard for them to keep up with a child. Often, I cried through the night, because I missed my mother. Nana was a stickler for cleanliness and on a hot night I remember her sweating as she bathed me—her neck and thick, dark hair wet, probably the way it was on that fated night she decided she had had enough. She called my father to come get me. He was not around. She called my father's parents to come. My paternal grandfather was not around either. So my grandmother called my uncle, who came for me in the middle of the night and took me to his apartment. He carried me and I held on to him. The next morning for breakfast, my aunt made me two scrambled eggs and two pieces of toast with butter and strawberry jelly and a large glass of chocolate milk.

One constant for me was—you guessed it—food. When I was four, my paternal grandmother bragged that I could eat a whole chicken by myself. Was it heredity or learned behavior? I really don't know.

During my first summer home from college, I worked at my family's successful car dealership in upstate New York. After I reported to work on the first day, my dad took me aside and said, "The other employees are gloating, because you have everything going for you: you're beautiful, smart and rich and yet you're FAT."

The dye was cast. Food became very important to me. I used food as a punctuation mark for everything: celebration, sorrow, boredom and friendship. Food became friend, elixir and anesthesia all wrapped into one. Legal and relatively safe, food was a bargain at any price. So it is no surprise that I have struggled with weight all my life.

For many years, I recalled what I believed to be my finest moment, which occurred during college. I observed an eighteen-day period of fasting, having nothing to eat or drink but two quarts of water daily. I lost twenty-two pounds during that period. I was ecstatic. I shopped. I bought. I really looked terrific. Until, gradually, I gained all of the weight back (and got very sick as well).

One particularly painful dating experience occurred when I was dating a guy who was a yuppie type. He was one of four friends who were very close and considered themselves so cool. We dated for almost a year. In my family, New Year's Eve is pretty important, and so, having a date for that night is very important as well. The four couples had big plans to spend one New Year's Eve together at a rather exciting nightspot. As I prepared for the big night, I tried to find a fantastic outfit but could not. I just felt heavy, unattractive and, frankly, just not as good as the other girls. I called my boyfriend a few nights before New Year's Eve and made some lame excuse indicating I couldn't keep our plans. He responded, "Don't worry; your chair won't be empty." It appeared that we both shared the same opinion of my worth. Then I lied to my father. I just couldn't bear to tell him I would be alone on New Year's Eve. I mustered the courage to leave my apartment and went to a movie theater. When the movie was over, I walked over to a café and ordered food "to go"—a big piece of quiche followed by an éclair. I returned to my apartment to eat my pain away. Trust me, that wasn't the only evening of its kind.

Trying to compensate for being overweight led to other negatives as well. I could reveal those character flaws to you here, those moments of desperation, but you probably already know and understand. Outside my area of expertise, they are better left to professional counselors to unravel. However, I will say more about one fallout that became the impetus for this book: Shopping and spending money became my compulsion to compensate for my unhappiness about body figure. Before I was married, I spent all of my money and used credit cards irresponsibly to buy clothes that I thought would either make me look thin or give me stature through wearing designer labels. This behavior ultimately led me to file for bankruptcy. The double meaning and application of the term *bankrupt* internally and externally was not lost on me.

Many years later, a work in progress, I feel I have learned a lot and have something to share. Passionate about looking good, I have turned a compulsion into a hobby and, I believe, an art form. I am still a heavy, plus size woman and yet I feel I look sensational every day. I have learned that for some people, looking great comes easily. For others, including myself, it requires effort and insight. Some, disillusioned by our thin-obsessed culture, will say that's impossible. I believe it is possible. It just takes a little longer.

I am married to a wonderful man who makes me feel like a goddess. He is the smartest, funniest, sexiest, most handsome guy in the world. He is also a man who likes curvaceous women. We have a terrific teenage son who does well in school, loves sports, stays out of trouble and, thankfully, is built like his dad. We have a house in the country and a Golden Retriever named Holly.

I have a business called Big Girls Won't Cry, which is an image maker and shopping service for plus size women and teens. I like to say that my clients can have their cake and eat it, too.

I have two best girlfriends, Anne and Marie, who have emboldened me to think I have something to say in this area of angst for so many. We live in three different cities, so once a year we get together and do makeovers or rebuild our wardrobes. We laugh, talk, eat, drink, sometimes cry a bit, laugh some more and shop! They are beautiful, curvy women and, at the end of our weekends together, they are even more beautiful and self-assured for the world to see.

I would be irresponsible if I said, "Follow my tips and organizational plan, look great and forget the health side of being heavy." I am not a medical doctor, but I think extra pounds probably do compromise good health (not to mention emotional well-being as well).

With *Pretty Plus* you will have the information and secrets to become an insider to much of the fashion industry that has previously eluded you by understanding its terminology. The terms are defined in the text and presented in a glossary at the end of the book. The opportunity to understand the fashion industry is a powerful tool: We can undo the marginalization that casted us as "outsiders" in fashion and reduced us to desperate buyers as opposed to sophisticated shoppers.

Marginalization is the social process of becoming or being relegated or confined to a lower social standing or outer limit or edge, according to the dictionary. Historically, examples have included the marginalization of the underclass, the marginalization of the single mother and the marginalization of literature. I suggest the marginalization of the plus size woman fits into this paradigm as well.

The possibility of severe social and material deprivation exists as a product of marginalization. According to Bob Mullaly, author of *The*

New Structural Social Work, while sociologists who coined the term were referring to life sustaining resources such as employment, food and shelter, I believe the casting out of plus size women is not outside this concept. Maximally there is a plethora of psychological, social and economic consequences of this concept for plus size women. However, for the purposes of this book, the concern is limited to the consequence of being an outsider to fashion. It is the intent of this book to reinstate plus size women's access to the world and joys of fashion.

There is every reason to live life beautifully while carrying twenty, fifty or even one hundred extra pounds, whether you intend to shed them or not. Comfort and style need not be mutually exclusive. Being plus size and being fashionable need not be mutually exclusive either. This is often hard for plus size women to see. One reason is that when perusing a fashion magazine, family magazine or clothing catalog, plus size women rarely see any clothing to which they can relate. There is a disconnect between those pages and their lives. I've never read a discussion of chafing even once! It is cruel for the fashion industry to show only thin women: either thin women in thin clothes or thin women in purportedly plus size fashion. Come on—we're not blind! However, often we are myopic; we assimilate these portrayals and hate ourselves. But, as my husband says, it doesn't have to be that way. The options we, as plus size women, see available to us often cause us to lose interest and energy about our appearances. We acquiesce, yet that is the attitude we must avoid. Looking good does require a tonic of time, attitude, knowledge and money designated for that very purpose. In the future, I hope to see the fashion industry, especially the recreational clothing and shoe businesses, respond to our needs and respect our dollars. We're buyers too! Women size sixteen or larger represent half of the women in this country.

That being said, my friend Marie, whose phraseology has erupted more than a volcano or two of laughter over the years, has labeled the reason for all of the problems associated with being overweight as the "ass factor." She used it when we couldn't get dates in college, buy nice clothes or stay on a diet. As I was developing a working title for this book, the

acronym A.S.S. came to me, because that is my claim: being assured, sexy
and sensational no matter what you weigh, transcending the "ass factor"
and infusing it with new meaning.

Here are a few principles that have guided my own evolution to
looking great:

- Apply the principles of fade and focus: Camouflage the negatives
  and accentuate the positives.
- Create your best feature.
- Buy less and buy better to build a complete wardrobe.
- Don't try to look too young; instead, look svelte and energetic.
- Wear what's right for you, not what's trendy or currently in style.
- Use an accurate three-way mirror.
- Keep the tags on new garments and the receipts in a designated
  shoe box and mull over the purchases until you are sure of them.
- Let jewelry and other accessories make your fashion statement.
- Have two go-to outfits (or clusters) at the ready for various occa-
  sions so you can dress appropriately and proudly.
- Wear clothing that fits you flatteringly and comfortably.
- Dress in a way that reflects an expectation of running into someone
  you care about seeing.
- Love what you wear.
- Choose comfort, both physical and emotional, as a foundation to
  looking good.
- Never discuss dieting; it's boring and nobody cares.

My family and friends have encouraged me to write this book for
years, because over the past decade they have seen how my secrets have
changed the way I look, the way I carry myself in the world and how
others reach out to me for help in this area. In fact, my business as a
fashion consultant for plus size women and teens is precisely about
transforming the pity party into a pretty party.

The summer day I started this book my husband and I were sitting
in a tree-lined neighborhood shopping center sipping iced lattes. A plus

size woman dressed in gray sweatpants, a nondescript T-shirt and green rubber garden clogs passed us. "There's a buyer for your book," my husband said with a wink. Five minutes later, she emerged from the delicatessen carrying a sandwich or two, walked right over to us and asked me about the skort I was wearing. Gratified, I took a few minutes, told her a few things, explained why a skort was a good choice and told her where she could get one. She was mesmerized. You would have thought I was revealing the secret to a long and happy life. Maybe in a small way, I was. I took that meeting as an omen.

Think of me as your big sister when you are reading this book. You know me, I know you and I know my plan will enhance your well-being. Reading this book will give you the necessary information and confidence to develop the following skills:

- Transform the pity party into a pretty party with one concept and three tools (which will be discussed more fully in chapter 9):
    - Fade and Focus: Camouflage the negative and accentuate the positive.
    - The Pretty Party Portfolio: A collection of pictures of clothing and accessories you admire and whose distinguishing features you will implement in your wardrobe.
    - The Essential Inventory Card: An index card of your entire wardrobe and cluster outfits that indicates what pieces you are missing and helps you focus while shopping.
    - The Go-To Guide: A binder of pictures of complete outfits created from your wardrobe to facilitate dressing for different occasions.
- Organize your closet.
- Create your prettiest face.
- Design and spotlight your best feature.
- Use fabric, color, proportion and shape to be your sexiest and to look curvy but svelte.
- Reframe the traditional elements of fashion design to enhance the large woman.

- Use accessories to uplift your mood and image of yourself.
- Purchase shoes that will boost your style quotient and be comfortable, too.
- Select bathing suits and sports gear that flatter and feel comfortable.
- Request alterations for a perfect, slimming, youthful and comfortable fit.
- Develop a wish list for others to aid them when they are shopping for you.
- Depend on go-to outfits (and clusters) for dressy, work and casual occasions.
- Use body language as a secret weapon.
- Cope with and minimize the personal challenges of being heavy in terms of fashion.
- Identify items that fade and focus, camouflage and attract.
- Save money.
- Respect the limited time you have available to spend on your appearance.
- Use fashion terms that have previously made you feel like an outsider to the industry.
- Transform yourself from a desperate buyer to a sophisticated shopper.

I won't offer political or judgmental comments and I don't have any answers about slimming down. Rather, I hope this book becomes a springboard for plus size women to converse with one another about challenges and solutions. Stick with me, because I offer these tips as a woman who copes with the same realities and frustrations you do. Each day when I dress, I utilize the tools and methods presented here and my beauty emerges. I'll respect your fashion preferences, lifestyle and comfort needs as well as your budget. By the end of reading this book, you will have the secrets that have eluded you for years. I promise you will look better than ever. You will be well on your way to dressing sexy, sensational and successful no matter what you weigh. As George Eliot said, "It is never too late to be what you might have been."

CHAPTER 1

Best Silhouette

DIAMOND IN THE ROUGH

"Fashion is architecture: it is a matter of proportions."
~Coco Chanel

There's a line in the movie *The Devil Wears Prada* that I love to hear every time I watch it. Andy, the new assistant at a high-end fashion magazine, is whining to her co-worker Nigel about not getting credit for her efforts. He retorts that she just doesn't get it; her job at the magazine should be coveted as an opportunity and privilege: "Don't you know that you are working at the place that published some of the greatest artists of the century? Halston, Lagerfeld, de la Renta. And what they did, what they created was greater than art because you live your life in it…" That line played over and over in my head after I saw the movie the first time. It haunted me. It taunted me. Deep in a pity party, the implication was that that type of sensuous, artistic experience was outside the grasp of those who wear plus size. It represented the love-hate relationship that had grown between me and the fashion industry. I guess it is human nature to love the things outside your reach and hate yourself for not fitting in. I felt this way for many years. I often bought garments that would fit if I lost ten pounds. I bought clothing that had the right designer label if it was close to working for me. I bought a lot of makeup with designer labels, because it completed "the look."

My second epiphany came when I worked with a personal shopper named Sandra. I badly needed a coat. Ten years ago, the availability of quality plus size garments was deplorable. My husband called ahead to the best department, not the plus size department, and made an appointment for me. He told Sandra I needed a coat and perhaps a few more details. I arrived a bit early and started looking at the merchandise alone. I was sure that there simply was not one coat that was going to fit me. Trust me, I had an attitude brewing. I just knew I was going to be embarrassed. Sandra walked up to me and began the introductions. She stood about five feet tall and weighed about a hundred pounds. She asked me one or two questions about what primary purpose the coat would serve. Looked me over. She walked over to one of the racks of car coats, which are three-quarter length coats, and picked the one in back (they are ordered by size, the largest one at the back). She unbuttoned the coat and helped me slip it on. We looked at it together in a three-way mirror; it looked great. I said, "Thanks. I'll take it."

With no more talking we walked over to the checkout desk and I paid for the coat. Then it dawned on me: maybe I could get more than a coat out of this experience. So I asked a question: "How did you know that coat would flatter me?" Then Sandra articulated what became my awakening. She explained, "I begin by looking at a client's frame and then her size. It is your frame, the basic shape of your body, that determines what clothing will look good on you—more than size."

"The next step is to avoid problem areas," she went on. "In your case, the size of your arms would prevent you from wearing most of the coats in this department. I wanted a coat that would show off your hourglass figure, I looked for one with raglan sleeves." Raglan sleeves are wide with larger armholes. We didn't say more. I left with my stunning camel hair coat with great lines, four large tortoise shell buttons and sewn-in scarf at the neckline plus a whole lot more. In fact, this was the beginning of developing the concept of "fade and focus"—camouflaging the negative and accentuating the positive—which transformed me from a desperate buyer into a sophisticated shopper.

I went back to see Sandra several times and was usually happy with what she picked for me. However, it wasn't too long before I came to believe I knew more than she did in terms of what worked for me and my selections were less expensive. I learned to trust what I knew would work and realized that I was the one who could fully understand the fashion realities of being a large woman.

Body Frames and Body Diamonds
Your frame is the basic shape of your body, the size of one body part compared to others, regardless of how much you weigh. Let's begin with this and determine which of the following shapes represents you best. Did you know that your body frame can be likened to the shape of a diamond?

In my opinion, there are five body types. Sometimes this determination is harder to identify than others. Often a heavy woman is heavy all over. When this is the case, decide if one body part is disproportionate to or larger than other parts; this will be the key.

Pear Shape Diamond
Smaller through the arms, shoulders and breasts than the lower half and has wide hips, buttocks, thighs and calves.

Round Shape Diamond
Round and full through the arms, shoulders, back, tummy, hips and thighs and has a noticeable waist.

Heart Shape Diamond
Broad and full in the arms, shoulders and through the ribcage but narrower through the hips, thighs and legs.

Marquise Shape Diamond
Thinner arms, shoulders, hips, buttocks and legs and has a large tummy.

Emerald Shape Diamond
Wide and full from the shoulders and arms through the hips, thighs and legs and has no appreciable indentation at the waist.

To begin the journey to a more dazzling you, a woman needs to decide to which diamond she can be likened. I would love to see every woman celebrate this acceptance by wearing a diamond of her shape every day, whether real or faux—a facsimile of a pure material—as a reminder of both her shape and that she is indeed a diamond, perhaps for now, in the rough.

Sandra began my understanding by determining the shape of my frame. Later, I began to formulate the concept that I was a round shape diamond.

Principles of Design
Once you figure out the shape or frame of your body, you will be able to strategically use the principles of fashion design to look your best. This section provides a preliminary understanding of the six classic principles of design: shape, line, color, balance, proportion and texture. I then reframe these elements to help you enhance and embrace your body shape as a large woman. All of the elements should be in conversation with one another. This knowledge will be the basis for every clothing purchase you make from now on; it will become your clout. You need not become an expert or memorize the design elements per se, but you will need to become familiar with them to look great. Further, you will see overlap between the elements, but you will not be too confused as long as you stay focused on the goal. The goal is to capture your longest, most streamlined, shapeliest figure using these tools to emphasize and camouflage, drawing attention to your attractive features and drawing attention

away from what you consider to be less attractive. It is an art; the French dubbed it *trompe l'oeil,* which means "to fool the eye."

Shape
The outline of an outfit or its silhouette is what is meant by shape as a design element.

Shape Reframed for a Large Woman
The shape of a garment allows you to spotlight the areas of your body that you feel are attractive and to downplay the ones that aren't. Shape allows you to pair the shape of the garment with your frame. For example, if you are a pear shape diamond, heavier on the bottom than the top, you should choose an outfit with a simple, skimming A-line skirt that gradually widens from waist to hemline and a fitted top that shows off the attractive features of your upper body. Pencil skirts, which are narrow and taper at the knee, are great for round, heart or marquise diamond shapes, because these body types tend to have shapely legs. The pear and emerald shape diamonds benefit from gentle A-line skirts and dresses. If you are an emerald shape diamond, full from the shoulders through the knees, choose an outfit that has contour and definition built in, like a cocoon style coat or dress, which is full through the shoulders and middle but narrows toward the knee. The same style looks great on a heart shape diamond. Alternately, the round shape diamond benefits by wearing an outfit that has princess seaming—vertical shaping panels in the torso—built in, paralleling the body's hourglass figure.

Look at the garment and ask yourself this question: Will the shape of this garment be flattering for my shape? Put another way, does the shape of this garment compensate for or disguise an unattractive area? It may take a few tries, but soon you will know what styles will work best for you, your eye will be drawn to them and you will not waste time trying on things that will be unflattering.

Line
A woman looks her slimmest when she looks her longest. The line of an outfit should be continuous, fluid and vertical.

Line Reframed for a Large Woman
Streamlining should be the goal of the plus size woman. You should try to look your tallest or longest. The buzz word here should be elongate. The clothing pieces that are put together should not seem intermittent; there should be a continuous, vertical quality to the outfit. The use of color, monochromatically (a single color) or tone-on-tone (shades of one color), is one means to this end. Wearing shoes that offer some additional height, even a kitten heel of one to one and a half inches, is another means that will elongate your look. Another means is to keep embellishments, color and trim near the face or in an area that does not detract from a continuous line of color or detail through the center of your body.

Color
In fashion, color is a key element in enhancing the skin tone, hair and eyes of a woman. The placement of the right color near the face is important. Equally important, the design element of color can be used to focus and fade, meaning camouflage parts of your body strategically.

Color Revisited for a Large Woman
While I don't like a lot of frills on large women, the use of color to look vibrant, fresh and pretty is critical. I wear a lot of black, it's true, but I use white for contrast and drama or color for interest close to my face. I often use a monochromatic palette or tone-on-tone from top to bottom with the addition of a colorful or interesting vest, jacket, cardigan or duster. I believe this is slenderizing, because it is elongating. However, there is another use of color for pear and heart shape diamonds that I think is underused. Use softer, darker colors to erase your larger areas and use bright, flattering colors to draw attention to more flattering areas. This uses the design element of color to balance the body.

Color is a wonderful way for the plus size shopper to be part of designer grandeur and trends. Miranda Priestly, Andy's hard-edged, demanding boss in *The Devil Wears Prada*, speaks condescendingly to Andy when she gives an instructive soliloquy about the color of Andy's sweater. Miranda explains the color is not just blue, but a shade called cerulean, featured in collections by Oscar de la Renta and Yves St. Laruent. She describes the process of a certain color becoming popular: "And then cerulean quickly showed up in the collections of eight designers. Then it filtered down through the department stores and then trickled on down into some tragic casual corner where you, no doubt, fished it out of some clearance bin." If I found that cerulean sweater, clearance bin or not, it would be my Oscar de la Renta and I would value it as such.

Balance
The element of balance seeks to align the various fragments of an outfit to the end of a harmonious whole.

Balance Reframed for a Large Woman
In order to complete a streamlined presentation of ourselves we need to use the other design elements to promote the illusion of balance. The goal for every outfit each day is a smooth, shapely, linear composition. When you determined your essential shape or frame, you will recall it was a comparison of body parts in relation to one another in terms of size. Balance, as a design element, allows you to compensate using the other design tools. Here is a glimpse of "fade and focus": an emerald shape diamond could wear a black duster over white slacks, creating contour through shape and color. A duster is a coat-jacket or cardigan that comes just above the knee. Another example is a pretty color twin-set of a matching shell and cardigan over a dark, simple A-line bottom for a pear shape diamond or the reverse, a dark twinset over a skirt with a pattern or embellishment detail, for the heart shape diamond. If you are larger on the top half of your body, a heart shape diamond, be sure to keep the length of your skirts a bit longer; it will serve to elongate the

appearance of the leg, thereby keeping your whole body in better balance. By now, you should be seeing the overlap among the design elements as they work together. It is important to strike a   balance by downplaying larger, unattractive areas and simultaneously focusing attention on your flattering attributes.

Proportion

The manipulation of proportion as a design element is the seasonal spice of the designer's recipe. It is what makes things interesting, different, trendy and fun. Proportion calls upon scale to do its bidding. One season it is a full cape or poncho over a pencil skirt or narrow slacks. The next season it is a cropped jacket and wide, cuffed trousers. The next season it is an hourglass fitted ensemble, dress or pants suit.

Proportion Reframed for a Large Woman

Proportion, like balance, can strategically emphasize and hide a lot. However, this is one area in which the plus size woman must not succumb to trends. A cropped jacket, which has a boxy cut and short length, is unflattering on me, a round diamond. In fact, where a cropped jacket ends is right at my stomach. Not where I want the eye to fall; remember, the eye falls where the garment ends. Wide, cuffed trousers are unflattering on any plus size woman, especially a round diamond, because the cuff cuts the line of the leg. We want to elongate, especially heavy legs. Therefore, this style, though trendy and good-looking, is not attractive on me. I'd be wasting my money if I bought it and it would probably hang in the back of my closet. Give me the Marilyn Monroe proportioned outfit, fitted for me and with the right undergarments, and I'll look great year to year, season to season. The proportion of the outfit dovetails with my body's proportions. Marilyn Monroe and I share the same frame type.

A poncho or long asymmetrical skimming thigh-length tunic over a slim skirt or tulip skirt, which has a gentle balloon effect through the hips, is great for round, heart and marquise shape diamonds. The proportion elongates the upper torso while drawing attention to shapely legs.

Texture

Texture and fabrication are elements that allow the designer to distinguish his or her collection from others utilizing similar trends and proportions of the season. The drape of an outfit or the way a garment hangs or falls, can represent pleasure or embarrassment to the wearer and is determined by texture and fabric choices.

Texture Reframed for a Large Woman

Knowledge of texture and fabric is truly a gift to the plus size shopper. I will give you two lists of fabrics: one of fabrics to avoid and one of those to seek.

In general, look for fabrics that are thin and add no bulk, but are firm and hold a shape. Crumple and squeeze a portion of the garment in your hand. If it is wrinkled when you release it, give it a pass. If it feels stiff and thick, keep looking. Specifically, you should avoid linen, stiff cotton, brushed cotton, velour and heavy wool. The reason is that they either add bulk or do not drape or skim your body. Stiff or heavy fabrics contribute to visual weight. Visual weight means that a garment makes you look larger than you are, because it appears that you fill it, that you are as big as the expanse of the fabric. Similarly, do not choose fabrics that shine. Embellishments that shine are fine as long as they are placed in an area to which you want to draw attention. If the majority of the fabric composition is linen or stiff cotton, it will not be flattering. Finally, unless you enjoy the symphony of your thighs rubbing together when you walk, run away from corduroy.

On the other hand, look for sumptuous soft cottons with Lycra or spandex blended in. Tencel is a great fabric for casual clothing, because it has a great drape to it. Denim, as long as it fits well and has a soft quality to it, is a great choice. Seek out matte jersey, thin knits, silks and tropical weight wools. Fabric, synthetic or natural, combined with Lycra or spandex is best. It doesn't stretch out, looks good from wearing to wearing and feels soft and sexy. Look for synthetic combinations such as viscose/nylon, viscose/spandex, rayon/spandex, polyester/spandex and rayon/nylon.

Crochet, luxurious trim, ruching (fabric gathered for a puckering effect) and interesting embellishments are textural elements that can draw attention to and away from an area if strategically placed, either by original design or by your own alteration. Using texture, while staying in the same color scheme or tone-on-tone from top to bottom, is an interesting and rich way to stir things up without giving up the elongating benefit of the monochromatic palette.

Good fabrics will skim and drape your body while holding their integrity (not stretch out or wrinkle excessively) and not adding bulk, either in natural fibers or synthetic. Embellishments, as an element of texture, should be used to draw attention and make an attractive area a focal point.

CHAPTER 2

Undergarments and Lingerie

BEAUTY COMES
FROM WITHIN

"If love is blind, why is lingerie so popular?"
~Source Unknown

My beautiful friend Anne called me one day to say she was quite anxious about a wedding to which she was obligated to go. It was the wedding of a business acquaintance of her husband's. She wasn't happy. She wasn't particularly close to the groom or his stylish, thin wife. Anne dreaded going to the occasion. Thus she procrastinated in getting an outfit for the affair. A week before the wedding, she asked me if I would help her. She bluntly said, "If I feel I look good, I'll go. If not, I'm going to make an excuse and get out of it." I couldn't let Anne avoid the wedding when I knew I could help her. "Meet me at the mall at 10:00 A.M. tomorrow and you shall go to the ball," I replied to her plea.

Unbeknownst to Anne, I arrived for our shopping date the next day armed. I brought something I knew she had never considered wearing before: a longline bra, which begins at the bust and extends to the waist or a bit below. Sometimes it is boned and wired to be worn without straps. I didn't tell her I had it in my handbag. We looked at a few items in the store and she tried some things on. Some looked better than others, but nothing really impressed us. The clothes, pretty on the hanger, looked dowdy on her. Anne, a round diamond, is very busty and full through her midriff and arms. Disillusioned, she said, "I'm just not going."

That's when I reached into my bag, pulled out the black longline bra and, since we are about the same size, said, "Try this." She acquiesced. I revisited the sales floor and selected a few fitted dressy tops. When Anne tried the tops on with the longline bra, the difference was uncanny.

Here's why it worked. First, it is essential to remove or at least minimize bumps, lumps, back fat and shapelessness from top to bottom. This is the "fade" part. Second, it is essential to uplift the bust and create a waist. This is the "focus" part. Third, the key is smoothness and firmness with no bulges from the waist down. To do this, the undergarments must not be too tight. This is critical; if an undergarment is too tight, it will simply redistribute the extra skin, creating an unattractive bulge—just what we're trying to avoid.

I said to Anne, "Now you have options. Let's keep shopping." So, we went to another store. Everything was different in her approach to the merchandise. The bra opened up some fun, sexy and exciting choices that would not have been options before. Finally, Anne selected an outfit made of separates. She chose a sheer, stretchy black top adorned with colorful, stitched ribbons in a circular design with a very pretty silver zipper. She combined the top with dressy narrow black slacks made of cotton and Lycra that had a sheer full-length skirt made of black chiffon over them, providing a sexy illusion of a trim, shapely body underneath. Then we went to a shoe store that specializes in comfortable, lovely shoes and selected graceful metallic-toned heels. Anne already had an evening bag that would be stunning and she always wears spectacular diamond jewelry.

Anne had arrived to our shopping venture wearing a well-worn minimizer brassiere made to flatten and smooth the chest. It provided very little support and shape and not a lot of contrast (indentation) of her midriff and waist. Therefore, to avoid clothing clinging to unattractive bulges, she was forced to choose larger tops that provided coverage but little shape. The garments, although pretty, looked mature, out-of-date and heavy.

On the other hand, the longline bra did two main things for Anne: First, it lifted her large chest nicely and it trimmed her tummy, creating a refreshing contrast between her bust and midriff/waist area. She looked younger and slimmer. There was almost an athletic quality in the firmness of her midriff and waist. Second, her posture improved, because the bra supported her back. She held herself taller and straighter. Not being too tight, the bra was comfortable as well. Overall, the bra gave Anne a very hot look: sexy, trim, firm and, frankly, a little kinky! As I watched Anne look at herself in the mirror, I could tell she saw that too and projected that aura!

More than a bit teary, she thanked me and, after giving me a hug, returned home fully intending to go to the wedding looking sexy, sensational and successful! Indeed, Anne went to the wedding and received a host of compliments. At the top of the list was her husband, who was not only pleased that she attended but also very proud of his beautiful wife. I had a ball as well. It was enormously gratifying to know and share a secret: the black longline bra, which provides a firm, smooth, uplifting shape and thereby presents options many women would never have considered before.

The object is to find undergarments that shape, smooth and firm and are made of soft, substantial, stretchy materials. A few points to remember: First, undergarments that hold you in too tightly in one area usually create an unattractive bulge in another area. "Being held in" is less beneficial than being "smoothed out." Second, try to buy undergarments that have no seams or laces that show though clothing. You want a smooth garment. Third, do not buy an undergarment too small for you thinking that it will make you look slimmer and better. It won't. Fourth, if an undergarment shrinks or if you get larger, get rid of it. Buy a new one in the correct size. Simply put, it is counterproductive to wear an undergarment that is too small. Finally, if a garment loses its firmness and shape due to wear and washing or if you change sizes, replace it.

Sexy, Sensational and Successful Foundations
When you find a brand you like, stick with it. There are significant variations in how different products fit.

Bras
After your face, your breasts may well be the area that gets the most attention. Therefore, it's important to view purchasing and wearing bras as an opportunity to look beautiful and sexy. Wearing a well-fitting bra and a matching pair (same color) of panties makes you feel pretty right from the start of your day. Treat yourself to attractive undergarments and you'll be surprised how it makes you feel about yourself. I'm happy to report that there are numerous stores, inexpensive as well as pricey, that have a wide range of appealing items and sizes to choose from.

It is important to be fitted for a bra properly. Go to a specialty store or the lingerie department of a good department store and ask the sales professional to fit you. This is important for two reasons: you want the right size and style for your bust. No part of the breast should spill out of the bra, either on the side or on the top. If it does, it is not the right bra for you. Either the size or the style is wrong and it will create an uncooperative point of focus, negating all that we are working to achieve. Look for bra straps that are wide, padded and comfortable. Even if you have large, heavy breasts, you don't have to suffer those painful indentations on your shoulders. You should purchase bras in two colors, nude and black.

Today, bras can serve more than their original purpose to uplift and support breasts. Bras are important tools in manufacturing shape and providing your best overall silhouette.

The Minimizer Bra
The minimizer bra is not new to the landscape of bras, but it still deserves some discussion for full-busted women. The minimizer bra does two things better than the traditional bra: It creates a more youthful bustline and it smoothes out and covers bulges. There are many

brands to choose from. Personally, I enjoy minimizer bras from two brands. The first bra is by Olga (style number 35069) and second is by Le Mystere (style Renaissance Dream). The bras are in the medium to upper price range, thirty and fifty dollars respectively. Try to choose a bra with four hooks. Bras with fewer hooks provide less support and often create an indentation exacerbating back fat. The fit of the bra as it encircles your ribcage, more than the straps, should provide most of the support.

The Padded Bra

Women have been wearing padded bras for a very long time. Some plus size women who are smaller on top would look better and more balanced with a fuller bustline. This illusion can be created easily with a padded bra. There are countless options. Some allow for two sizes of pads to be placed inside the cup, giving the woman a choice as to what looks more flattering, that is, how much padding is desired. In other bras the padding is built into or sewn into the cup. The idea here is for the plus size woman to use this option to create a curvy, hourglass shape and to balance her top and bottom.

The Longline Bra

I hope I've convinced you with Anne's story of the significance of creating shape in the upper half of a woman's body. The silhouette we try to achieve must celebrate curves by providing contrast from full areas to narrow areas, minimizing bulges and promoting firmness. The longline bra helps us to do this. Although they have improved in comfort, longline bras are still not as comfortable as three or four hook bras, so it is understandable to use a longline bra when you want to look particularly sexy and assured, but not every day. It is important to choose the best length for you. The best way to determine this is to sit down in the dressing room while trying bras on to be sure it fits comfortably. Next, lift your hands way above your head. Does the bra ride up? Elect to wear front closure longline bras when you can. There is no reason to struggle with this type of garment anymore. One brand I recommend is Goddess. Their line has regular bra straps and good midriff control, and they cost a modest forty-five dollars. The bra comes only in back closure, but can be altered at the store where it is purchased to make it a front closure, adding an additional fifteen to twenty dollars to the cost of the bra. It comes in white and black, but unfortunately, not in nude.

The Posture Bra

Posture and the way heavy women sometimes carry themselves can be deal breakers. (I will discuss this more fully in chapter 16, "Body Language.") There are bras that are specifically designed to support the back. And they do! They feel great. I know this may sound improbable, but this new generation of bras is almost energizing. These bras allow women to stand straight and sit up tall. They are made of substantial stretchy fabrics but are not too restrictive. Posture bras do not have the traditional bra straps. They can be compared to a stretchy, fitted sleeveless blouse that, of course, closes in the front. An added value is no more back bulges. The fabric supports, firms and flattens the back. The posture bra that I love is made by Cortland, costs about thirty-eight dollars and closes in the front! It is my absolute favorite bra.

There are other products on the market that claim the same benefits and should be tried if you are open-minded. One such product is the Control Vest by As We Change, which is basically a long vest with a twelve hook front closure that is worn over a bra. It keeps your back straight and your tummy in.

The Camisole Bra

An overall guideline for looking smoother and longer: seek less bulk and clinginess in the clothing you select. The camisole bra helps you do that. The bra has a sexy lace insert between the two cups, providing the appearance of an additional garment, a camisole. A camisole is a straight top trimmed with lace or embroidery. Wear the camisole bra under a blazer or shirt to give a layered look. The beauty is that there is no bulk or clinginess that you would necessarily have by wearing an additional garment underneath. It's a sexy, youthful option; you feel the jacket against your skin with no shirt or camisole in between. One brand you may enjoy is Carol Wright Gifts, which can be purchased online and costs only eighteen dollars. It comes in black, white and pink and a wide range of sizes.

The Shoulder Pad Bra
The shoulder pad bra offers shape and balance to your whole silhouette. The shoulder pads are small pads used to create the illusion of a better defined shoulder. The pads are attached to the bra straps and remain there comfortably throughout the day. Many heavy women benefit from this type of bra. Women who are pear shape benefit from the balance this bra provides, widening their shoulders to offset wider hips. The incidental benefit is the appearance of a smaller waist. This is one way to manufacture the hourglass figure. Women who are fleshy and round at the shoulder and arms areas (round shape diamonds) benefit from the contour established from the shoulder pads, too. The visual line is extended off the shoulders, creating a more graceful drape for the fabric of the garment. Once again, contrast and therefore shape is being manufactured. The shoulders are broader, which makes the rest of the body appear to be narrower. These are not the shoulder pads of the 1980s; they are more subtle, but still provide a slenderizing and refreshing silhouette. This style bra can be found in the Bloomingdale's catalog and costs fifty dollars. If, however, you cannot find this style in your size, simply purchase a pair of shoulder pads from a fabric store and have your seamstress sew them under the bra straps of a bra you will permanently designate for this purpose.

Shapers, Panties and One-Piece Support Garments
Remember, the goal is not so much to hold you in, but to smooth you out, with a measure of firmness along the way. The intent is to be bulge-free.

Shapers/Girdles

There is a new generation of girdles called shapers. These new shapers are less restrictive. There is no need to have nightmares about your mother's or grandmother's girdles anymore. Most notably, the fabric that shapers are made of is very different; it is lighter, softer and gentler.

As the mother of a baseball player, I have come to liken shapers to "sliding shorts." And while I don't think you will be sliding into second base any time soon, they have a similarly protective quality. What am I talking about? Chafing. These sliding shorts—others liken them to biker's shorts—allow you to put skirts and dresses back in your closet and choose to wear them! They protect the areas between your thighs that rub together when you walk and create uncomfortable, if not painful, rashes and welts.

These garments come in varying lengths. I choose one that stops at mid-thigh, but there are garments that come to the knee and to the mid-calf as well. I'm very fond of a shaper product made by Rago of New York, style number 6206. It costs around thirty-five to forty dollars. Choose the product that suits the area you need to firm and smooth, depending on your legs and the garment you want to wear. Shapers allow you to wear slacks that might not have been attractive without the firming quality shapers provide, specifically white slacks.

SPANX offers support lingerie merchandise that women rave about and there are many products in this line that should be considered. I am a recent convert to SPANX. However, my friend Anne was wearing her own SPANX pants liner when we went shopping for the wedding she had to attend. This is a gentle stretchy garment that firms the body from the waist through mid-calf. It creates a fluid, firm shape for the lower half of a women's body. The key to wearing this undergarment is that it is not too tight, which can create bulges and make it uncomfortable to wear. This brand is probably the gold standard in the undergarment industry and deservedly so.

Importantly, these sliding shorts make panty lines and bulges a thing of the past. They are quite comfortable. Two important features to look for: fabric that will engender a gentle sliding action (zero friction) between the thighs as you walk and a band at the thigh that is comfortable but won't allow it to ride up through the course of the day. If you are going to start with one just to give it a try, choose a nude color in a mid-thigh length. That alone will bring skirts and dresses back into your wardrobe.

Panties

Look for panties that fit well and come up to your natural waist (the smallest part of your middle section). They are more comfortable and flattering. If you can get a high cut leg, it will elongate your leg and make you feel longer and slimmer. The fabric is a matter of personal choice. Some gals prefer stretchy materials and others prefer a nylon tricot. The important point is to have no bulges or panty lines. When you dress, try to wear a set of matching bra and panties, not so much in terms of brand or style, but in color. It sets a tone for yourself that you care from the start of your day.

The One-Piece

This is a garment that you step into and is a longline bra and a panty girdle combined, with three hooks under the crotch. It looks a little like a one-piece bathing suit. I do not recommend this for one important reason. I find it is virtually impossible to go to the bathroom and re-hook myself in this contraption.

Last year, my husband and son gave a birthday party for me at an elegant restaurant. I wanted to look my most svelte and so I wore a one-piece under a simple black dress. During dinner, I excused myself and went to the ladies' room not to return for what seemed like an hour. I could not re-hook the garment. There I was in this tiny stall, lovely marble and gold fixtures notwithstanding, struggling and perspiring, trying over and over to hook it again. I became nervous and embarrassed. Finally, I was able to get one of the three hooks closed and I returned to the table. For the rest of the evening the garment cut into me, because it was not closed properly. Not to mention that Prince Charles and the ever charming Camilla were at the restaurant that night. The irony of being in this chic place and struggling in the bathroom was not lost on me.

Hosiery
Remember, we always want to reduce bulk and awkwardness and promote a sexy, comfortable, assured feeling.

Pantyhose
Fortunately, hosiery options have widened for plus size women, both from inexpensive lines to expensive lines. That said, here is my suggestion: Don't waste your money on expensive hosiery; I don't. Select a product in sheer black or natural tones (what is natural for your skin tone) with some elasticity. The light support product creates a veneer that makes your skin look perfect. It also remains smooth and taut throughout the day or evening. Color on your legs can be good for two reasons: First, it makes you look healthy and slimmer. Secondly, it disguises veins and other things you would rather hide. If you really need to do some extra disguising, I recommend Just My Size opaque black tights. They look great, last forever and cost about five dollars per pair.

     Here's my trick: I wear my sliding shorts over my pantyhose, to smooth me out and to prevent chafing. I do not recommend control top or firm support hosiery. They tend to cause a bulge at the top and are difficult to put on. In addition, I have accidentally pushed my thumbnail through more than one pair, ruining the pair of support hosiery before ever getting out the door. Most importantly, they tend to cause chafing, because they are so tight. Besides, they cost more money and the use of the sliding shorts achieves the same goal: well placed firmness.

Thigh-Highs
Thigh-high stockings may be a sexy option for some women. Choose stockings that have a thick, firm elastic band at the top. Be sure to

get them long enough so you can place the elastic at the highest spot possible on your thighs. They will stay better if they are up high and in this location will create only the most minimal bulge. Sears carries two wonderful styles of thigh-highs and I personally recommend both. One has a thinner elastic band and costs about five dollars for two pairs. The other, the one I prefer, has a thick, lacey elastic band and costs about seven dollars for one pair. Indisputably, choose black!

Knee Socks
Sheer knee socks are heaven-sent. They allow you to have the look of stockings when wearing slacks without the hassle or expense. Some women today prefer the look of bare ankles (no hosiery). Only you can determine whether the use of hosiery adds to your daily comfort or not. This is a personal decision.

Buyer beware, there are two sizes of knee highs available: nine to eleven, which is for average size legs, and ten to thirteen, which is for full size legs. I wear the latter and no longer have these problems: that charming, deeply imbedded ring at the top of my calf where my circulation has been temporarily stopped; that constant dance of the sock slipping and my tugging it up throughout the day; my big toe popping through the hosiery, because the sock was pulled too tight to get it up high enough to stay. I do not recommend wearing knee socks with skirts or dresses.

Slips
If you are wearing a dress, a silky full-length slip may offer some additional shape and drape. The same holds true for half slips when wearing skirts. Choose pretty slips that are no bigger then you actually need. A slip should not be tight, but it should be fitted, which means it should skim your body.

Some women, in trying to reduce the friction associated with chafing, wear split half slips (sort of like culottes). Personally, I find that the split slip rides up my inner thighs and I need to adjust it about every third step I take. If you need to adjust, readjust and tug at a garment throughout the day, it is not the right one for you.

For several reasons, a sexy black slip is hard to beat, if you catch my drift; if you don't, read on.

Lingerie

Plus size lingerie has come a long way, baby! First, it transforms the plus size woman, beautiful on the inside and the outside. Second, much of today's plus size lingerie is beautiful to look at, rich with flattering detail on the outside, but also ample with figure support and helpful fabrication in terms of its very construction on the inside.

There is every reason to purchase and wear sensuous lingerie. There are many brands that offer beautiful sexy lingerie in plus sizes. Fredericks of Hollywood is one. Lane Bryant's own brand, Cacique, has many lovely and sexy things to choose from as does the brand Always for Me. I recommend ordering by catalog or from a Web site and trying things on in the privacy of your own home. Be discriminating, take your time and only keep what you think you will wear. Start with only one or two items. Great garments to begin with are a slip-style nightie, tap pants, a bustier, a tempting bra and matching panties or a pair of thigh-high stockings. Store pictures of things you may want to try in the future in your Pretty Party Portfolio and revisit it from time to time.

Selecting wonderful, flattering lingerie that also sizzles is as easy as steps one, two and three: camouflage, flaunt and play. Camouflage or conceal what you choose (fade), flaunt the good stuff (focus) and play with garments that reflect your style using detail and color.

Camouflage

Okay, remember you are talking with a big sister, so be honest: What do you need to conceal to feel unencumbered, open and playful? If it's your legs, choose a long gown made of sheer, beautiful fabric with great embellishments at the bust. If it's your thighs, choose long line baby dolls or bi-level skirts with moving hems. Tummy concerns? Select a flapper style blouson chemise, which has lots of tummy coverage, because it is full through the middle, but narrows at the hip with a jaunty, flaunty skirt. Need to manufacture a waist? Bustiers and corsets, which tie or hook around the mid-section to create a waist, are not for everyone, but for those who are willing to experiment, big time payoffs await. Think about an Old West saloon corset or a Victorian inspired, beautiful floral tapestry or jacquard. Issues with your buttocks? Choose longer, sheer, scarf-like hems (gypsy style) or tap pants, which are styled like shorts and have a flare at the hem.

Many of today's garments have wonderful support already built-in. Underwire bras with demi and full cups, molded and sheer lace bra support cups and traditional and adjustable eye and hook closures abound. In addition, crisscross back straps and double straps do double duty: they look great and add support to the bust.

Here's why these supports are so important. Yes, they make your breasts more attractive. Here's the value added: When your bust is firmly defined, it creates a more flattering drape for the rest of the garment and manufactures an indentation in the bodice for a shapely figure (recall Anne's story).

Flaunt

It pains me that this part doesn't come more easily to many big sisters, but the media and culture in general have taken its toll on us. So here's a remedy. Take a private moment—perhaps ten minutes—and look at yourself in the mirror lovingly. Here's the important part: pretend you are seeing your best girlfriend in the mirror and you want to build her confidence. What features are her loveliest? Which would you suggest she emphasize? Those are the features you must flaunt when it comes to lingerie.

Play

The playground should be of your own choosing. Open your mind but be true to yourself. There are many types of lingerie to choose from, ranging from sensual to statement, your own personal one. The styles you can select from include baby dolls, chemises, gowns, bras, corsets, panties and tap pants.

Play with rich details that flatter and are strategically placed, such as front and side slits, moving hems, shape-defining side panels, deep V–necks and pleats that cover and tease.

Choose sophisticated detailing or embellishments, such as ruffles, jewels, charms, bows, ribbon, lace and sequin trim, that draw attention to the areas you want to flaunt. Select fabrics that are figure-flattering, such as microfibers, stretch laces, support stretch satins, jacquard mesh and other soft sheer synthetics. No collection of lingerie is complete without something made of silk, which has enough weight to drape well and feel sumptuous and rich on your skin.

That being said, when plus size women look at plus size lingerie via models, even models that purport to be plus size, it is easy to become disenchanted. We compare ourselves to the tiniest fraction of the female population. Let me assure you, real women have curves, bumps, bulges and cellulite—and don't get thrown out of bed because of it. By the way, real men have bumps and bulges, too.

The time has come to be our own best girlfriend. The exercise I suggested using your mirror, combined with an online lingerie catalog is a great place to begin. Forget the pity party and embrace the pretty party.

Extending the Lifespan of Your Undergarments

1. Wash all lingerie in a laundry bag either by hand or on the delicate cycle of your washing machine using Woolite or a similar detergent. Make sure to separate by color (all black together, all white and nude together). Hang all of your garments to dry in your bathroom. It is well worth the extra effort and inconvenience. Do not use the dryer for lingerie—ever. You would be compromising the integrity of the garments, reducing their lifespan and throwing money away. There

are women who will tell you to wash all lingerie by hand only. I must admit I use the delicate cycle of my washing machine and a mesh laundry bag.

2. If a bra gets too tight around the back, try bra extenders before you throw it out and purchase a new one. Bra extenders are a little patch of hooks that link into the hooks on the back of the bra. They come in a variety of colors and number of hooks. Remember, I never recommend fewer than a four hook bra anyway. They cost around three dollars per pack, so it is always worth a try.

3. A product known as Comfy Straps (one pair is about fourteen dollars), available from As We Change, will cure the problem of slipping bra straps as well as painful indentations in the shoulders from bra straps.

4. No See 'ems is a neat product that closes the gap between buttons on a shirt. It is a two-sided tape that works around the button on the inside of the shirt to prevent embarrassing "peep shows." A set costs fourteen dollars and can be purchased from As We Change.

5. Know your favorite brands and your sizes. It will reduce stress when you need to purchase an item. Write them down and keep them in your Pretty Party Portfolio.

6. If you choose to shop via catalog or online, check out Lady Grace for one-stop shopping. They have a great selection, a wide array of sizes and reasonable prices.

CHAPTER 3

Activewear

TOUGH TO
BE A SPORT

"If I were a cat, what would make me purr?
A pair of really comfortable blue jeans, and massages."
~Cinnamon Stomberger

As a baseball mom, I spend a lot of time at games and tournaments and find that there is a lot of downtime. So, what does a voyeur like me do with downtime? I watch. I observe. I evaluate. I have found that many women of all sizes struggle with creating appropriate and flattering activewear outfits. I believe a woman's goal should be to look casual, comfortable, pretty and well-turned out. It appears that this is easier said than done.

The challenge for plus size women is the limited availability of attractive, appropriate and comfortable clothing for recreation. How can I say this when there seems to be no shortage of plus size casual clothing available to purchase? I say this, because I feel very few manufacturers "get it" and therefore there is very little opportunity to purchase separates that "fade and focus." There appears to be little or no understanding of what larger women need to look great while pursuing recreational activities, including participating in warm weather sports, such as golf or tennis, as well as attending warm weather sporting events, such as your child's lacrosse game or a professional baseball game.

In regard to virtually all other types of garments, designers and manufacturers are identifying a need by producing a wide variety of attractive items for larger women from which to choose. Not so in the activewear area. Don't they know we want to have fun, too? An item that is simply large, colorful and washable is not good enough! I'm going to describe what you should search for and buy as well as what to avoid.

Flattering Activewear

This section will be threefold: fabric, garments and brand names. While there is not a plethora of strategic items from which to choose, the well-dressed woman does not need dozens of outfits to be well-dressed. Needing an abundance of clothing, I believe, is reminiscent of the insecurity this book seeks to assuage. Instead, having a half dozen or so separate pieces that work well with one another will provide a constant stream of "go-to" good looks without compromising your bank account.

Fabric

There are five activewear fabrics that work best for plus size women. The first and best fabric to look for in activewear is polyester combined with a dry-weave fabric (such as COOLMAX) in an approximately fifty-fifty proportion. This will have the slimmest drape, provide contour, look current, feel cool and crisp and wash easily every time. This fabric is most often found in skorts, shorts, capris, slacks and skirts. To be fair, there are many other innovative fabrics on the market today that also do a great job, such as Supplex® Nylon, Arizona Sun Supply Inc. and Double Dry Cotton.

The second fabic is Tencel. Similar to the polyester/COOLMAX fabric, Tencel has great drape and can be cut to offer contour and shape to a garment. It is a little heavier and actually a generation older than COOLMAX, but it has great weight for casual clothing. Not to mention, it is better for you to wear as a spectator, not as a participant. You will see tops and bottoms made of Tencel.

The third fabric is a flat, stretch knit, tightly woven, obviously made of synthetic material. This is where you must be careful that the garment will retain a flattering shape. It is imperative for the fabric to resume its original form after washing. Keep the dryer time to a minimum, maybe fifteen minutes, then hang up the garment to dry completely. If the garment is disappointing after the washing and drying process, return it. This type of fabric is found in sporty knit separates, jackets and bottoms (think refined warm-up suit).

The fourth fabric is cotton combined with spandex. Look for 5 percent spandex if you want the garment to look good after the first washing. Cotton is still the best fabric choice for T-shirts and polo shirts.

Finally, denim, in blue, black, white or any other colors, can look slenderizing and be fun. Again, look for 3 to 5 percent of spandex or Lycra combined with the cotton to retain the shape of the garment. Denim jackets are a favorite of mine, but mostly you will look for denim bottoms, skirts and jeans.

Garments

A good choice for the backbone of your recreation wardrobe is the skort. It looks like a pencil skirt, but has slits on the sides for ease of motion and shorts sewn in for comfort (no chafing). If you are heavier on the bottom, choose a dark color skort. If you are slimmer on the bottom, opt for a lighter color or pattern. A blue denim or khaki color skort is versatile, too.

While skorts are a great choice for plus size women, they have one problem. Many manufacturers make skorts that are not long enough and don't fall into a pencil style shape skirt, narrowing slightly and hitting at (or even slightly below) the knee. They tend to be wide mini-skirts. Not good! Here is a solution I use that will allow you to wear skorts more and more, which will single-handedly transform your casual and sports wardrobe.

Purchase two of the same skort. Take them to your seamstress and have her use the fabric from one to enhance the other. Have her elongate and shape the skort so that it narrows slightly at the knee, with a slit at both sides. "How expensive is this?" you may ask. Let's say the skort costs twenty-nine to thirty-nine dollars; double it and add fifteen to twenty dollars for the alteration. Now, you have invested about one hundred dollars in a garment that you will wear all the time. When you wear it frequently, you'll come to view it as a great bargain, because the cost of each wearing will become less and less. Buy less, buy better, buy wisely and have a go-to item from which you will derive not only aesthetic and physical satisfaction but also emotional contentment as well. I think one hundred dollars is not too much to pay for a great fitting skort you will love and wear often.

When shopping for slacks, look for refined, lightweight slacks made of polyester and a dry-weave combination, which is very flattering on plus size women. A pair of blue, black or white jeans, worn with a pretty, flat shoe is always a good choice.

The polo shirt, refined T-shirt and "baseball style" shirt (black panels along the sides of the body to promote a slender silhouette) are very important. The key is to select three or four tops that really fit well, are long enough, are made of cotton with spandex and have great color. That doesn't mean you should not have polos in white and black. You should have these two basic colors, but you can also choose one or two other colors that are threaded throughout your wardrobe. For example, coral is a frequent accent color for me. I have a few polo shirts, a pair of sandals, a handbag and jewelry in that color.

The sports vest is a wonder item. It is slenderizing and provides a finishing touch. It can bring separates together and complete an outfit. It will also allow you to leave your handbag in the car, because it has great pockets, sometimes with zippers. Those of us with heavy arms appreciate the ease of movement in a vest. Often, vests come in beautiful colors, which echoes throughout the designer's line as accents on tops and bottoms. You may choose to purchase several pieces from the line for this reason. However, a vest in a great color worn over a monochromatic backdrop will always make you look well-dressed and put together. Look for extra value in a vest that is reversible, which is essentially two looks for the price of one.

A jacket, either polyester with polyurethane lamination or just plain denim, also completes an outfit and provides a bit of protection from the elements. I like outer garments that serve as rain gear in the form of a jacket, wind shirt or vest. The anorak, a waterproof, hip-length, hooded jacket, is a great addition to the sportswear scene for fall and spring.

A refined warm-up suit with its matching jacket and pants, a T-shirt or polo shirt and cropped slacks or a skirt and an empire waist dress are three outfits that also work well if the fabrics have firm drape and retain their shapes.

Brand Names

This section is short and sweet. I have found that Liz Golf produces the richest, best-fitting line of recreational separates in plus sizes. In fact, this brand is the backbone of my sports wardrobe. The look is classic and friendly. I ride around in the golf cart and spend time with my husband who plays golf quite regularly. This brand provides the clothing I want for spending time on the green.

Bette and Court, Lands' End and Talbots also produce great recreational clothing for plus size women who want to have some fun.

Activewear to Avoid

The majority of sporty clothing on the market today will not make it through the first washing. Often, but not always, the price of a garment matters in terms of maintaining its integrity through the washing and drying cycles. In general, more expensive clothing will hold up better. If you are attracted to a garment in the store and choose to buy it, clip the tags before you are about to wear it and save them in a designated shoe box with all your clothing receipts. If you become disappointed with the garment after washing it, return it for your money back. Many stores will honor this policy.

Fabric

First, unless you are a coed, the worst things you can buy are sweats—sweatpants, sweatsuits, sweatshirts. They are big, bulky and unfashionable. Certainly, a sweatshirt as a vacation souvenir has its place, but promise me you will wear it only over a refined bottom like a skort or pair of well-fitting slacks. Second, the cotton T-shirt, no matter how pretty the color, is off-limits unless it has at least 3 percent spandex or Lycra combed into the fabric and fits well (it should skim and drape your body, not just cover it with room to spare). Third, lightweight knits that have no spandex in the fabric content have no chance of maintaining their shapes and should be left on the rack. Face it, they have no chance of surviving the first washing and you'll be disappointed. Fourth, tightly clinging, shiny Lycra bottoms such as shorts or capris miss the opportunity inherent in a draping fabric to improve your silhouette and worse, call attention to heavy legs.

Garments

Please don't wear garments that show too much; use your own good judgment to decide what is appropriate. Items that are too small or too revealing should not be worn to public sporting events and facilities. Women of every size should heed this advice. It is inappropriate to wear too small or too revealing clothes at children's activities.

Brand Names

It is not my place to criticize a specific company. I will, however, say that it is difficult and misleading to choose clothing when companies do not use real plus size models to model plus size clothing. If it looks too good to be true, it probably is. Remember to buy less, buy better and recreate!

CHAPTER 4

Beachwear

NO KIDDING!

"Is not the most erotic part of the body wherever the
clothing affords a glimpse?"
~Roland Barthes

There is a bathing suit that will make you look thinner and more attractive. There is at least one style for each diamond shape plus size woman that will make her look better than ever before in a swimsuit by applying the concept of "fade and focus." Choose firm fabrics and good bra support, because it is these two factors that will create the drape you desire in the suit. I still understand that, like me, you are not comfortable parading around in a swimsuit and I will offer some great cover-up options as well.

Bathing Suits
Pear Shape Diamond
The mini-swim dress has an A-line design and is a good choice for the pear shape diamond. The fitted empire waist, just under the bust, provides a good point for the fabric to gather and drape down gently over the full tummy and backside. A full skirt is necessary to create balance and proportion over full hips and legs. Use all dark coloration throughout with interesting details, such as a pretty gold or silver buckle or an

interesting knot in the fabric, at the high-waist for a good fade and focus technique. Additionally, a vibrant floral, ethnic or geometric pattern top portion over the bust (focus) with a dark skirt covering the bottom half (fade) is beautiful as well. With smaller shoulders and arms, the pear shape diamond can choose a halter top or other intriguing details to draw attention to the shoulders via the straps.

Round Shape Diamond

The round shape diamond should choose a swimsuit that shows off her hourglass figure. She probably has a beautiful bust to show off, too. For this shape, it's hard to beat the swim dress. Choose a top with a comfortable surplice wrap style, eye-catching color or other interesting details for focus. The high waist creates a great drape over a full tummy and backside for the fade effect. The coloration of the lower half of the suit should be more subdued to continue the fade. The length of the swimsuit depends on how much thigh you want to expose.

Additionally, the hourglass figure looks good in a tankini, a two-piece bathing suit with an empire-waisted, A-line top, as long as a skirt is chosen for the bottom half. The skirt is key to establishing attractive proportion over large thighs. I love suits that are monochromatic and use great details for embellishment, specifically in places to which we want to draw the eye.

Heart Shape Diamond

The two-piece tankini is a fantastic look for the plus size heart shape diamond. By wearing a longer, solid, dark color top, the larger upper torso will be minimized—fade. The heart shape diamond should choose a skirt as the bottom of the tankini for balance. In addition, choose a vivid coordinating pattern or color for the bottom to boost the balance and overall proportion of the look—focus.

Marquise Shape Diamond

The marquise shape diamond also benefits from the tankini; however, she may choose a traditional bathing suit bottom, fitted at the crotch, instead of a skirt. The benefit of this style is that a long tankini top with an empire waist (high, just under the bust) can cover a large tummy—fade. A strategic selection of color or pattern is important too. The dark color should be at the tummy for fade and the bright color at the bust and hips—focus.

In addition, the marquise shape diamond can also enjoy the traditional maillot, again with well-placed color. Choose a bathing suit that has a vibrant print of color for the background of the suit and a ruched (gathered, pleated effect), dark (preferably black) band sweeping across the middle of the suit diagonally for a fade effect.

Emerald Shape Diamond

The emerald shape diamond benefits from the swim dress. It is a very beautiful bathing suit that boasts a longer length, sometimes down to the knee. It offers great shape, drape and coverage. Importantly, given strategic insertions of color or vivid pattern against a solid dark backdrop, curves and contour can be styled into the swim dress for a flattering curvy look employing fade and focus.

Cover-Ups

The concept of the cover-up is terrific. To begin, find the shortest length cover-up your leg will permit; that is, show the most leg you can and still be attractive. Every woman's best length is different. Then add another inch or two of length for movement and sitting comfortably. No one wants to have to think about being covered up and looking appropriate, but you want to show as much skin as possible. Please recall the concept of visual weight. The more leg you show, the better. The more fabric, the more you will appear to fill it out.

The T-shirt dress, which is usually knee-length, makes a great cover-up. More and more, I see women wearing a gentle trapeze style, which has an exaggerated A-line and is very forgiving. Again, only choose as much "swing" in the trapeze as you need. Do not opt for more fabric than you absolutely need; have the garment skim your body.

Cover-ups with an empire (high) waist are another beautiful option, especially if you coordinate the color with your swimsuit. They tend to be flattering and youthful. Often they come in beach fabrics such as gauze, terry cloth or cotton jersey. Made of natural materials, they breathe well and are therefore cooler.

Another popular style is the cocoon style. This style has a zipper running the length of the front of the garment that offers an up and down visual line and interesting trim. Here's a tip I discovered from personal experience: This style is particularly helpful because it allows you to put it on more discreetly. You can actually start to put it on while sitting in your chair at the pool or beach. When you begin to stand, it is already on your arm or arms and it just falls into place as you stand. Then all you need to do is zip it up. The other styles force you to stand up and put the cover-up on over your head, which many women want to avoid doing.

The traditional beach shift, also called beach dress, that matches the bathing suit in terms of fabric or print should not be overlooked either. It makes a well turned out look every time.

Choose wisely when it comes to your cover-up. Give it almost as much thought as the bathing suit itself. It will become your "go-to" garment at the pool or the beach. In fact, it will bring you hours of comfort and ease, because you will know that you are appropriately covered and looking good. All of the styles I referred to look great on all of the diamond shapes.

Beach Accessories

Beach shoes, a hat, sunglasses and a tote are part of the complete picture. Choose one complete set that is coordinated as opposed to several unrelated pieces, no matter how good-looking they are. Pick a color scheme or unifying detail. We'll discuss choosing and coordinating accessories more in depth in chapter 8.

This type of purchase is an area where Target and Wal-Mart can't be beat. Choose colorful straw, plastic or fabric accessories, which tend to be inexpensive but a lot of fun. There is no reason you can't look better than ever at the beach or pool this year.

CHAPTER 5

Petite Focus

TALL TALES

"I have often said that I wish I had invented blue jeans: the most spectacular, the most practical, the most relaxed and nonchalant. They have expression, modesty, sex appeal, simplicity—all I hope for in my clothes." ~Yves Saint Laurent

First of all, let's be clear about the term petite. Petite refers to height and, of course, not to weight or circumferential body measurements; it doesn't matter what size you are around the bust, waist or hips. Women who stand five feet four inches or shorter are considered petite by the fashion industry.

It's a little ironic, because the average height of American women is five feet four inches. The real distinction for a petite woman compared with her "average" height counterparts is not so much her total height, but usually the distance between her bust and waist; many petite women are short-waisted. A woman can be five feet seven inches tall and still wear petite clothing. Why? Because the measurement that doesn't fit with average women's clothing is the length between her bust and waist. A woman like this can go a long time before she realizes that this is the reason clothing doesn't fit her well without significant alternations and, sometimes, not even then.

A telltale sign is the sleeves. Do you always feel you need to roll up or shorten the sleeves of a jacket or dress? If so, this may be the issue you need to address when purchasing clothing. There is no law stating that you can't buy plus size petite tops and jackets and plus size regular skirts and slacks.

Other petite women are short-measured between the waist and the crotch. The distance between your waist and crotch will make it very difficult for slacks and jeans to fit well. Often the fabric will bunch up around your tummy adding visual weight, which you obviously don't want. This alteration is very difficult to perform effectively. Therefore, my suggestion is that you shop for plus size petite bottoms, especially in slacks and jeans.

If you fall into either of these two categories, you may need to seek petite clothing, too.

Elongate

The mantra throughout this book has been to elongate your silhouette. If it was true for taller plus size women it is even more imperative for petite plus size women. Always seek a vertical line in an outfit. The goal is to achieve a long vertical line but still be able to see legs and skin.

The Vertical Line

Vertical lines are not limited to stripes and coloration. Vertical lines in zippers, buttons, single-breasted jackets and coats, stitching, seams, cut, embellishments as well as the drape of the fabric are effective ways to establish a vertical, elongating line.

When the eye sees a vertical line it perceives a taller and more slender image. Diagonal lines, especially when they are draping more north to south than east to west, are flattering too. However, stay away from horizontal lines; the plus size petite woman just can't afford it.

Small-scale prints are fine as long as the vertical quality dominates the pattern. However, if an item has a print, it is often best to keep it near the face, although this is not always necessary. In fact, a small-scale print with a dark background can hide a few flaws, like a tummy bulge, often more so than a single-colored garment.

Narrow Silhouettes

Plus size petite women can layer garments for a richer look. Keep the first layer closely fitted to the body. Use lightweight fabrics that drape. Be sure the drape of the garment skims the body but doesn't cling in an unflattering way. You may want to add a colorful accent; keep that underneath and let only a small portion of the color show.

Avoid stiff fabrics, because they will look boxy and project visual weight. Similarly, avoid shiny or bulky fabrics. Always opt for a matte finish; it is more forgiving and offers a flattering drape. Think *soft* when you touch the fabric: does it feel stiff or soft? Scrunch the fabric in your hand; if there are no wrinkles when you release it, it is probably a soft, flattering fabric. On the other hand, make sure it has enough weight to drape.

The plus size petite woman will look her best in simple, well-tailored clothing. You are after the sleekest, most well turned out look possible. Avoid a lot of trim and embellishments. You have less height to achieve the elongated silhouette and can't afford distractions on your clothing. It may be important to select high quality clothing that lends itself to alterations. Princess seaming and excellent vertical lines imbedded in a garment will be more important to your overall look than anything else. Seek elegance and simplicity, a sentiment perfectly captured by the Yves St. Laurent quote at the beginning of this chapter.

Visual Weight

If you choose to wear a skirt or dress, keep it at or just below the knee. This involves the concept of visual weight. If a garment hangs low, it will appear that you fill up the whole thing. It will make you seem imbalanced. Plus size petite women must show skin: neckline, forearms, legs or ankles. However, you do not need to show all of those areas at the same time, so pick the area that would be most flattering to allow skin to show. It will balance your whole image. Similarly, keep slacks hemmed just touching the instep of the foot. Any excess length will make you seem shorter.

Keep the tone-on-tone concept in place for finishing touches. If you are wearing a black knee-length skirt, wear black hosiery, a black heel with a pointed toe and a black handbag that suits the shoe. If you are wearing a camel colored skirt, wear nude hosiery, a camel toned pump with a low, sweetheart throat and a light-colored coat.

Monochromatic and Tone–on-Tone

Avoid contrasting colors between your tops and bottoms. Why break the body in half? Monochromatic and tone-on-tone combinations achieve the elongated look you're after. There is, however, nothing wrong with wearing two shades of the same color. This will offer a little more interest without sacrificing the vertical line. Also, as long as you remain in the same color scheme, a textural distinction between the top and bottom is a welcome change as long as it doesn't add bulk.

Dark neutrals achieve the leanest vertical line. If you feel you want to add color, position the color on the inside of the top, closest to your face. This allows you to enjoy the slenderizing effect of the dark color but has the impact of color where it counts most, at the face. Another look is to wear a dark neutral top and bottom with a vest or open jacket of color over it.

Plus size petite women may not benefit from light neutrals, even if worn on the top and bottom. However, if you love white, beige and cream shades, work them into the first scenario just described: Wear the color under an outfit of dark neutrals.

Shoes

Petite plus size women must choose their shoes wisely. Select shoes that elongate the feet and the legs. There are three ways to achieve this. The first is coloration. Choose shoes whose color echoes the outfit, especially the lower half. Wear hosiery that is a tonal bridge between the skirt, dress or slacks and the shoe. The second factor has to do with the cut of the shoe. Choose a shoe that has a V-shaped or sweetheart shaped throat, allowing the instep to be seen, and a pointed shoe box. Importantly, the shoe must fit well; it must not appear that the foot is spilling over. The third factor is the heel of the shoe. Choose heels, either a stacked heel or kitten heel, that are graceful and not too tall. Too high of a heel will cause you to look out of balance.

Where to Shop

I have found that the Talbots stores offer the widest range of sizes and styles for plus size petite women. The styles they offer run the gamut too. While Talbots stores have mostly updated classic clothing, women whose style runs from luxurious to artistic will find great pieces at their stores as well.

CHAPTER 6

Coats

THINK
GIFT WRAP

"One should either be a work of art, or wear a work of art."
~Oscar Wilde

Have you ever received a gift impeccably wrapped and couldn't believe your good fortune? The anticipation of the treasure inside forced you to hold the package respectfully and even affectionately. The presentation of the outer wrapping called you to make a judgment: something very worthwhile was inside and it must be treated accordingly. Think of the coats in your wardrobe in this way. People will judge you in a nanosecond; your coat is your wrapping that creates the first impression others have and will likely keep of you.

Outerwear is important and usually expensive; however, it presents one-stop shopping for "fade and focus." The cut or shape of the coat will provide much of the "fade." The style details will provide the "focus." In essence, as you will see in the examples below, the shape and style details are the consummate "fade and focus" team. A well-dressed woman needs to have the following outer garments in her closet:

- Trench-style raincoat—a waterproof, all-purpose trench coat
- Dressy overcoat or topcoat (below the knee length)—a lightweight coat designed to wear over a suit jacket

- Car coat—a sport coat of a shorter length, especially comfortable for wearing while driving
- Blazer or jacket—a single or double breasted sport jacket
- Vest—a sleeveless jacket that extends to the waist or below

The weather of the city in which you live will affect the materials and the specific qualities of your selections. If you live in an area where the temperature never dips below eighty degrees, of course you won't need a dressy overcoat or a car coat, but the raincoat, jacket and vest will still be indispensable. If, however, I could only purchase one coat, it would be the trench-style raincoat. I encourage each diamond shape to read this whole chapter, even the tips for the different diamond shapes. There is good advice throughout the chapter and it often overlaps, reinforcing certain concepts such as balance and visual weight.

In order to make the best selections for these important purchases, it is necessary to revisit the five diamond silhouettes that reflect the body frames I presented in the first chapter. Recall my second epiphany, taught to me by my knowledgeable personal shopper, Sandra: It is the frame of a woman, more so than her size, that determines what clothing will look good. Once you determine this, you can identify problem areas and apply the fade and focus concept.

Pear Shape Diamond
Trench-Style Raincoat
Shape
The coat should gradually flare to the hemline; this is the essential shape you are seeking. This means that a style belted at the waist will not be a good choice. However, an empire waist, which indents just below the bust, is a good choice, because the flowing vertical line begins from a higher place on the body, allowing more opportunity to gently expand as the coat covers your hips. Look for an armhole that extends just beyond your natural shoulder line. This is intended to create the illusion of balance against your larger lower half. The length should be just

below the knee. Avoid a longer style, as it gives the illusion of visual weight.

Style Details
Choose a light neutral color such as British tan, khaki or cream; it is richer and more fashionable than a dark raincoat. Seek soft materials that drape and well-placed lines that support a graceful and soft expansion. While the traditional belted trench coat will not be the most flattering option, you can and should seek embellishments that recall the traditional trench coat. You can accomplish this with a wool collar, leather covered buttons, epaulets (shoulder ornaments), hacked pockets (pockets cut on a diagonal), fabric and color.

Keep embellishments at the top of the coat. Your overall goal is a coat that comfortably fits your upper body and gently camouflages your wider lower half.

Dressy Overcoat and Car Coat
Shape
The best shape will be the same as the trench coat style. You may be able to find a style where vertical panels afford an optical illusion of length as well as ease of movement. A gentle swing coat may be a good option.

Style Details
Look for soft, rich wools. Here is your chance for a fur or velvet collar or even a shawl collar. The pear shape diamond can afford rich embellishments at the top, thereby balancing her lower half. Choose beautiful buttons but keep the details at the top half of the coat.

Blazer and Vest
Shape
The pear shape diamond wants to take the focus away from the difference in proportion between her upper and lower halves. A traditional long blazer ending below the buttocks can actually do more harm than

good. This is because it magnifies the imbalance by not fitting well. To counter this, choose a cropped jacket that falls to your high hip, just below your waist. It will fit better. Do not hide yourself in excess fabric to cover the lower half of your body. Your goal is to put the focus on the upper half of your body with a well-fitted, terrific jacket.

A second option is a rounded shirttail hem that provides some coverage for your tummy and creates the illusion of a longer torso. This should fit well through the shoulders and not give you excess fabric, which you must avoid.

A third option is a sweater coat with a swing style. This style has an exaggerated A-line shape and is very full at the bottom. Choose fingertip-length in a dark or rich color.

Style Details

Use rich style details that broaden your upper half, such as wide lapels. Velvets, metallic trims and brocades with their woven designs from rich yarns work well. A denim jacket or vest cropped to your high hip or even a shirttail style could become a casual staple in your wardrobe. Pear shape diamonds are blessed, because they can use color on a jacket or vest to boost their overall looks as long as the garment does not extend too low, which would magnify their larger lower halves.

If you choose the fingertip-length sweater coat, keep the color dark and rich (as it is now covering your lower half as well). Opt for flat wools like matte jersey, merino or cashmere. Again, the key is a soft drape. Vertical details, like leather piping—decorative trim on the seams—and other tonal embellishments, are interesting and slenderizing.

Round Shape Diamond
Trench-Style Raincoat
Shape

The round shape diamond can wear the traditional style trench coat. This is a style that can take you anywhere, from a casual football game to a dressy occasion over a dress or pants suit. There is a reason that this style raincoat has been copied every which way; it works! To wear this coat well, the woman should have a noticeable natural waist.

I am a round shape diamond and although I can wear a belted style, I often prefer the comfort of a beltless or half-belt style. However, if you have a waist, show it off.

Style Details
Keep the details traditional. There is no improvement on perfection, the wool collar, leather covered buttons, hacked pockets and epaulets. You may opt for a single-breasted look (the traditional look is double-breasted, which has two parallel rows of buttons) and of course, there is no reason to buy the name brand synonymous with this style—many designers have replicated the style beautifully and for much less money.

Dressy Overcoat and Car Coat
Shape
I often choose a balmacaan style because of the sleeve. It is an easy fit with raglan sleeves that are not confining. There is a generous quality through the bust and down through the hips.

Any coat with princess seaming is beautiful on the round shape diamond, such as chesterfield (semi-fitted and straight cut), reefer (based on British brass-buttoned Navy coats) or wrap (closed with a sash) styles.

Contemporary versions of the traditional peacoat are very flattering as well. They tend to be fitted, but with ease, and they are longer in length than they were a generation ago. This provides coverage and confidence through the hip, covering the backside.

Style Details
This is an area where less is more. Choose substantially beautiful materials for the coat's construction and avoid too much embellishment. Go for a classic, bold but elegant look. To me, this is very sexy. Good coats in soft rich wools remind me of the sirens of old movies—think Kim Novak in Alfred Hitchcock's *Vertigo*.

Blazer and Vest
Shape
Choose a shaped blazer. The traditional riding coat is the best choice. It is single-breasted, skims the hourglass figure and its longer length is more flattering. It also extends the vertical line below fuller areas (tummy, hips and buttocks).

A cardigan style jacket or sweater is also a good choice, because it offers a vertical line through the middle where the sweater opens. Keep the fabrication flat and soft.

Style Details
Again, I prefer to keep the details to a minimum. Princess seaming in the construction of the garment is detail enough. Single-breasted is a much more slenderizing option than double-breasted. The single vertical line of buttons is an elongating detail or you could choose no buttons at all.

Vests have become the backbone of my casual wardrobe. I have several. Interestingly, all of them are reversible, which, of course, gives me two options per vest. Usually one side is a more vibrant color. In that case, I'll wear a dark, monochromatic top and bottom with the vibrant side of the vest showing. In the alternative, I'll wear the darker side of the vest showing with slacks or a skirt of the same color and a white T-shirt or turtleneck sweater underneath.

Heart Shape Diamond
Trench-Style Raincoat
Shape
The heart shape diamond is opposite of the pear shape diamond. Some of same principles will apply, but in reverse. The goal is to achieve the illusion of balance between the upper and lower half of the body. I recommend the trench style raincoat. The balmacaan style, full through the shoulders and bust and then straight through the hips and legs, creates the impression of grace and balance.

Style Details
Where the pear shape diamond wants attention at the top through embellishment, the heart shape diamond does not. The heart shape diamond is looking for elongation and simplicity. One way to achieve this is through a mandarin collar, which extends the vertical line upwards. Another way is to use leather covered buttons and leather trim though the entire button placket thereby imposing a vertical, lengthening line in the raincoat. I recommend choosing a traditional fabric and color, British tan or khaki. The fabric should lie flat and, of course, be waterproof. This must be a beltless style.

Dressy Overcoat and Car Coat
Shape
In addition to the balmacaan style, the cape style is a good choice, especially a three-quarter length, which displays the heart shape diamond's slender and shapely legs.

Style Details
Since the heart shape diamond is full through the shoulders and chest, keep the details to a minimum. However, choose rich flat fabrics that are dark in color.

Blazer and Vest
Shape
The heart shape diamond can wear a loosely-woven (called hopsack) or unstructured jacket well. Falling to the lower hip, just past the tummy where the body begins to narrow, these style coats cover the fuller area of the body and show off the more slender lower half. Most vests are cut in this shape as well and so this garment should be a staple in the heart shape diamond's casual wardrobe.

Style Details
The heart shape diamond enjoys the benefit of pairing a dark toned upper garment, jacket or vest, with a more lively color or print below, skirt, skort

or slacks. This is a great look and will achieve balance through the strategic placement of color.

Marquise Shape Diamond
Trench-Style Raincoat
Shape

The marquise shape diamond, narrow in the shoulders and hips but with a full tummy, can wear several styles well. A favorite is the Chesterfield style trench coat. Not only does it have princess seaming for a graceful style, but it also begins its indentation and shaping just under the bust, which allows more room for a gentle A-line effect, gradually widening over the tummy and through the rest of the coat. Also, because it is a classic design, it tends to be more tailored and fitted, which works well for the marquise shape diamond's shoulders and hips, where she doesn't need extra fabric and size.

Style Details

The traditional details—wool collar, leather covered buttons, epaulets and hacked pockets—in the traditional color can create the look you are after without the traditional belt, which should be avoided.

Dressy Overcoat and Car Coat
Shape

The Chesterfield or Reefer style coat works well. The marquise shape diamond needs to cover a full tummy with a total, uninterrupted vertical line. Any style that is fitted in the shoulders but gradually widens just under the bust is flattering. Additionally, the marquise shape can wear a seven-eighths swing coat as long as it closes with buttons and not a belt or sash. This is an area your seamstress can help. If you love a style that comes with a belt, take it to your seamstress and have her remove the belt loops and add two pretty fasteners at the bust.

Style Details

Choose embellishment at the collar and cuffs, but keep it simple through the middle. Fabrics that lay flat and drape will always be more flattering. Avoid fabrics that are stiff, like some canvases, suedes and leathers, as they will cling to your tummy and protrude out from that point, suggesting that you are full all the way down.

Blazer and Vest

Shape

Depending on the size of her tummy, the marquise shape diamond may be able to wear a fitted jacket or vest. However, if this is not an option, the advice provided to the heart shape diamond applies: a hopsack or unconstructed jacket works well. As the body begins to narrow past the tummy, these style coats will highlight slender hips and legs, which will look very attractive. Most vests are cut in this shape as well and so this garment should be a staple in the marquise shape diamond's casual wardrobe.

Style Details

Because the marquise shape diamond is more slender though the shoulders and the hips, she should look for vibrant coloration in those areas. Color blocking, the strategic use of large squares of color, contrasted with darker, more subtle tones can be a very complimentary effect.

Emerald Shape Diamond

Trench-Style Raincoat

Shape

The emerald shape diamond must look for coats that fabricate shape, as she tends to be wide and straight from shoulder through the hips. Fortunately, shape is not too difficult to find in coats. Look for a trench coat in the reefer style with a gentle A-line from the bust through the hemline, which is very shapely.

In addition, the balmacaan style, graceful and straight from the shoulders through the hemline, is a great style to choose. Similar to the round shape diamond, who is not comfortable wearing a belted style, this style coat provides coverage and comfort while looking very elegant.

Style Details

Choose a style with the traditional trench coat details: capelet at the shoulders, epaulets, leather covered buttons, hacked pockets and detail at the cuffs in the traditional colors of British tan, khaki or cream.

Dressy Overcoat and Car Coat

Shape

Pick the same style for your overcoat or car coat as your trench coat, either a reefer or balmacaan style, as you'll never go wrong. In addition, a seven-eighths length swing car coat works well too. The contemporary version of the peacoat is attractive on the emerald shape diamond too. It offers shape, a gentle A-line and length several inches below the back-side that is flattering. For the emerald shape diamond, I recommend the double-breasted style, as long as the buttons are placed fairly close together and the vertical quality is dominate.

Style Details

Keep the coat collarless and the fabric softly skimming the body. Soft suede or leather and draping wools are flattering. The trim should be vertical; leather piping or a simple placket of buttons may be enough.

Blazer and Vest

Shape

Jackets can be worn open and should be fairly simple in design and embellishment. Whatever is worn underneath must fit close to the body and not add any additional bulk. A tailored look is very attractive. In this way, the wearer is fabricating both shape and style.

Style Details

A collarless, draped design for knit jackets, sweaters and vests works well too. In addition, the blouson jacket, worn open, is a terrific option. Match the tone (not necessarily the exact color) of the blouson jacket with the slacks, jeans or skirt you choose for a vertical effect.

If you choose a vest, keep it long. A tunic style works well. Keep all embellishments (zipper or buttons) running down the center of the garment to enhance the vertical effect.

CHAPTER 7

Shoes

FIND YOUR
SOLE MATE!

"I don't know who invented the high heel, but all men owe him a lot."
~Marilyn Monroe

I am now going to offer a perspective that may seem harsh, but remember, I am a curvy woman, too. If you are heavy and weigh around the 200 pound mark or upwards, this chapter will skyrocket your sex appeal, because it will radically change your knowledge about shoes and will empower you to purchase and wear drop-dead gorgeous and, at the same time, comfortable shoes. I will discuss specific brands as well as the elements of a shoe's design and construction that you need to be knowledgeable about in order to make good choices. This chapter intends to do three things for you: Dismiss the notion that style and comfort are mutually exclusive, empower you to select comfortable and stylish shoes and help you build your shoe wardrobe immediately.

There is no way to appear assured and sexy when your feet hurt. It changes everything—from an aching body, feet, legs and back to an aching and disillusioned spirit. Heck, it even hurts to put on uncomfortable shoes when you get dressed in the morning. Anticipating the entire day in uncomfortable shoes is a painful experience in and of itself. Uncomfortable shoes change the way we walk, how much we walk and how much we complain about walking. Bad shoes, no matter how beautiful they are, are just that—bad.

The corollary is bad, too. Many women have opted out of choosing good-looking shoes and instead wear shoes that should be restricted to gardening or work as a correctional officer in a maximum security prison. This brings me to an interesting comparison.

Look at how men's shoes are constructed. Hold the shoe in your hands. Feel the weight. Look at the stitching, the sole (bottom) and the heel (the part that elevates the foot). Pinch the leather between your index finger and thumb. Press down on the arch, the built-up portion that supports the arch or center of the foot, and feel its construction. Rub your hand along the leather of the insole, the portion inside the shoe where the foot rests. You can see and feel how a man's weight is well distributed, stabilized and supported in shoes.

Now take an attractive shoe (other than a sneaker) out of your closet and do the same thing. Note the differences between the two shoes, in terms of its construction, weight, stitching, sole, heel, arch and insole, as well as the leather of the upper area (above the sole). I think you see my point. While we, as curvy women, weigh substantially the same as our male counterparts, our shoes are flimsy, lack support and stability and are basically inadequate to perform the task assigned: to make us look good and feel good. Often we succumb to the two options we know: Wear shoes that make us physically ache (and thereby we look dreadful) or wear dreadful shoes that cause our spirits to ache and diminish our style before we even get out the door.

Only Good Shoes Worn Here

To begin, buy good shoes. This is the most important area in which to spend your fashion dollars, especially initially. It's better to have three pairs of good shoes than two dozen pairs of cheap shoes. This is a good example of where less is more. At the conclusion of this chapter you will be able to purchase three pairs of shoes that will change and improve your appearance immediately; it will also change how you present yourself as a consumer forever. In addition, I will offer a few options that will save you money in both the short and long runs.

Cheap shoes cause you to present yourself unenthusiastically, whether you are aware of this or not. Firstly, inexpensive shoes begin to look bad very quickly. Secondly, heavy women are hard on shoes for obvious reasons: weight and posture. Thirdly, it makes curvy women look particularly heavy and unkempt when they shuffle or walk in a way that projects discomfort. This is one of the gross inequities of life. If a thin person appears to be uncomfortable when she walks, it is attributed to her shoes. If a heavy person appears to be uncomfortable when she walks, it is attributed to being slovenly, out of shape and untidy.

First Step

Go to a quality shoe store or the shoe section of an upscale department store and ask to have your feet measured. Stand up straight and stand firmly on the measuring device. To get an accurate measurement, do not shift your weight to the foot not being measured. If this stirs up feelings of being weighed publicly, get over it. This is not about pounds; it is about shoe size. Now do it with the other foot. Yes, both feet need to be correctly measured by a professional. Don't try to do it yourself. How do you know if you were measured by a professional? She will give you more information than just your shoe size.

First, she will give you the length and width of your left foot and your right foot. You may notice they are not the same. Second, she will give you insight about the width of your foot at the ball of your foot, the widest part, and at the heel of your foot. Third, she will tell you about the length of your toes. She may also discuss the arch (or lack thereof) of your foot. You may be thinking that this seems complicated and wondering if it is really necessary. Yes it is, if you want to make a good selection of shoes for yourself. Why? Because shoes are manufactured for average feet. Yet who among us is average? Shoes are manufactured assuming both feet match. Yet they rarely do.

In my own case, my left foot measures 8.75 inches wide. My right foot measures 9.5 inches wide. The forefronts of my feet are wide and I have a severe bunion at one of the joints of my right foot. My heels are relatively narrow, and my toes are short. You can see the challenge I face every time I buy shoes.

If you were measured but weren't told the type of information I just revealed about myself, you don't have the right sales professional. You must seek this person out. Go to a store that carries the brands I refer to in my following discussion and find a person there with many years of experience in the shoe business. Years ago, there was a different level of knowledge and responsibility associated with fitting shoes properly. That is one of the things we have lost in our quick-paced, quick to throw out society. In other words, find a salesperson who evokes knowledge and confidence. You will also be surprised by her knowledge of style, too, but we'll discuss that later in this chapter. Establish a relationship with a knowledgeable salesperson in a store whose shoes you love. She'll give you good advice and alert you to upcoming sales. She will do minor repairs and adjustments. Further, shoes often come in a wider variety of sizes and styles than the particular store carries; she can locate and order them for you to try on at no additional charge.

When you have found a salesperson who can give you the type of information I shared about my own feet and whom you feel you trust, you can begin to shop for beautiful, comfortable shoes. Importantly, this person will know the tricks of the trade and will use padding, placed and glued under the insole, to give you the best possible fit for both feet. There should be no extra charge for this service.

Be a Name Dropper

"To name is to limit" is a common saying, but that is certainly not my intention here. Rather, these brand names encompass a change in our thinking as consumers about what a shoe must accomplish to deserve to be purchased. The reciprocal is true as well: These brands reflect a changing respect some manufacturers are developing to compete for curvy women's shoe dollars. What I present here is a beginning, but certainly not an end, in the quest for comfortable, great-looking shoes.

Casual Shoes

Casual, comfortable shoes are naturally easier to discuss, so let's begin there. By casual shoes, I mean shoes to be worn with slacks, jeans, shorts, skorts and sporty skirts and dresses.

This is probably where most of your life will happen—in casual, comfortable shoes—so it is important to think about three things to the end of comfort and style: the shape, the materials and the construction of the shoe.

The casual shoe should be stylish, pretty and feminine. The shape of the shoe can be either tailored or a bit chunky, but nevertheless it should be flattering to your legs. I make this distinction, because while some shoes are pretty in and of themselves, they may look too slight on the feet in terms of balance for the larger woman. While other shoes— the sporty clog with its thick sole and open back, the mule with its loafer style or wedgies with wedge-shaped heels connected to the arches, for example—may not look feminine on the shelf in the store. However, when worn, they give great shape and balance to your overall contour. When a sport clog is done in pretty materials, it is a very acceptable option and also gives the added bonus of height. This type of shoe often has thick polyurethane soles and will give you great comfort and shock absorbance too.

There are a host of great looks in the marketplace today. Some use fun fabrics, finishes and embellishments, some reference rich leathers, others evidence a sports inclination and still others remind us of a sporty mule. The materials used on the upper portion of the shoe must be durable and must continue to look fresh and clean for at least a season (if not several). This has implications: Can you wipe them off with a damp cloth? Will dirt show? Will the embellishments fade or fall off? What about color? The best color for a casual shoe is a neutral shade that is consistent with your skin tone to elongate the leg. If, however, you wear a lot of one particular color, the casual shoe is a great place to continue your personalized look. While I wear a great deal of black in my clothing, black casual shoes can look harsh and heavy. A black sole on a casual shoe of another color looks, in my opinion, like an orthopedic necessity. Instead, look for materials that are lighter, softer and prettier in inference.

Some of the brand names I have tried on and wear myself include Aerosoles, Merrell, Privo by Clarks, Dansko, ASGI, Sofft, Munro, Pikolinos, Mephisto, Cole Haan-Nike Air and Stuart Weitzman.

First, Sofft, Munro and Stuart Weitzman offer different widths: narrow, medium and wide (Munro offers a double wide size as well). Aerosoles offers a few styles in wide widths. Pikolinos and Dansko reflect European sizing, so while they only offer a medium width, they tend to be cut fuller.

Recently, I purchased a pair of Dansko clogs that are enclosed at the heel and patent leather leopard print on a two inch platform. Why was this a good choice? I had been getting quite a bit of arthritic pain in my hip and back, going down into my leg. Then I realized that the problem was that I needed to better stabilize and distribute my weight with additional support for my foot as I walked. These clogs are a pair of "industrial strength" shoes. My husband thinks they're attractive, but likened them to shoes a cartoon character would wear because of the "bubble" effect in their toe box. This feature is helpful for women with bad bunions, but they narrow through the instep, creating contrast and shape for style. The construction is very solid, almost stiff, but still allows my foot to move and bend as I walk. In addition, the materials from which the shoes are made are fun and pretty. Yes, the shoes are chunky and I probably wouldn't wear them with a skirt, but they do give me a two-inch lift and some style to wear with slacks. This is an example of compromise: you give and you get.

My custom is to gently wear new shoes around the house, leaving my option to return the purchase intact. I found with this pair that my feet felt as comfortable as slippers. Further, they offered support to the rest of my body (mainly my back, hips and legs) that gave me overall comfort that was very valuable. This brings me to an important point about shoes that are comfortable to the foot, but compromise overall posture. When a shoe is large, floppy and shapeless and offers no support, the wearer tends to compensate and walk in a way designed to keep the shoe from falling off, whether or not the wearer is conscious of this. This is a significant detriment to the overall alignment of the body and creates an unattractive quality of loping when walking.

Pikolinos, Merrell, Munro and Clarks Privo offer soles that purportedly boost energy, absorb shock and offer a type of reflexology treatment when you walk. I can't confirm all these claims, but they do feel quite good. Aerosoles offers extra cushioned footbeds with breathable leather linings and flexible rubber soles. ASGI offers a new shoe design called pods, which look rather futuristic; they are protrusions from the sole of the shoe that claim to support and distribute weight. Certainly, an admirable goal.

Munro and Pikolinos have removable insoles that allow you to put your own orthotics in the shoes. For those of us with real foot challenges, this may be among the most important breakthroughs in shoe design and construction. Having your own orthotics in your shoes allows you to have a fully customized fit every time you go out your door!

One more word about Munro: Some people may think Munro shoes are not trendy or "in." However, they more than make up for it with classic, trim, good-looking styles, a great use of microfiber stretch fabrics (which wear great and comfortably) and height through sporty heels, usually one to two inches. In terms of internal construction, they are superb. Munro shoes offer a metal shank (under the arch) for support and stability, include removable sock liners (insoles) for your own orthotics, boast latex bottoms and, made in the United States, are a great value at about ninety dollars per pair. If you are really shoe challenged in terms of fit and fashion, you can't go wrong with Munro.

What are these great casual shoes going to cost? Aerosoles, Merrell and Munro are the bargains here, costing seventy to ninety dollars per pair. Clarks Privo, Dansko and ASGI, are the medium priced lines, costing between one hundred dollars and $130 per pair. Pikolino, Mephisto and Stuart Weitzman are the higher end lines, costing $150 to $250 per pair. To price the cost and obtain details of orthotics, contact a podiatrist or conduct research online. In addition, some health insurance companies will offset the cost of orthotics. Remember, use the same orthotics in all of your shoes of a similar category, be it casual, dressy or sporty, which requires enough depth in the shoes to accommodate them.

Dressy Shoes

You need to wear heels to slenderize and balance your proportion by creating a leg lengthening effect. I am not talking about four-inch or higher stilettos, but rather a range of heels from kitten heels one inch high through sculpted and stacked heels of two to three inches. Sculpted heels have a broad, medium heel and stacked heels have layers of leather or wood creating a thick heel. I have not forgotten my promise of comfort: physical and emotional comfort is foundational. The fact is that heels are beautiful and sexy and not antithetical to comfort. I will agree, however, that there is a tradeoff: some comfort for some style.

Foot structure may be hereditary, but that doesn't mean you need to wear shoes that resemble your grandmother's. When shopping for dressy shoes it is important to wear hosiery and a skirt or slacks that approximate the outfit you want to complement and to look in a full-length mirror to see the entire effect. Go to the store armed with your Essential Index Card listing outfits you need shoes for and be prepared to try on several pairs of shoes in order to be a discriminating buyer. Buying heels should be a joy, because you can boost your style and sex appeal as quickly as it takes to slip on the "glass slipper."

When buying heels, you need to look for several criteria. The first is heel height. How high of a heel can you wear without giving up comfort? Begin with this, because it will limit and focus your selection right way. No matter how beautiful or how much of a bargain the shoe is, if you can't walk comfortably, you won't look good in it and you will be wasting your money. On the other hand, don't stubbornly say, "I can't wear heels." Yes you can. Try a kitten heel first; it may only be one inch high. But if the shape of the heel is pretty and feminine, it will give you a lift to balance your proportion.

The second criterion has to do with the shape of the heel. Look for a sculpted heel, which, as the name implies, has a gently rounded shape. A sculpted heel tends to reflect your own curves in a pretty way. Moreover, a stacked heel, often made of wood, is a good choice. Not covered in leather, it tends to wear better and you won't have those awful gashes and digs that leather heels get after only a few wearings. A chunky, square heel can be attractive too, if it has modern lines and some height. In fact, if it has good proportion to the rest of the shoe, it can be an excellent balance to a larger frame. However, here is the key detail: Some portion of the shoe design has to be sleek and have an architectural quality, otherwise it will look dowdy and outdated.

The third criterion is the shoe's throat or vamp (the part that covers your instep and toes), how the shoe frames the instep of your foot. Look for shoes that have a sweetheart throat (a line that follows the letter V), which lengthens feet and slims ankles. Another good choice is the classic shorter vamp, because it shows some toe cleavage, the separation between toes—very sexy—and, again, lengthens the foot. The latter is not usually a good option for me, because a short vamp tends to hit right on my bunion—ouch! My point is to watch where the cut of the shoe hits your tricky spots.

The fourth criterion is the toe box, which is the portion that covers the toes. The classic, gently pointed toe box is the most flattering universally. Why? Because it elongates the feet and therefore the legs. Remember when I mentioned that I had short toes? By knowing this, I also know my toes tend to fit in a pointed toe box and I can often benefit from the sleeker look. Knowledge is power, or in this case, knowledge yields a slimming effect. However, other toe box shapes work well too: rounded, square, open toe or closed. My suggestion is to keep it simple and updated yet classic and clean.

The fifth criterion is the sole of the shoe, platform or flexible. Shoes built on platforms give you a boost in height. It actually absorbs up to an inch of the heel height in terms of the contrast between the height of your heel and the rest of your foot. Personally, I like platforms for this reason and several other reasons. Platforms gives me stability when I walk, I don't feel every pebble on the ground and they give additional cushion that absorbs shock between my foot and the ground. Sometimes they are in the form of wedges (wedgies) and sometimes chunky heels.

However, some people prefer flexible soles. Flexible soles allow the shoes to "break in" faster. They also allow more movement and flex in the insteps. This is a matter of personal preference. If you are seeking to achieve a graceful and elegant style, flexible soles will be your best bet. Make sure that there is material and cushion on the bottom of the shoes as well as under the insoles of the shoes to absorb the shock of each step taken. In addition, look for shoes with arches that distribute your weight. Otherwise, the front pads of your feet will burn with discomfort.

The sixth criterion involves the materials used to construct the shoes. Recall the discussion of men's shoes. Women's heels need to be made of substantial materials, offering support and durability. I have several manufacturers to recommend that use the same good materials again and again.

The bargain shoe is Sofft. They have a good selection of high quality shoes, good design, substantial materials and shock absorbing features. The shoes come in varied widths of narrow, medium and wide. The toe boxes tend to be rounded and pretty, but not sleek. The price is about seventy to ninety dollars. This is an admirable high heel for work and can transition well for evening events, if needed.

Vaneli offers a huge selection of dressy shoes in a wide range of widths: AAA, AA, B, W (very narrow to wide) and a few styles in extra wide. The shoes are lovely, stylish and executed in current colors and fabrics. The construction is decent and the prices are between one hundred dollars and $130.

The next brand rises in cost, but is esteemed: Cole Haan-Nike Air. These heels are very attractive, modern and a bit more comfortable than others. There are many models to choose from, classic and modern designs and vivid and neutral colors. I saw a display of several models in fire engine red the other day. These shoes purport to have superior construction and good padding at the forefronts of your feet. The median price for this brand is $275. Unfortunately, the shoes are offered only in medium width, so I can't wear this product and thus can't personally vouch for their comfort and wear.

In terms of appeal, my personal favorite is Stuart Weitzman. These shoes come in various widths: narrow, medium and wide. In my opinion, they are among the most beautiful shoes in the marketplace today, even compared to the more expensive designer lines. Stuart Weitzman uses classic, luxurious finishes. Though these shoes are expensive (approximately $225 to $275 per pair), with some luck I have been able to buy them on sale at Nordstrom. Here's the downside: the soles are not usually very thick. For more comfort, I buy them a half size larger than I need and have padding in the form of additional insoles glued under the original insoles. The shoes from the brand Ferragamo tend to be similar to Stuart Weitzman shoes in all of the areas I just mentioned.

A discussion of high-end comfort heels would not be complete without mentioning Taryn Rose, a relative newcomer to the scene. Taryn Rose shoes are beautifully constructed, made of soft comfortable materials and have built-in arches (I believe they are the only product that can boast this). They are very stylish and fresh. Mostly outside my price range, they cost about $300 to $450 per pair.

A word of caution: I bought a pair of silver wedgies from an unnamed manufacturer in an expensive shoe boutique, charming to look at and they felt comfortable in the store. Suffice it to say, they were not so comfortable an hour after wearing them to work.

Footwear Favorites
- Nude (nude for you), soft tones in both color and texture elongate your feet, legs and body. Any time you can select shoes that are consistent with your skin tone or hosiery tone, you will create an

optical illusion of an additional couple of inches of height. Be sure the bottom half of the shoe matches the upper half. Choose a nude color over black or dark brown shoes.

- Metallic finishes also elongate and lighten the appearance of your feet, your step and, frankly, your whole persona. They are softer and richer and will enhance anything you are wearing. Use soft, burnished tones rather than loud, high intensity finishes. Think about replacing several pairs of shoes with one pair with a metallic finish.

- Sandals and pedicured feet go hand in hand. Sandals are an open, fresh and sexy look. Wear platform sandals for additional height. Try on different sandal styles until you find one that slenderizes your feet and legs while still respecting the peculiarities of your foot, thus giving you lots of comfort. I buy the same style year after year. I prefer a thong style with a cork sole, which is very shock absorbent.

- Good-looking black mules or clogs (think an updated trim look) and black opaque hosiery (Just My Size, five dollars per pair and they last forever) give you instant longer, slimmer legs. Wear a black pencil skirt made with Lycra or a skort. With this combination of shoes, skirt and opaque hosiery, say goodbye to varicose and spider veins and say hello to a youthful, sporty and casually comfortable staple.

- Some boots also elongate and slenderize the legs. Choose ankle boots with stylish, comfortable heels. Hem your slacks or jeans so they touch the boot at the insteps (or even a quarter of an inch more). Choose simple, good quality tall black or brown leather boots that come up just a bit higher than where your skirt ends. I recommend Silhouettes for boots (about one hundred dollars to $150 per pair). They have extra wide calves (seventeen inches or nineteen inches) and many widths, sizes and heel heights to choose from. Make sure to choose the correct height of the boot too, as tall as fits you well (usually thirteen or fourteen inches). Keep it simple; buy the best leather with the simplest lines.

- Shoe inserts improve the comfort level of high heels, such as the products from Foot Petals, Divine Drops and Heelmates (about nineteen dollars for a few pairs). These are a must—try them out! They are often displayed at the checkout counters of upscale shoe departments. You must cushion the forefronts of your feet or the reality is you will not wear high heels—and that would be a pity.

Footwear Faux Pas

- Don't wear shoes with ankle straps. Cutting the legs at the ankles does the opposite of what we are striving for. Remember, you are always seeking to lengthen your look; don't chop it up.
- Don't wear shoes that have high vamps; it thickens ankles and legs. Think about showing skin and elongating your look!
- Never wear white shoes with dark hosiery. Visually, it cuts your legs off and makes you look shorter and heavier than you are.
- Don't wear shoes if your feet spill over or seem to bulge out. If this happens, it is not the right style or size for you and you don't have to settle for that. Consider shoes with microfiber stretch to give you the coverage you may need.
- Don't allow shoes to appear uncared for and worn. Find a cobbler who will perform at least three routine jobs on a regular basis. The first job is to attach taps to the tips of your new, unworn shoes to reduce scuffing and signs of premature wear. The second job is to replace lifts on a frequent basis, every two to three months if needed. The third job is to replace the entire soles of shoes annually, if needed. Cobblers can also do miracles by stretching a particular part of a shoe to improve fit. They also repair shoes and other leather goods to keep you looking sharp while spending minimal amounts of money.

Moreover, there are a few jobs you can do at home. If the shoes are made of fabric or suede, you should condition them against the elements to keep the shoes looking their best for the longest period possible. You can purchase conditioning sprays at the checkout counters of shoe stores or shoe departments for about eight dollars and condition them yourself. Also, there are other wonderful shoe care products for use at home. One in particular is a small sponge infused with a light shoe polish, used to clean and buff for a great, fresh finish.

If you are alarmed by the costs of the shoes I mentioned, you will be happy to know that with minimal care and rotation (don't wear the same shoes every day) your shoes will last for a few years. This is the basis for building a wardrobe of shoes: general maintenance, restoring good shoes and replacing shoes only when necessary. Often your cobbler will be the best judge of when it is necessary to replace shoes.

Off and Running—Building Your Sexy and Sensational Shoe Wardrobe

If I was told I could have only four pairs of shoes in my closet for fall, winter, spring and summer or that I needed to rebuild my footwear wardrobe from scratch with an approximate budget of $500, here is what I would buy from the brand names to which I have already referred:

1. One pair of pumps with a metallic finish, sleek, pointed toe boxes and two inch stacked, sculpted heels—or kitten heels—for all professional and dressy needs.
2. One pair of mules or clogs in black suede on thick rubberized platform soles with about two inches of height for casual wear with jeans, slacks, skirts and skorts. (I chose black, because I wear a lot of black and the continuous line from my slacks or hosiery to my shoes elongates my leg line.)
3. One pair of Munro wedges, which would serve double duty as sandals and pumps, in a somewhat enclosed style with subtle copper metallic microfiber stretch fabric for casual and professional wear with all types of clothing.
4. One pair of black (or brown) leather boots, knee high in a classic, unadorned style with two inch stacked heels and a subtle latex bottom underneath both heels and soles for casual and dressy wear with slacks, jeans, skirts and dresses.

CHAPTER 8

Accessories Rock!

THE WEAR-WITH-ALL
TO LOOK GREAT

"Remember that always dressing in understated good taste is the same as playing dead." ~Susan Catherine

A woman needs to be clear about her style. Style is about attitude and the image you want to present to the world. For us curvy women, much of fashion, in terms of clothing, is dictated by fit, and shoes may be limited by comfort. But when it comes to accessories, the sky's the limit and the opportunity to create "focus"—meaningful attention and expression—abounds. The plus size woman should revel in this opportunity.

Create your image. This is where the Pretty Party Portfolio comes into play. Become aware of the things you admire on other women when you're out and about or when perusing a fashion magazine. I'm a bit of a voyeur, I must admit. I love to watch people. Perhaps this is where the teacher in me surfaces; I'm continually grading those I observe, especially on their accessories. I assess two distinct objectives. First, does she use accessories in a fun and uplifting manner or just a perfunctory one? Second, does she use accessories effectively to present a clear image, whether it is luxurious, feminine, sexy, preppy, athletic, ethnic or artistic?

Strive for consistency—this is how you build a wardrobe. A little of this and a little of that or "this is cute" won't get it done. Do not make an accessory purchase until you can identify the image that you want to make your own. Do not take the tags off an item until you build a matching set of accessories and keep the receipts in a designated shoe box.

Here's a tip from my interior designer that may be helpful. If you are seeking a new design when redecorating a room (colors, style or function of furniture and treatments), do not make new purchases that serve as a bridge between the old and the new. Only purchase items that clearly contribute and are necessary to the new design, even though you will not execute it in full immediately. Said another way, restrict yourself to purchases that reflect your new, clear style.

Ladies' accessories include handbags, shoes, small leather goods, key fobs, scarves, eyeglasses, sunglasses, totes, umbrellas, luggage, coats and jewelry. In this book, shoes, coats and jewelry are covered in separate chapters, but their roles should be considered in the context of developing your individual style and in developing a matching or consistent set of accessories as well.

In chapter 1, we discussed the design elements of shape, line, color, balance, proportion and texture. An understanding of these concepts is critical to making wise accessory purchases. While I tend to keep my clothing simple and classic, I love to use accessories for a vivid touch of the fabulous. I don't buy a lot, because I already have developed a wardrobe of accessories. Importantly, this is an area where I think a woman can get a lot of bang for her fashion buck without breaking the bank. A woman who has done her research can replicate designer accessories by recalling the six design principles. The key to doing this successfully is consistency. Cut out pages of accessories you love from magazines. Circle the design elements you see with a marker pen and label them: "squared gold tone hardware," "hammered silver tone hardware," "tan mock-crocodile," etc. By doing so, you are implying that this is the distinguishing element of the item and will serve as the common denominator for all of the accessories you will select.

You can purchase accessories that have elements similar to the expensive items you covet, but spend a fraction of their cost. The malls are full of stores with terrific accessories. Target, H&M, Loehmann's, TJ

Maxx, Marshall's and Sears all have terrific options when you shop with an informed eye. Obviously, if you can afford it, upscale accessories will boost your wardrobe a great deal, but the same rules of design apply regardless of what you can afford.

At first, you do not need several of one item or sets of accessories. Begin with a stylish handbag, tote, umbrella, scarf, pair of sunglasses, raincoat, pair of leather gloves and hat (seasonally). Strive for items that are bold, impressive and strongly evidentiary of your emerging style. Use color, designer characteristics, striking hardware or details to unify this group of accessories. You do not need a matching set of accessories in the obvious way; for example, the Burberry nova check black and tan plaid. However, there must be a distinctly unifying influence among all the accessories. This set of accessories can pull your look together at any given time. There are times I have to run out on an errand and don't have time to dress the way I want. Give me a pair of black jeans and a well-cut black top with a colorful vest or a warm-up suit, matching top and bottom with a set of accessories such as described here and I'll appear well-dressed and pulled together, casually and effortlessly.

Handbags

Many women, including myself, have love affairs with handbags. I love good handbags for many reasons. Firstly, they never suggest they would look a lot better if I lost ten pounds. Secondly, I trust my handbags to carry and even organize my busy life. Thirdly, good handbags allow me to make a statement about my lifestyle or, frankly, the lifestyle of which I dream. There is a saying, "you never get a second chance to make a first impression." I believe that and I'm willing to bet my pocketbook on it.

Before you shop for a handbag, please consider a few things: size, function, straps, durability and style. Large women need large handbags. The concept of proportion is not only important in terms of the comparison of the elements within an outfit but also in terms of how the proportion of the item relates to the wearer. Small handbags on a large woman make her look awkward and unrefined as well as magnify her size.

The function of a handbag is important, too. How many things does a women need to carry in her handbag? Will she be able to use an additional tote bag or briefcase or does the bag need to be large enough to carry everything? Will she need to choose a bag that has organizational features, such as cell phone, business card and pen pockets, zippered compartments for makeup or medicine or outside pockets for papers to be tucked away neatly?

Comfort between a woman and her handbag is critical. This is where the straps come in. The first thing I look for in a handbag is whether it has double straps. Sometimes I like to carry my bag in the grip of my hand, other times I like to put it on my shoulder and still other times I like to put it across my body and let it hang to one side to free my hands completely. Straps should be wide and durable but soft enough to be comfortable.

The handbag needs to look fresh and in good repair for at least one entire season. That said, there is nothing wrong with a distressed look in a handbag as long as that is the intended look. Also, handbags can be carried for several seasons. I'm using my fall/winter bag for a fourth season. Some of the dressy bags I own I have had for more than ten years. Therefore, consider the construction of the bag. Is the leather or fabric durable? Can it be wiped or easily cleaned? Does the zipper or hardware seem sturdy? Do the straps seem likely to be able to carry the weight of the contents of the bag without appearing stretched?

Now, for the fun part, the style of the handbag is your playground! Your fashion statement will be a combination of how you select the shape, fabric, color, texture and embellishments of your handbag.

Shape

For everyday handbags there are essentially six shapes that handbag designers work with, all of which look great on the plus size woman assuming the supporting features are large and impressive enough.

The drawstring bag tends to have a soft and supple finish. It is a bag that has a more casual quality. The shape is somewhat cylindrical and it usually has a pretty string or tassel at the drawstring that is a great finishing touch. I find that personal effects tend to fall to the bottom and are not easily retrieved. However, to counter this, you can use delightful small accessories for organization, such as cases for eyeglasses, makeup, business cards or a checkbook. The strap has about a ten-inch drop and the bag usually falls around your waist. For this reason, pear and round (with defined waist) shape diamonds will enjoy this style bag, because it will draw attention to their main feature: their waists.

The hobo bag is similar to the drawstring bag and has a soft, casual finish. It is even more unconstructed (floppy) than the drawstring bag. It tends to be larger and the drop from the shoulder is often shorter, about seven to eight inches. With the hobo bag you might trade the pretty embellishment of the drawstring for exterior pockets or great stitching and a rich, supple exterior material such as suede. In terms of organization, the same is true as the drawstring bag: items will fall to the bottom. The hobo bag tends to fit snugly under one's arm, thereby drawing attention to the bust. This type of bag is flattering for pear and marquise shape diamonds, but not for heart and emerald shape diamonds. Wearing a bag at a higher point of the body will serve to balance the larger hips of the pear shape diamond and not draw attention to the larger middle area of the marquise shape diamond. However, the drop of the bag may not be comfortable for many plus size women, because their arms and shoulders are larger. Walk around the store wearing the bag for a few minutes to see if it works for you.

The shopper style bag tends to have depth, but it also has firmer construction than the drawstring and hobo styles (it is not floppy). It is often rich with organizing features built right in: cell phone, business card and pen pockets and zippered compartments. It has short handles, usually a five-inch drop. This means it will be particularly attractive for heart, marquise and emerald shape diamonds, because when gripped in the hand, the bag will fall around low hip height, emphasizing the point at which the bodies of these diamond shapes become more slender. This is one style bag that may have double straps and an additional, longer shoulder strap. A variation of the shopper style is the dome shopper, which can be very beautiful. The materials of which it is made are even firmer than the regular shopper style and may be more formal and luxurious as well, with a zipper at the top to secure the contents. Often, the term tote style is used interchangeably with shopper style. However, when I use the term *tote* I am talking about a large bag that does not really close at the top. Therefore, while it is an important accessory, to me it is not a handbag; I consider it similar to a beach bag but made of more refined materials. Nevertheless, you may come across the term when shopping for a handbag so be prepared to recognize its characteristics in that context.

The satchel, a soft, casual style, is usually very rich in detail. This style is wide but not deep. Many women enjoy this, because when you open it and look inside, everything is visible and accessible. It has relatively short straps, usually a seven or eight-inch drop. For the pear and marquise shape diamonds, this style may work when carried on the shoulder. However, for most other plus size diamond shapes, larger women are not comfortable carrying this style and strap length on the shoulder; instead they carry it on the elbow or by a hand grip. More and more, the satchel style boasts the organizational features of a deeper bag such as the shopper.

The messenger style bag is a traditional beauty. It recalls the English countryside. The materials from which it is constructed tend to be firm and supple: Rich leather, suede and canvas, alone or in combination with one another, are the customary materials for this bag. Brass hardware fittings often enhance its rugged good looks. Usually a long shoulder strap comes with this bag. More and more, this strap is adjustable, because not everyone likes their bags to hang low on their hips. This adjustment is especially welcome for petite plus size women. This bag looks particularly good on emerald, heart and marquise shape diamonds, because it elongates the figure and doesn't add width in an unflattering place.

The final style is similar to the distinguished Birkin bag. This has been the "it" bag for a few years. It is a showstopper, to be sure. It has a hard, square body that gently narrows to the top and a well-constructed flap boasting beautiful hardware details to close and secure the contents of the bag. It is not uncommon to see double straps, a four-inch drop handle and a long shoulder strap, too. Due to the long shoulder strap, this bag compliments any of the diamond shapes. Moreover, it tends to have size and depth, so even if a woman were to carry the bag by its short handle on the elbow it would drop and draw attention to the low hip area. I can't imagine a woman in the world whose style wouldn't be enhanced by a replica of this rich bag. In fact, many variations of the bag have been named for movie stars. For example, the Kelly bag, a cousin of the Birkin bag, was named after classic film star Grace Kelly.

Coloration

In terms of clothing, words like monochromatic, tone-on-tone, dark, neutral and black are the buzzwords. That's because they work; they make women look longer. But these terms are not true when it comes to accessories. There is every reason for plus size women to purchase accessories that show off varied, vivid and striking coloration. In fact, when displayed against a dark or monochromatic background, namely your clothing, they pop even more. It is a win-win combination: A plus size woman gets the benefit of looking svelte in the darker colors of her clothing, but gets the added benefit of "wow" as her accessories contrast against that background Therefore, pick a color scheme for the season and stick with it. Your choice for the fall/winter may be different than the spring/summer colors you choose, depending on where you live.

Some of the colors that really pop are rich blues, greens, pinks, purples, yellows, oranges and reds made of leather or fabric, genuine or synthetic. Other color schemes involve collections of bold silver or gold tone hardware and treated leathers. Similarly, the use of bold pop art color schemes and designs lend excitement or individuality to one's style. Magnificent use of quilting and woven fabrics and leathers give maximal impact in terms of the coloration of a bag. If you choose traditional leathers, be sure the tone is sumptuous, deep and serves as a great backdrop to rich details, which provide striking coloration to a bag. Another great application of color is a patchwork of leathers.

Texture

A plus size woman especially benefits from the look of significant texture and interest when considering the materials of which handbags and other accessories are made. One reason is that materials that are bold and interesting seem commensurate with her overall stature. This way, if you choose leather, make it rich, supple and thick. Patent leather is a great option: it is durable, can be wiped off easily and comes in vivid colors. If you choose suede, opt for a firm, fine quality and one that begs to be touched. If you choose snakeskin or another skin (genuine or faux), make it daring and dramatic. If you choose an animal print or calf hair, select stunning, clear representations. (Calf hair is leather with short, firm animal fur/hair.) If you choose tapestry or quilting, the fabric needs to be plush and vivid. If you choose nylon, the fabric needs to be sleek and strong. If you choose rattan and natural weaves, choose firm, well-constructed applications.

Embellishments

Embellishments are the detail, trim and hardware that make each handbag special. Often it is the embellishments with which a woman falls in love. They catch the eye and make the fantasy soar. On handbags, embellishments take the form of buckles, closures, joints, labels, tags and heels. (Heels are the little protrusions good handbags stand on; often the addition of heels is a trick that makes less expensive handbags appear to be of higher quality and cost.) Heels serve a function, but add beauty and distinction as well.

To begin, choose a tone of hardware, either gold or silver. For example, some accessories that my preppy-style younger clients seem to favor include the use of bold silver hardware details on handbags and other accessories paired with striking silver jewelry. The bold silver tone hardware, then, serves as the unifying influence among their accessories. Another example are my clients who love bold gold tone (including brass) hardware details as the unifying element among their accessories, including their wallets, checkbooks, makeup cases, pillboxes, sunglasses, gloves and hats. It's not uncommon for them to add a Hermes-style silk scarf echoing gold trim as well. Hermes is a designer famous for silk scarves with opulent designs of floral, graphic, equestrian and gold chain themes.

Terrific embellishments include faux jewels, crystals, animal prints, pleating, ruching, ruffles, zippers, grommets, braiding, three-dimensional enhancements and designer logos or recognizable features unique to the brand name (this, however, is not my favorite, because I feel it sells your own sense of creativity short). Some women, with avocations that lend themselves, utilize theme for embellishment, which provides an important unifying influence, such as an equestrian theme.

Dressy Handbags
When your lifestyle calls for dressy clothing, the appropriate handbag is needed to complete the outfit. Often, plus size women, disgusted with the matronly clothing available to them for dressy occasions, go a step further and cheat themselves out of the sheer delight of carrying evening bags. Eveningwear calls for a clutch bag, which has no handle and is carried under the arm, or something similar. This type of bag is usually made of dramatic, high-impact materials, such as satin, silk, beading, stones, calf hair, snakeskin or crocodile, be it real or faux. When selecting an evening bag, keep impact in mind as much as size. Evening bags are obviously smaller than daytime bags. Therefore, to be appropriate for the larger woman, the bag needs to be very beautiful and significant. Traditionally, clutch bags and wristlets (features a small hand strap at one corner) tend to be about twelve inches wide by six inches high and usually a rectangular shape.

The audiere, a small and luxurious evening bag, is a variation on the theme. This little jewel box of a pocketbook is very small, maybe five or six inches, is usually a unique shape, often an animal, and is completely covered in crystals or some other high intensity material, such as hammered gold or silver. A woman carries the bag nestled in the palm of her hand; the appearance is more like jewelry than a handbag. The reason a large woman can get away with such a small bag has to do with punch more than size. It is the impact of the evening bag that must be proportionate to a large women's stature.

A graceful shoulder bag made of similar materials is a great option too. Often eveningwear shoulder bags have long, thin satin cords or gold chains as the straps and jeweled closures. A woman may still choose to carry the bag under her arm, like a clutch, and let the strap dangle.

Small Leather Goods
When I first received my business cards for Big Girls Won't Cry, I took a bunch of cards out of the box, wrapped a rubber band around them and stuck them in my handbag. Not the impression I want to make when handing out my cards.

Elegant women have small leather goods and matching accessories (like a business card case), not rubber bands. My advice is to select a wallet and checkbook case, key fob (similar to a watch fob, attached to a key ring), eyeglass case, makeup case, pill box and business card case that share a unifying influence. Add leather gloves, a hat, a scarf, an umbrella and a tote bag and you're all set. If you choose gold tone hardware, strive to find a raincoat and shoes that have consistent details. Most of these accessories will work from season to season; obviously some are not needed in warm weather. The important thing is that they work together to contribute to the overall image you have selected for yourself. While they need not match exactly and certainly do not need to be from the same manufacturer, they need to have a unifying influence; often, that it is in the detail or color of the item.

Sunglasses
Sunglasses hide a multitude of sins. They make a woman look chic, mysterious and sexy in about ten seconds. The discussion of proportion and detail in terms of handbags holds true for sunglasses as well. Large women need to select sunglasses that appear bold and important. Select frames and lenses that look like the classics (think Ray Ban Olympians or aviators) or even what's trendy, just as long as it fits you well. With

these details in mind, refer to the section on eyewear in chapter 13 to select a frame flattering to the shape of your face.

Sunglasses are an area where you can save some money. Designer sunglasses can cost $200 to $400. If you want a specific designer or logo, be prepared to pay for it. But if it's just the style you're after, you can find it for a fraction of that amount. Check out Loehmann's and Target for stylish, inexpensive sunglasses. I do not recommend buying sunglasses on the Internet, because I believe you need to try them on and judge them for both look and comfort. An excellent pair of sunglasses should become one of your go-to items when you need to run out of the house quickly; without makeup, sunglasses are your best friend. Remember to buy sunglass with UV filters to protect your eyes.

Scarves

If your clothing palette tends to be dark and monochromatic, scarves can add color and a burst of interest or beauty very quickly. Choose long, rather flat scarves. The best scarves to choose are made of silk (genuine or not) or soft, fine, sheer woven fabrics. Let the scarf drape long, either in front or in back. The important thing is the burst of color or pattern near the face. Avoid bulk. A great look for plus size women is a brooch (large, distinct pin) affixed to the knot of the scarf or just under it. The three-dimensional quality is high-impact and the tone of the brooch, gold or silver, will be a polishing touch that brings together all the accessories you have selected. An example of how I used a brooch for impact is with one of my raincoats. The coat has a placket of hidden buttons and it seemed naked. So I added a big brooch and a scarf pinned under the lapel that hangs long without a knot at all, permanently.

Hats

If you look good in hats, you've got an edge. First, a hat gives height. The taller you look, the slimmer you look. Second, hats are a finishing touch that frames your most important feature: your face. Third, given the infrequency of ladies wearing hats, it is high-impact.

If you can pull it off, try a fedora. It is a felt hat with a medium size brim and high crown with lengthwise crease from front to back. These hats are often made in vivid colors or animal prints with beautiful details.

The beret style should not be overlooked either. It is a soft hat without a brim that is draped and tilted to the side of the head, usually made from a knit. The beret lends itself easily to a matching set of accessories, such as gloves and a scarf, umbrella and tote bag, for a warm, youthful, inviting look.

Gloves

Expressive, beautiful hands are an asset to anyone. Gloves, especially leather gloves, are instant refinement for a woman. Just look through magazines and see how many "indoor" outfits are featured with models wearing gloves. While I don't necessarily suggest that you wear gloves indoors, the elegance and the finishing quality should not be lost on you. Gloves are another fashion accessory that polish and complete your look. Again, look for distinct colors or finishing details. Gloves come in sizes, so be sure to get a good fit to avoid tearing or discomfort.

Wearing one or a combination of these accessories is a great way to easily create a focus point on your body and achieve a complete, "pulled together" look. Try a set of accessories with different outfits and see how it creates a different look with each combo. Just remember to apply the design elements and have fun; let your style shine.

CHAPTER 9

Building a Pretty Party Wardrobe

INVENTORY YOUR
CLOSET RUTHLESSLY

"To be a fashionable woman is to know yourself, know what you represent, and know what works for you. To be 'in fashion' could be a disaster on 90 percent of women. You are not a page out of *Vogue*." ~Author Unknown

Shopping for the plus size woman can be either exhausting or exhilarating. Without a plan it can be exhausting, unproductive, demoralizing and expensive. However, if you want to make shopping a positive experience, don't leave home without a sassy attitude and knowledge of what's right for you; that is, "fade and focus" customized for you.

This brings me to my third epiphany that called me to write this book: "To thine own self be true," to borrow from William Shakespeare. Simply put, there is no one who knows you better and therefore, no one in a better position to advocate for you and your fashion needs than you. You must determine what you need to look your best, follow the advice in this book and seek it out. Saying you have nothing to wear or you are embarrassed by the way you look are no longer valid reasons for declining invitations and passing on activities. You must embrace yourself lovingly, accentuate the positive, camouflage the negative, be realistic about your lifestyle and get up and go.

By the end of this chapter you can begin to utilize three tools that will change forever how you purchase clothing: the Pretty Party Portfolio, the

Essential Inventory Card and the Go-To Guide. The costs are minimal: The portfolio will be about six dollars, a pack of index cards and sleeves will be about eight dollars and the binder and photo pages will be about the same.

Pretty Party Portfolio
The Pretty Party Portfolio is a plastic accordion envelope with twelve compartments. This becomes the place where you identify and organize the things you love. Building from the bottom up, the twelve sections are shoes, bottoms, dresses and suits, tops, coats, activewear, swimwear, lingerie, accessories, hair and cosmetics, jewelry and miscellaneous (catalogs, resources, business cards). Shoes and bottoms will be the anchors of your outfits.

Each time you come across something that intrigues you from a magazine, catalog or elsewhere, cut it out and put it in the correct section of the portfolio. Sometimes you will not be able to get the item you have identified, but more often than not, you can replicate the style or feature of an item that appeals to you with an item appropriate for you.

You don't need to become a designer or an artist, but I do think it's important to maintain a collection of looks you love. You do not have to limit yourself to plus size fashions. As you peruse magazines and clothing catalogs, tear out the things you love and file them accordingly. Periodically, probably one time per season, edit your portfolio. It is helpful to maintain this, because as you shop you become mindful of items to look for. Perhaps you won't find the items exactly, but you will be an informed, discriminating shopper and you will develop ideas on how to use certain design elements and trends in ways that will work for you. This is called interpretation. Recall the cerulean blue anecdote I mentioned from the movie *The Devil Wears Prada*. If I were to see a cerulean blue military jacket in a magazine, I would cut it out and file it in my portfolio. Then one day I might see a shell (sleeveless top) in that color. I could buy it and wear it under a well-fitted black pantsuit. Maybe I could find a monochromatic outfit in cerulean blue. Another application is a bold necklace or handbag in that color. Three interpretations of a designer's signature that would work for me!

When your portfolio reflects the lessons in this book, you are ready to hit the stores. Your portfolio should be a source of inspiration and should allow you to think beyond the limitations you have heretofore imposed; namely, buy it if it fits. Rather, the items you have inserted in your portfolio should reference the six design elements discussed earlier as they pertain to your frame and reflect your emerging style.

My friend Marie, whom I introduced to you in the beginning of this book, is a good example. She continued to buy short tank tops for years and didn't understand that she was buying the same unflattering style over and over again. When we were in college, Marie, a pear shape diamond, could wear abbreviated, sexy tank tops. But over the years her body changed slightly, although her habits for buying clothes didn't. Here's what I recommended for her. Her arms still look good and she should continue to wear sleeveless tops; however, the tops should be long enough to skim her hips and buttocks and have embellishment at the neck to keep the eye focused there. This will keep the look sophisticated and worthy of her. I have sent her several Michael Kors ads of well-embellished sleeveless tops to put in her portfolio. Hopefully, as she peruses the contents of the portfolio, the more appropriate application or interpretation of this style will become her new shopping habit and she will seek it out.

Inventory Your Closet Ruthlessly

I have heard that many people wear only 20 percent of what's in their closets. Go through every piece of clothing you own (including shoes, jewelry, accessories and handbags) and make a decision about it: trash it, donate it, fix it or keep it. If it is too worn or has a stain, trash it. If it is still wearable but is too small, too big or otherwise unsuitable to the wardrobe you are developing, give it to a worthy organization. These days, the containers in some shopping centers make it easy to give items of clothing away to less privileged women who will be glad to have them. Only keep clothing items that you love, that fit well, that can be altered to fit well or that are immediately usable. Don't keep things that you haven't worn in over a year. Make room for beautiful new things that you will wear right away. Recently, I took eleven pieces that had been hanging in my closet but I hadn't worn in a very long time to my seamstress. They needed simple alterations (hemming, cuffs shortened, tapering at the knee, let out a skirt and dress). When I picked them up, the bill was $110. A little hefty, yes, but I scored eleven "new" pieces of clothing that I started to wear immediately.

If, at the end of this purging effort, there isn't much left in your closet, don't panic; you will fill that closet soon enough. It's insanity to keep the things that have made you feel unattractive and expect a different result. Use good judgment and be honest with yourself.

Organize the clothing you are keeping by category: slacks, jeans, skirts, skorts, tops, sweaters, jackets, dresses and coats. Within these categories make subcategories based on color. For example, slacks: black, gray, brown, khaki; jeans: blue, black, white; camisoles: black, white, cream, navy, red, etc. Separate things that are very special. Enclose them in a garment bag with a sachet. Keep shoes in boxes and label each box clearly. Wrap handbags in felts and place them in a basket or container on a closet shelf. Remove items that are specifically seasonal and store elsewhere with cedar chips or bars. It is important to have a well-laid out closet plan to facilitate dressing.

The Essential Inventory Card

The Essential Inventory Card is an index card (or cards) carried in a perfectly fitted plastic sleeve and tucked neatly in your handbag at all times. On this card, you list your Go-To cluster outfits and circle in pencil items that are missing to make outfits complete. Prepare sections for dressy, work and casual occasions. In addition, change the card seasonally. I am able to record my whole wardrobe on one five-inch by eight-inch card, back and front. For me, the only section I need to change seasonally is my casual wardrobe, because it reflects summer sports events, like golf and my son's baseball games. When you shop, you are armed with this tool. It helps you shop with a particular focus.

Begin by thinking about the types of occasions for which you need to be well dressed. For me they are dressy (out to dinner or a show), work (appointments and meetings), casual (attending ball games, shopping, errands around town) and sports (golf, tennis, seashore vacations).

Build from the Bottom Up

I recommend that you begin creating an outfit with the anchor piece: slacks, skirt, skort, dress or suit. Most women have more difficulty with bottoms, slacks or jeans, so this is the first thing to consider as a building block for a complete outfit. To create the Essential Inventory Card, first take all of your bottom pieces out of the closet and lay them in a clear area, perhaps on your bed. Pile the ones you have decided to keep by occasion. Be sure they are flattering. Start with three five by eight inch index cards. Label each one of the three cards with the occasion (dressy, work and casual). List on each card: anchors, tops, footwear and accessories. List the bottom pieces under the anchor column and begin to build. You may want to develop abbreviations for items or use mine to save space.

Second, take out your significant tops: blouses, T-shirts, tunics, sweaters, vests and jackets. Does each item work well with at least one bottom? Pile the tops next to the matching pile of bottoms. Now, start to create outfits and actually try them on in the privacy of your room with a good mirror. On the index card labeled with the occasion (dressy, work or casual), list the tops next to the bottom for which they are intended.

Third, repeat the process with shoes by removing all pairs from your closet and placing them next to the bottoms they match. As you may know, shoes can make or break an outfit and for those of us who are plus size, shoes have to do double duty: support and distribute our weight and look drop-dead gorgeous. List the shoes that work with the anchor under the appropriate column, moving to the right of the index card.

This is where you will start to see Go-To cluster outfits emerging. Do you notice that with one anchor and pair of shoes you can substitute several tops (and accessories) to make great outfits that will work every

Abbreviations

Description	Technique	Examples
Color	Remove vowels and extra letters	black=blk, white= wht
Designer/Brand	Initial(s) capitalized in parentheses	Ralph Lauren = (RL) Misook = (M)
Several of the same type item to work into the cluster	Plus sign +	blk surplice tees+ =I have a few of this item
Need this item to complete the outfit	empty circle	n/a
Type of garment	Two to four capital letters	TS = twin-set DSTR = duster VST = vest JKT = jacket RC = rain coat BLR = blazer SWR = sweater SLK = slacks JNS = jeans SRT = skirt SKORT = skort SDL = sandals BTS = boots MLS = mules HLS = heels

time? So while I say you must have two Go-To outfits on hand, each outfit, in essence, is the cluster for a few more outfits rather effortlessly.

Finally, ask yourself: Are there any accessories that are needed for this outfit? I have sets of jewelry for specific outfits, because I believe so firmly in the power of jewelry as an accessory. Write accessories down next to the top column. This could also include foundations (undergarments). This is the column on the right side of the index card.

Put the clothing back in your closet, ordered by type of garment and then color, as you did when you inventoried your closet. You will see that you have put pieces back into your closet that you have not listed on your Essential Inventory Card. This is acceptable for now, but if in a year you haven't worn any of these pieces, remove them from your closet and donate them. Too much in a closet truly detracts from and confuses your pretty party wardrobe plan.

Look at your Essential Inventory Card and identify items you need but do not have in order to complete the outfits. Write the names of the items you're missing in pencil and circle them. For instance, say you have metallic pumps, a black skirt and a metallic cardigan, but you are missing a black camisole to complete the outfit. You would pencil in the words *black cami-sole* and draw a circle around them, indicating this is what you are looking for the next time you shop. This is the beginning of your shopping plan.

If you see that you have a great anchor piece and shoes to match, pencil in the words reflecting the idea for a new top, camisole and jacket combination and circle them, indicating you want to develop this Go-To cluster into an additional outfit once you purchase the correct pieces.

Next, if you see that you need another outfit or two in a particular category, such as dressy outfits, draw a large wide circle in pencil indicating the need for a complete outfit. Incidentally, you will already see many of the pieces and shoes you have on hand reflected on the card so if, while shopping, you see a terrific A-line dress, you can note that you already have metallic pumps that would work well.

Less is more. It is not necessary to have ten outfits for each type of occasion in your life. I certainly don't. In fact, once you get this template going, you will be able to use tops or sets of jewelry that you already have with a particular outfit and change your look just enough to keep it interesting but in a subtle way that still gives you the confidence to know that it will work.

As I said earlier, I am able to keep my whole wardrobe on one index card, front and back, with the exception of a summer casual card. I keep it in my handbag so it is always with me and I refer to it often. If I am considering a new piece, I look to see if it will fit in one of my cluster outfits. Unless it is a completely new look, I know right away whether I have the other pieces needed to make it work. In fact, one of my benchmarks is how quickly I wear a new purchase. If I wear it quickly, I am sure that it was needed and was a good decision. If it sits in my closet for a long time, I will probably return it. I keep the tags on a garment until I put it on my back to wear and the receipts in a shoebox designated for that purpose, so returns are easy.

Only buy clothing that fits now, notwithstanding reasonable alterations. Don't buy something that will fit "in ten pounds." Don't put that kind of pressure on yourself. Here's why: "In ten pounds" suggests that there is something wrong with you now and that you are putting your life on hold until this event occurs. There is nothing wrong with you right now. Find the looks you love then edit and alter. Buy the right garments for your frame in the right sizes and go out looking your best today.

The Go-To Guide

The Go-To Guide is a pretty three-ring binder containing plastic photograph pages. Take a picture of each complete outfit—and I mean complete—and tuck the photos into the plastic slots. When you are ready to dress, you can refer to the book for expedience, if you need to. With two four-inch by six-inch photos per page, you can see two Go-To outfits for each occasion (casual, work or dressy) at a glance. You can add more pages as you need to, but in the beginning be content with two Go-To outfits for each category of your lifestyle so that you're good to go at a moment's notice.

Every woman needs at least two Go-To core outfits for each occasion of her life (dressy, work, casual). Keep in mind the Essential Inventory Card you just developed. You should have created, at all times ready to go, two outfits that you can count on. These outfits always look good, are always comfortable and are ready to be worn at a moment's notice. All aspects of the outfits are available and in good condition, including the necessary undergarments, shoes and accessories.

Here's how to develop the Go-To Guide: On the back of a door, place a bi-level hook and hang the top and bottom of an outfit so you can see both. Place a small table nearby, slightly to the side, and lay out the shoes, accessories, jewelry and special undergarments, if needed. Now take a photograph. Place the photo in your Go-To Guide. Organize your photo pages by category: dressy, work and casual. I remind you that less is more; it is better to have a few terrific and complete Go-To outfits for each occasion of your lifestyle than a closet stuffed or over-stuffed with a lot of random clothing, shoes and accessories that you are overwhelmed by.

There is never a time when I have to decline an invitation because I do not have something wonderful to wear. Wonderful is a relative term. I prefer streamlined, well-constructed and well-fitted clothes and accessories that are the backdrop for me. Yes, people tease me that I wear black a lot. Until I'm shown otherwise, I'm sticking with Donna Karan and a host of other fashion landmarks who understand the power, grace and svelte effect of black. Use your own Go-To Guide to dress quickly and appropriately for any occasion, knowing you will look sexy, sensational and successful.

My Essential Inventory Card
These are examples of my Essential Inventory Card. I have spelled out more than I would on my own card so it makes more sense to you. As a general note, I wouldn't wear my skorts and sandals in the winter, because I live in the mid-Atlantic region of the country, but most of the rest of the items would be year-round.

Casual (spring, summer, fall)

Bottom/Anchor	Top	Footwear	Accessories
blk jeans (NYDJ)	rd crochet jacket (M)wht tee/blk vest+blk tee/pnk vestblk/leopard tunic	blk mules metallic sandals blk clogs metallic sandals	red set silver set pink set silver set
wht jeans (RL)	blk jacquard duster wht twin-set wht tee/tan vest	blk boots metallic sandals metallic sandals	silver set silver set red set
blk skort (LIZ)	blk surplice tee+ coral polo s/sl V-neck (St. J.) wht tee/blk vest	metallic sandals coral sandals blk tights/clogs metallic sandals	pink set coral set silver set silver set
blue jeans (NYDJ)	navy polo multi wrap (MSN) navy twin-set (DB) fringe jacket (CHNL)	metallic sandals tan suede clogs tan clogs tan clogs	red set coral set red set silver set

Work (year-round)

Bottom/Anchor	Top	Footwear	Accessories
blk slacks+	cream twin-set blk blazer beaded green blk cashmere t-neck blk tee/vest+	blk boots metallic boots blk boots leopard heels metallic boots	coral set, raincoat(RL) coral set green set red set silver sct
wht slacks (RL)	navy/wht sweater wht/tee/duster blk blazer (DB)	metallic boots leopard heels leopard heels	silver set green set red set
blk pencil skirt+	blk knit-gold trim (M) blk/pink knit (M) blk/teal stripe jacket/scarf (H) glen plaid jacket	leopard heels black tights/wedgies blk tights/wedgies leopard heels blk tights/wedgies	red set pink set turquoise set red set coral set
metallic quilt skirt	blk t-neck+ blk blazer (DB) camel blazer (DB)	leopard heels leopard heels leopard heels	red set turquoise set red set
red dress (DVF)	n/a	blk tights/wedgies	red set
blk knit dress (M)	n/a	leopard heels	turquoise set

Sports (spring, summer, fall) I'd wear casual clothes to winter sporting events, which are noted on my first Essential Inventory Card.

Bottom/Anchor	Top	Footwear	Accessories
blk skort (LIZ)	tees+ polos+ tee/vest+	flat sandals golf shoes flat sandals	coral set pink set silver set
cream skort (LIZ)	navy twin-set blk twin-set blk surplice tee+	metallic sandals metallic sandals metallic sandals	red set turquoise set silver set
khaki skort (LE)	polos+	flat sandals	coral set
coral/wht print skort (LE)	coral polo s/sl wht sweater	coral sandals coral sandals	coral set coral set
wht skort (LE)	wht tee/vest+ blk surplice tee+ navy twin-set	golf shoes flat sandals flat sandals	green set pink set silver set

Dressy (year-round)

Bottom/Anchor	Top	Footwear	Accessories
halter dress/slvr/blk	blk silk jacket	blk heels	dressy silver set
pink tweed knit skirt(M)	blk twin-set (M)	pink suede heels	dressy pink set
wht slacks/jeans (RL)	blk duster (M) green sweater (St.J.)	metallic heels leopard heels	dressy leopard dressy green set
blk pencil skirt (MR)	pink halter top & blk leather blazer	blk heels	dressy pink set
black tuxedo suit (RL)		gold heels	dressy gold set

Treasured Clothes

I have some pieces that are the real deal. Mostly, I bought them on sale. However, there are other pieces I own and refer to as my designer jacket, sweater, suit or dress even though I didn't buy them at a designer store. Why? These special items make me feel great and remind me that being a plus size woman does not exclude me from being sexy or part of the stylish landscape.

There's no reason that I can't extrapolate or interpret. Many of these designs and fabrics are not only beautiful, but are appropriate for the image I choose for myself. I store my treasured clothes in a garment bag in a special area of my closet and treat them as the real deal. When I put them on and go out, I know I look fabulous!

Less is More

This is especially true for the woman who is building a *Pretty Plus* wardrobe. A few core outfits per category reflecting your lifestyle is the way to go. Why? Because while color matters, so does the shape of a garment, shoes and undergarments. It's easy to get confused in all those matters, so keep it simple. Develop a few core outfits and clusters and always have them in perfect condition with all of the pieces ready.

Why Do I Have Nothing to Wear?

When I begin to work with a client I often visit her closet first to determine:

- What's in there?
- How much is in there?
- How is it displayed?
- What style does she like?
- What works well for her?
- What must be removed?

Most of the time here is what I find. By the way, it is often the same for all of the diamond shapes.

- **What's in there?** Extraneous stuff, things not wardrobe related and things just being stored.
- **How much is in there?** Way too much. It is often difficult to see what's in there or how the pieces are related to one another to make outfits.
- **How is it displayed?** Not in an organized manner. A poor choice of hangers and lighting are common too.
- **What style does she like?** Often there is not a dominant style but rather a little bit of everything.
- **What works well for her?** Many garments do not fit well. This means mostly they are not selected for wear but just hang there taking up space.
- **What must be removed?** Anything that hasn't been worn in over a year, anything stained or torn, anything not wardrobe related and anything that needs to be altered.

Closet Snapshot
Remember, if you're not wearing it, remove it from your closet. Organization is key. When you couple your closet plan with the Go-To Guide, you'll always know what to wear and it will be right there for the taking. This is a liberating experience for the plus size woman. If you have passed up invitations because you had "nothing to wear," you'll understand why less is more.

Organization
Organize the like items in your closet in groupings and designate specific areas for the different categories. Keep the floor of your closet clean and clear of junk. Everything in your closet should have a designated place:
- Outerwear hangs together
- Boots on boot trees or in original boxes, labeled, on the floor
- Shoes on top shelf, in original boxes, clearly labeled
- Handbags in boxes, labeled on top shelf
- Dresses and suits
- Long jackets
- Blazers, jackets, toppers

- Slacks (ordered by color)
- Jeans
- Skirts
- Tops (ordered by color)
- Knits folded on shelves
- Undergarments on or in specific shelves or drawers
- Accessories on specific shelf
- Jewelry in a hanging bag
- Playtime clothing together (skorts and tees)

Here are a few closet organizers and accessories that I personally recommend:

- A hanging jewelry bag. This hangs on a heavy-duty hanger and has clear plastic pockets (looks a little bit like a shoe bag only much smaller and finer). The benefit of this is that you can see all of your jewelry at a glance. You can mix genuine and faux. There are two sides to the bag, usually about thirty-three pockets per side (www.lillianvernon.com).
- A hanging, flexible set of fabric shelves. This is great for sweaters or knits. The garments are folded and therefore do not stretch while hanging, especially in the shoulders. The benefit is that it is open and you can see it while looking at the rest of your clothing.
- A hanging belt or scarf rack or a heavy-duty rubberized set of hooks on a hanger. This allows you to see these types of accessory at a glance.
- Fabric lined baskets. These are great to store small leather goods and handbags.
- Hangers that are a thick plastic and have a rubber coating. These hold tops better than plain plastic hangers. This is important to the plus size woman, because tops are wider at the neck and shoulders and tend to slip off plastic hangers. Place the shoulder seams neatly on the hanger and the garment will be perfect every time you wear it. These hangers hold slacks better too. They can be purchased at Wal-Mart, Target or a similar store. Anticipate and buy a suitable amount so that

you have a matching set of hangers in your closet.

- A wicker or a woven plastic hamper. Use it in your closet to hold fragile items until you are able to wash them separately. Do not just throw them in the family laundry basket and expect you will remember to treat them differently. I have forgotten many times and the result is a shrunken garment no longer suitable to wear. Money wasted.
- Excellent lighting. When you wear a lot of dark toned garments, it is not always easy to distinguish one from the other. Good lighting in your closet also helps you to see if a garment has a stain or needs repair.
- Shelf liner. Line the shelves of your closet with scented paper, the same one with which you line your dresser drawers.
- Clothing hooks. Locate a place in your closet or on the outer door and install substantial clothing hooks. Over-the-door hooks or wreath hangers will accomplish this too without being installed. Place the hooks at two levels so you can see what the top and bottom of an outfit will look like together. This will be the place where, you can look at and evaluate an outfit or just hang your clothes for the next day or occasion. This bi-level hook is also where you will place your complete outfit to photograph for the Go-To Guide.

If you feel particularly energetic or motivated, redecorate your closet. Paint it a favorite pale shade, install good lighting and purchase closet accessories (hangers, baskets, shelves and hooks) that match and are really special. I confessed earlier to being a bit of a voyeur. I love peeking into the closets of the beautiful people in magazine spreads. Then it dawned on me that type of closet euphoria is not outside my reach or your reach either.

Similarly, customized closets are not out of reach either. In addition to expensive companies that will come to your home and measure your available space to maximize storage options, companies such as ClosetMaid sell hardware packs that have a complete system in a box for under one hundred dollars. This organizational system is critical to the plus size woman who has previously approached dressing with trepidation; it will make dressing options clear and accessible.

CHAPTER 10

Shop, Feed Yourself

NURTURANCE

"Just around the corner in every woman's mind is a lovely dress, a wonderful suit, or entire costume which will make an enchanting new creature of her." ~Wilhela Cushman

As I have examined my relationship with food over the years, I have come to the conclusion that I have often nurtured myself with it, sometimes a good thing and sometimes a bad thing. Often, I have heard phrases like, "Treat yourself to something else besides food" and "Find other ways to care for yourself and treat yourself lovingly." I think those well-intentioned people might have meant indulging in a bubble bath, a manicure or yoga class. Who could argue with those pearls of wisdom? They are certainly good suggestions. However, those ideas seemed simplistic to me then and now. Ironically, I have come to equate presenting myself beautifully as an act of love and nurturance for myself. I couch the shopping experience in that context for you now.

Think about preparing yourself to shop to set yourself up for success. First, dress nicely and comfortably, wear good foundation garments and wear or bring shoes that will correspond with the clothing for which you are shopping. Second, go shopping with a specific focus. What are you looking for today (slacks, jeans)? Third, bring the Essential Inventory Card. That is your insurance policy against making mistakes and wasting money on things you don't need. Fourth, if you want to buy and fill in the gaps on your Essential Inventory Card, shop alone. Meet up with a friend for lunch if you miss the social side of shopping, but do your work alone, focused on yourself.

Personal Shopper

A personal shopper can be a terrific ally when setting out on your shopping mission. She will know the various departments in the store and she will know the merchandise in her department well. Also, she is an expert shopper and can put outfits together with ease. The services of a professional shopper are imbedded in the cost of the items you buy, so there is no additional cost for her services. This is comparable to getting interior design services for free at certain well-established furniture emporiums. Certainly a good deal in and of itself, because a reasonably priced interior designer charges about $200 per hour. The same concept applies for the time they are with you. They will probably spend about an hour or two with you and that time is completely focused on you.

The second time I worked with Sandra, my personal shopper, my fashion focus was slacks. I arrived at the appointed time and she showed me to the dressing room. The largest, most sumptuous dressing room in the store was prepared for *me*! Hanging neatly were about a dozen pairs of slacks from her department and from a few of the other departments in the store. I left with three pairs of slacks that I would never have treated myself to before that experience. They were expensive but beautiful and I wore them for several seasons.

I have worked with a few personal shoppers and have observed others in action. They seem to be friendly, accepting and genuinely enthusiastic about their assignments: to help you buy clothing and earn a commission based on your purchase. It is my opinion that generally you will buy more expensive items when you work with a personal shopper than you would if you were shopping alone. That is not necessarily a bad thing. I would rather have one good item that I love and am proud of than three lesser items. In the beginning of stepping up your fashion sensibilities, this may be a push you need.

If you are going to use a personal shopper, be sure you have called ahead, have an appointment and have shared what specifically you are looking to buy. Although this may be obvious, there is no reason to feel pressured by a personal shopper. For now she may know a bit more than you do about fashion and the merchandise in her department; this is her job and what she is paid to do via her arrangement with the store. But in effect, she works for you.

Tell her about your Pretty Party Portfolio and Essential Inventory Card or even better, show her. More importantly, do not lose sight of what you have learned in the previous chapters about line, shape, balance, proportion, color and texture. Evaluate her selections based on your knowledge and the style you have been cultivating in your portfolio. Do not defer to her. You know more about you than she does. She knows more about what merchandise is available in her store today.

A word of caution: Unless you are absolutely certain about her recommendations, do not allow them to be altered. A wise move may be to take them home and mull. Once a garment is altered, it cannot be returned. Since the merchandise may be pricey, you want to be removed from any intimidation that may have been exerted upon you, intentionally or not, before making expensive decisions. Further, not at the fault of the personal shopper, I have found myself caught up in the euphoria of indulging myself and being waited on and on occasion I have purchased more than I ought to have. Although it will require another trip back to the store for alterations and yet another trip to pick the items up when they are ready, trading some of your free time and a couple gallons of gas for the assurance that you did not spend money frivolously is satisfying.

There are two other advantages of developing a relationship with a personal shopper. First, she will probably develop a card for you in her file with your name, address, phone, email, size and style preferences. This allows you to call ahead when you have another fashion focus and get to work quickly. Second, she will notify you of sales even before they have been advertised, which gives you the jump on the best selection of sizes, styles and brands in the sales merchandise available.

Sharpen Your Eye

Shopping has become a fun experience for me. Here are some tips to make it a positive experience for you too. Begin in the best department the store or mall has to offer. I know they won't necessarily have your size, but they may have your fantasy. Look, touch and indulge your senses in the bounty that the best and the brightest of the fashion industry have put on the sales floor. Are there any fabrics, colors, styles, proportions, embellishments, trim, hardware and textures that you love and would like to incorporate (interpret) into your wardrobe?

Catalog and Online Descriptive Terms

Catalog and online shopping has become a favorite pastime of many women. First and foremost, with busy lives, they are convenient. Second, it may be more pleasant to try things on in the comfort of your own home. Third, it is more efficient in that you can better determine if the new piece "fits" well with the other pieces you own to make a complete outfit.

My biggest gripe, as I've mentioned before, is the use of thin models to display plus size clothing. At best, it's unrealistic and therefore unhelpful and at worst, it's a political and social criticism that we are not viewable.

As I peruse catalogs and online advertisements, there appears to be some phrases that seem to be particularly descriptive and responsive to plus size women's needs. Items that are described using this type of phrasing may be worth examining up close.

Dress
- Empire waist flows into a swingy six-panel skirt
- Unique hankie hem
- Cascading hem
- Removable ties at waist to customize fit
- Lined bodice

- Comfortable elasticized short sleeves
- Signature viscose rayon, prized for its comfort and forgiving drape
- Beautifully draped dress flows from a sequined scoop neck
- Fluid movement
- Slimming surplice empire waist
- Tone-on-tone embroidery

Pants
- Pretty drape and easy comfort (if "easy comfort" is alone watch out)
- Full-length stretch knit
- Wide leg design offers a slimming silhouette ("wide leg" alone may be too much fabric)
- Wide leg pant flatters every shape with its amazing "balancing" effect
- Detailed slant pocket
- Seaming details on the front of each leg add interest and shape
- Twill trim accents the vertical welt pockets
- Wide hem with side slits
- Bias cut band with side slits adds interest and drape-ability
- A-line shape
- Carefree white (will wash well)
- Memory stretch for comfort
- Smoothes and slims your shape without binding
- Perfect stretch jean
- High-tech pants wick moisture to keep you dry

Skirts
- Asymmetrical faux wrap
- Look of a dress but you select the sizes (top and bottom)
- Contour waistband sits at the natural waist
- Slimming stitched-down inverted pleats

Tops
- Stretch cotton tunic
- Figure-friendly waist shaping

- Three-quarter length sleeves
- Wrap neckline (surplice) collar with slight shirring
- Flattering square scoop neckline
- Surplice styling
- Back V neckline
- Slightly belled sleeves
- High side slits
- Touch of stretch in the fabric
- Wrinkle-free fit
- Mandarin collar
- Side slits
- Curve friendly shaping
- The longer length for which you've been asking
- Shape-friendly
- Jersey knit
- Side seam ruching (providing clever camouflage)
- Raglan armholes
- Wide strap tank
- Lettuce edged hem
- Flattering waist shaping
- Sweetheart empire waist
- Elasticized smocking shapes the neckline
- Underwire bra with removable molded cups provides reliable support
- Oversized novelty buttons
- Details that include a flattering jewel neckline
- Roomy shape and drop shoulders (not too roomy)
- Cotton gauze has a wonderful drape (if it has some stretch)
- Ultra-light, subtly stretchy and silky smooth with lavish beading at the neck
- Pointed front hem
- A-line fit
- More feminine shape and just two buttons that provide a more flattering silhouette

Gifts to Ask For

It is my recommendation that you buy your own clothing and ask your loved ones and friends to give you other types of gifts besides clothing. This is because you have a plan for yourself; you know your needs and wishes and you understand the design elements that suit you best. Of course, the exception to this would be if you were very specific. For example, "I'd love to have a navy blue cashmere turtleneck sweater, in size 2X." However, here is a wish list that I think you can adapt effectively if you offer information that reveals your preferences within each category:

- Jewelry
- Luggage
- Small leather goods
- Handbag
- Tote
- Umbrella
- Scarves
- Gloves
- Robe with zipper (not a tie belt) and matching slippers
- Bathroom accessories
- Monogrammed towels
- Closet accessories
- Gift certificates:
  - Favorite stores
  - Day spa: manicure/pedicure/facial/massage/waxing
  - Tanning
  - Makeup session
  - Hair salon
- Fragrance
- Lotions and creams
- Candles
- Pick up something on hold/layaway
- Alteration money
- Framed picture of you and a loved one looking great

- Leather bound journal
- Leather bound address/phone book
- Stationery
- Fancy shelf paper/liner
- Closet redecoration

Shopping does not have to be overwhelming for plus size women. Preparing ahead of time will ease frustrations and lead to success. Use tools like your Essential Inventory Card, a personal shopper and key words to find items you need to complete go-to outfits and that will enhance your figure. Shopping should be an enjoyable pastime. Limit yourself to time lengths you can handle and keep a positive outlook. There is clothing that will fit and flatter you. Keep your focus in mind and you will find the items you desire.

CHAPTER 11

Shop, Edit, Alter

MANUFACTURE YOUR
BEST FIGURE

"His clothes fit him so ill, and constrain him so much, that he seems rather their prisoner than their proprietor." ~Philip Dormer Stanhope

Usually, plus size clothing is made to be wide enough to cover our bodies. The philosophy seems to be maximal fabric, minimal shape. Heavy women believe large garments allow them to move around and sit comfortably and they believe tummy, hips, thighs, buttocks, arms and bulges on the back are disguised. However, often the bulges are enclosed, but not hidden; in fact, they may look larger than ever.

Big clothing also hides any shape we might want to display or manufacture. Visual weight is a term you need to understand well, so forgive the repetition. The less skin we see and the more fabric that exists create a concept known as visual weight. Visual weight is an illusion of sorts. It visually infers that the body is as big as the fabric or that the body fills out every square inch of the fabric, even when that is not true. Said another way, it makes us look bigger than we are. This is not what we need.

What you do need is to learn how alterations can trim down your appearance and create an attractive, feminine contour. Too often heavy women are just so glad to get something that fits (translation: is big enough) that the thought of altering the garment to enhance their shapes is elusive. Why? Because these women derive little joy and satisfaction from shopping; it can be a humiliating experience. Plus size women want to get new clothing in their closets as quickly as possible and be done with it. So to go through an additional step extending what feels like a degrading process seems unlikely. However, it is the intent of this book to change your thinking, right here, right now! To get the bang for your fashion buck, you have to commit to the process of seeking alterations.

Indeed, what may need to be altered first is your attitude. Right now you may feel that it's ludicrous to spend more money on clothes you don't deserve, that you can't achieve a perfect fit, that you won't look good anyway. *So what's the use?* you think to yourself. All of those notions are just not true. And if the truth be known, you don't think so either. Reading this book is an act of self-respect and optimism; it represents a willingness and openness on your part to try new things to the end of looking better. You know I pull it off daily and you can, too!

Let's talk about the alterations process. First you have to find a seamstress. Second, you have to get out of your car and take the garment in, get undressed in the little area behind the curtain and have some strange seamstress poke and pin you. Okay, not great. While I also had unsure feelings at the beginning of my relationship with my seamstress, I no longer feel that way. First of all, I'm a darn good customer. Second, she has gotten to know what I want. Third, she has learned a lot about creating illusion through alterations and has come to respect my knowledge. Sometimes when I wear a garment in the shop that she has previously altered, I can see her pride and satisfaction. They call that a win-win situation.

My advice is to find a nice, clean "mom and pop" cleaners that has a three-way mirror and a dressing area with which you are comfortable. Stand tall, don't hold your stomach in, take a deep breath and get to know the seamstress. Treat her well and you will get the perks of being a good customer. Make eye contact, smile, tip and say thank you!

Recently I purchased a stadium designer coat on sale. The sale price was seventy-nine dollars, marked down from $169. It is a very cool coat: black with polka dot trim on the outside, great silver tone hardware trim, great weight, some warmth but no bulk and reversible the polka dot side can be worn out. I took it to my seamstress and she needed to take in the coat in three places, because I was only able to get a size 3X off the sale rack, which is a size too big for me. She charged me forty dollars (which is fair, not cheap), but every time I wear it, it fits me great and makes me look shapely, slimmer and youthful—not a bad return on my investment.

I bought a few nice tops at discount stores. Each cost about twenty to twenty-five dollars. After one washing, I noticed that they shrunk in length, hitting my tummy in the middle in an unflattering way. This actually calls attention to something I would rather hide. I took a white T-shirt and the tops to my seamstress; I asked her to cut up the white T-shirt and add two inches of the fabric to the hem of each top, duplicating the fresh look of layering a white T-shirt underneath. In addition, I asked her to follow the A-line of the shirts and keep them a bit wider at the bottom, so as not to hug my tummy. She charged me ten dollars per shirt to make the alterations. It looks slimming, fresh and professionally done. I'm thrilled. It's become my signature to wear a white T-shirt "underneath" my top or jacket. But the beauty is there is no real T-shirt there, so no bulk or clinginess is added. It is an illusion. I doubt I would have worn those shirts much more had I not done the alterations. I would have wasted the money I'd spent on them completely, because I knew they were unflattering in the shorter length. To avoid future shrinkage, I also decided to wash the shirts in the washing machine but dry them only for fifteen minutes on air fluff. After that I hang them up to finish drying. This gives them an ironed look and saves me time.

Given that I alter most of what I buy, I'd rather buy fewer things, pay to have them altered and have them look great on me. Sometimes I'll alter things slightly; for example, I will lower a skirt hem only one inch, because that is all the fabric available, but it is just enough to make an improvement. Some people will think that is a waste of money, but if it helps me sit more comfortably and hits my leg at a more flattering point, I think it is the right thing to do. It costs about ten dollars to raise or lower a hem on a skirt. So, if it is a skirt that cost twenty-nine dollars, with the alterations it costs me thirty-nine dollars. If it is a full-priced skirt purchased, some department stores will alter it for free.

One additional point: Go to the seamstress with your own sense of clarity of what you want done. Together, you can examine how much or how little needs to be taken in or lengthened; in fact, you should let her show you at least two options, but know what your objective is in advance. Don't rely on her judgment. Some alterations I will suggest for you will be foreign to your seamstress or seem frivolous or difficult, because she has not done it before. Use my directions to explain the work to be done. If you find that your seamstress is having difficulty understanding what you want, be prepared to explain thoroughly.

The seamstress I work with is an immigrant and speaks English with difficulty. Her language uses tone as a means of communication. While we don't exchange many multi-syllabic sentences, we communicate pretty well. She seems to moan a lot when contemplating what I want done. I respond by gesticulating and speaking one word directions, staccato, louder than the previous word uttered. When she pins it correctly and we both seem pleased, she makes a lilting sound. That's when I smile and say thank you.

It may seem demanding, but have the seamstress pin the job completely for two reasons: so you can see it in a three-way mirror and suggest changes if needed.

When you work with a seamstress, you will both be clear about your expectations if the garment is fully pinned before alterations begin.

Make sure you receive your altered garments pressed and hanging, protected in plastic. There should be no extra charge for this. This is important for two reasons: Your clothes will be in perfect condition when you want to wear them and it reminds the seamstress that you value your clothing and expect a high standard of workmanship.

Top Ten Alterations

Here are the ten alterations I frequently request. I share the type of alteration I choose as well as the reason for it. By understanding the reason, you will be able to make good judgments about your own items and be able to explain your request clearly if asked. Use your understanding of demography to adjust for the costs of the alterations indicated. If you live in New York City, you'll probably have to double or triple the costs I suggest. If you live in a more rural area, perhaps the costs would be a bit lower.

1. **Shorten sleeves to a three-quarter or elbow length.** In my case, my best sleeve length shows my wrists and forearms. They're relatively slender and pretty. I also have attractive hands that are always manicured and I wear great jewelry. My upper arms are quite heavy and I am only comfortable when they are covered.

   Why choose an abbreviated sleeve length? You want to show skin where you can. Remember the concept of visual weight? More fabric, more presumed weight. Pare back the fabric and reveal pretty skin whenever possible. The exposed skin commands where the eye is drawn to. Each woman must find her own best sleeve length. The object is to show as much skin as you believe is appealing. My seamstress will hem knit sleeves too; don't let people tell you they can't do this. Find someone who will. Hemming sleeves usually costs about ten dollars or fifteen dollars if the garment is lined or is a knit.

2. **Taper skirts and dresses at the knee.** Many plus size women want skirts and dresses to be full for a few reasons: They have ample backsides, hips and tummies. But you can cover the negatives and still look shapely.

   Why taper? You want to create shapeliness and a trimmer looking lower half. Editing at the knee is one area on a women's body where we can manufacture a feminine, hourglass figure while losing no comfort. Skirts that are wide and full fall into the visual weight trap. While you may need the extra fabric to cover tummy, hips and backside, you need progressively less fabric at thighs and knee. This alteration should cost about twelve dollars for a skirt and sixteen dollars for a dress, because the editing needs to flow from a higher place on the garment.

Once, I purchased a Tamotsu suit, jacket and skirt. It is a black and teal pinstripe, fabulous acetate and viscose fabric. It fit very well right off the rack. However, I brought it to my seamstress and had her taper the skirt at the knee, one and a half inches at each side. She wasn't happy, inferring that it already fit well, but made the alterations anyway. The jacket is well fitted and generous through the shoulders. The contrast of the skirt, tapering in at the knee, provides a sexy hourglass effect and definitely shaved twenty pounds off of my appearance. It has become one of my Go-To outfits!

3. **Create an hourglass shape in slacks.** Avoid slacks that have a triangle shape when you lay them flat (the wide part at the waist and the point at the ankle). I understand the motivation for full slacks: We have heavy legs and we want them covered, we have cellulite and stuff that jiggles and want to sit comfortably. Respecting these issues does not preclude creating shape.

   Why take in at the knee? If you don't, they'll look like grandmothers' pants, make you look and feel "plus size" before they're on and look cheap. Editing at the knee is true for slacks, jeans and shorts as well as for skirts and dresses. I do not want you to alter to the point of the slacks being tight or restricted. Although it wouldn't be my first choice, an elastic waist may still be acceptable if the shape of the leg is flattering. I want you to taper and edit gently to create the illusion of a curvy sexy body while sacrificing no comfort or coverage. This alteration should cost about twelve dollars.

4. **Manufacture slacks that flare at the bottom as well as come in at the knee.** A broad upper half needs to be balanced at the bottom. Often, this occurs when you taper at the knee. However, what I am suggesting here is that just as you taper to the knee, you gradually open up the wideness at the hem.

   Why taper the knee and flare the bottom? The wideness at the bottom balances you from top to bottom. If you think about it, one of the problems of being plus size is a sense of disproportion. Poise and gracefulness is achieved by balance: Fashion is no different. Produce balance, proportion and an hourglass contour wherever you can and you will achieve that curvy, sensuous ideal. This alteration should cost about ten dollars.

5. **Hem pants for at least two types of shoes, comfort and dress.** There is self-respect and pride in this alteration. It conveys the message, "There are different facets of my lifestyle and I am worth having specifically designated items for each facet." Put another way, "I want to look great everywhere I go." Remember to bring in the shoes for the fitting.

   Why hem pants for different shoes? When pants drag on the floor or ground you look short and stubby, not to mention poorly dressed. Also, real life is having low heels for real life activities and you need to have pants that are similarly proportioned.

   Likewise, wearing a heel, as high as you are comfortable with, will do great things to improve your appearance through balance and proportion. For alteration purposes though, have a work or dressier pair of slacks hacked. This means they are hemmed on an angle. The part of the slack that covers the heel is longer than the part of the slack that breaks on the instep. The part that breaks on the instep of your foot should be a quarter inch longer than merely graze the foot; there should be a slight break. Hemming on an angle creates a more graceful walk and prevents that awful "high-water" look, which would add the appearance of thirty pounds to your figure. An unlined pair of pants or jeans should cost around ten dollars to hem and a lined pair about fifteen dollars.

6. **Choose garments that skim where they can**. Skim means to slide on and drape your body.

   Why have garments skim? When fabric clings to or stretches around fatty areas, it is unattractive. Also, with fabrics that skim you can create a silhouette that is more flattering. For alteration purposes, you need to buy garments with enough fabric to edit and alter. This means buy the garments large and long enough to cover your largest area and then take the garments in to skim and contour from that point of your body. This alteration can cost between ten and twenty dollars.

7. **Avoid bulkiness; remove or take in extra fabric on sleeves, under arms, back, hips, tummy, thighs and legs.** In fact, this is not so much about removing extra fabric but rather the opportunity to manufacture a curvy contour. The term *princess seams* refers to where the bodice of a garment opens at the bust, narrows through the midsection and waist and gently opens up an inch below the waist through the hips via vertical seaming. You can put princess seaming in garments through alterations. Make sure you ascertain your natural waist: it is the smallest area in your midsection regardless of what the garment or seamstress says. It is unique to each individual.

If you already have an hourglass figure, you can gradually open the clothing pieces to your larger point and gradually narrow them at your small areas. If you are bigger on the top or bottom, you need to gently edit to a point of balance. If you are seeking a sleeker profile, there is no need for more fabric than what is actually needed to drape your body gracefully. One more tip: at least one area of your body—top, bottom, arms, forearms, wrists, hands, legs, ankle, feet or waist—needs to appear graceful, trim, open and sexy. This is necessary to achieve contour, balance and proportion.

Why remove excess fabric? Extra fabric creates more visual weight, which makes us look bigger than we actually are. Another reason to remove it is that it sends to others the message that we dislike our bodies and just want to cover them up. Soon, you will appreciate that you don't need to sell yourself so cheaply. You can create the flow and contour of the top, slacks, skirt, dress or coat you desire to wear. It will be the fit that will enhance your appearance and style as much as the attractiveness of the item you have selected. The cost of this depends on how many areas of the item need to be altered.

8. **Add two inches to elongate/lengthen tops/jackets**. My signature is to add two inches of white T-shirt fabric to tops and jackets to cover

my stomach. Usually you would add fabric or trim in the same color or tone as the garment, making it look like an integral embellishment.

Why lengthen tops and jackets? To cover tummy and hip bulges. The worst thing is for a hem to cling and thereby draw attention to a bulge. Additionally, where a garment ends, is the point that the eye is drawn to. If it ends one inch above the widest part of your backside, it is not good. The same holds true for your arms, thighs, legs and tummy. The cost of this is about ten dollars.

9. **Shorten hems on skirts and dresses so they hit your legs in the most flattering place.** Know your best skirt and dress length. Most women, heavy or slender, will find that their most attractive place is the bottom of the knee. If your knees are attractive and you are comfortable sitting in a shorter skirt, you can hem as high as the top of your knee, especially for sports clothing. (If you are a teenager and have attractive, firm legs you can hem shorter.) If you don't like your knees and want to sit without being self-conscious, hem to the bottom of your knees and relax. However, be sure to hem just above the area revealing indentation or shapeliness on your legs.

    Why hem skirts and dresses? Everyone has a most flattering part of their legs. Show it off! Tanned legs or natural or black shades of hosiery are sexy. Don't allow a skirt or dress hem to add visual weight or dowdiness to your appearance. A hem costs about ten dollars— fifteen dollars if it is lined.

10. **Lengthen skirts and dresses to create sexy, sleek legs.** If the item has enough fabric to lower the hem and it is the type of fabric that won't show the previous hemline, just do it. It will cost about ten to fifteen dollars and will do wonders for your look, attitude and comfort level. However, if there is not enough fabric or if the fabric is the type that the previous hemline would make a permanent scar, consider adding trim that looks like an embellishment.

    Why lengthen skirt and dress hems? Similar to hemming skirts and dresses to the most flattering part of your legs, lengthening skirt and dress hems will help create balance and proportion. Lengthening hems can also introduce new pieces into your wardrobe that you were self-conscious to wear before.

Recently, I bought a couple of skorts. They were about two inches too short for my comfort level. Fortunately, they came with fabric belts that matched each skort. My seamstress added the fabric belts to the hem of the skorts and voilà! Each skort was now two inches longer. Recall also my discussion of buying two skorts to lengthen into one in chapter 3.

As I've mentioned earlier, I wear black a lot. Black trim is easy to find and add to the hems of garments. Working on the project of lengthening a black shirt, I went to the fabric store to buy black bias tape in a two-inch width (less than two dollars at any fabric store). From my trip to the store, I learned that bias tape comes in a multitude of colors and can be used to lengthen just about any color garment. Also, grossgrain ribbon is a great embellishment, comes in many colors and widths and is sold by the yard (buy two yards, two to three dollars per yard). This is where your own sense of fashion comes in. The trim you select should be consistent with your style: luxurious, preppy, feminine, sexy, athletic or ethnic.

I love the look of adding sheer fabric consistent with the color or tone of the item to a hem (or sleeve). It makes for a great illusion, gives coverage and shape and is sexy and enticing.

Sometimes it's easy to make big improvements with little effort. At first, I suggest you stick with the ten alternations we've discussed. Over time, you will learn what alterations work best and how to combine them. One time, I combined many of these alterations in one coat. Just before we were married, my husband bought me a designer trench coat and several matching accessories. The coat was a size eighteen, which was and is my size. But it wasn't flattering; it was too big, too much coat. He had spent a lot of money on it, but I wore it very infrequently over the years. A couple of years ago, I decided to remake the coat. First, I shortened the coat by six inches to hang about two inches below my knee. This is long enough for any dress or skirt I might wear and it immensely reduced the visual weight implied by the coat. Second, I changed the traditional belt in a subtle way: I raised it and created an eight-inch belt loop on the back of the coat from the fabric removed when the garment was shortened, which emphasized the smallest part of my back. This was the beginning of establishing a graceful outline. Third, I pared back the fabric through the back seam and the two side seams, establishing an hourglass contour. A generous fit is part of the coat's style and it was important to keep the feel of that while minimizing the bulk. Fourth, I left the time-honored wool collar, leather buttons and trim and of course the lining (which matches all of the accessories) intact. I now have a personalized trench coat. The alterations for this job cost well over one hundred dollars, but I wear it often now and expect I will have the coat for many more years.

This chapter is pivotal to looking great, because it strongly suggests a change in your thinking about acquiring and preparing your clothing. The extra time and costs involved in alterations may say "ready-to-wear" really isn't—but that's okay too. Perhaps, more importantly it says, "I'm worth it. I'm in control. I can shop, edit and alter. I can dress well by addressing my specific needs."

Emerald Shape Diamond

Casual

Illustrations courtesy of April Dukes

This sporty outfit creates shape with a double V neckline and buttons that create a lengthening effect. The tone on tone outfit has the slimming effect of mono-chromatic dressing but is spiced up by changes in hue. Black opaque hosiery and black ballet flats make her legs look great even with a raised hemline.

Dressy

The soft curves of the jacket create a sexy contour. Mondrian color-blocking allows "pattern" in the fabric to create the illusion of a curvy silhouette, while the dropped waist helps camouflage.

Heart Shape Diamond

Casual

Illustrations courtesy of April Dukes

This outfit uses a dark color on her larger top half and a lighter color on her slimmer lower half to balance her silhouette. The raised waist shapes and softens her largest area. The boots and slacks share the same light color, which not only lengthens her legs and makes her look taller but actually balances her broad top half, too.

Dressy

The soft, dark, open jacket creates the illusion of decreasing her full upper half. The drape in the jacket and the lighter underpinning create a feminine, shapely silhouette. The subtly revealed black camisole underneath the jacket further minimizes the wide horizontal line of her chest area and adds some sensuous interest as well.

Marquise Shape Diamond

Casual

Illustrations courtesy of April Dukes

This duster uses color blocking to draw attention away from her large tummy. The empire waist creates indentation and shape and allows the fabric to drape from a higher point, disguising her middle. The continuation of the color at the bottom of the long jacket through the slacks to the shoes creates a long, streamlined silhouette.

Dressy

The empire waist creates a flattering drape and shape, enhanced by the fabric, a soft jersey, which will move nicely. The open skin at the neckline frames her pretty face and exposed forearms draw the eye away from her larger mid-section.

Pear Shape Diamond

Casual

The jersey dress is flattering by its shape and use of trim. The details are kept to the top of the item—neckline and chest pockets—while a set of buttons provides a long, visual vertical line. The fabric is thick enough to provide coverage but still supple enough to drape well.

Dressy

This pear shape diamond has attractive arms and shows them off! The dress is a simple, sexy, A-line cut that keeps the majority of the embellishment at the neck, where the eye is drawn. The use of black hosiery and heels yields long sexy legs, lengthening and balancing the whole silhouette.

Round Shape Diamond

The soft surplice top is flattering to the top of her body. The high waist and longer length of the top disguises her round tummy. The whole outfit—top, boot cut slacks and shoes—uses a tone-on-tone coloration providing a slenderizing vertical line.

Dressy

The use of the surplice neckline and long peplum top is very forgiving, flowing from the raised waist. The pencil skirt tapers to show off shapely legs. Lots of skin is shown, down to the peep toe, making the retro outfit stylish and sexy.

Petite

The outfit uses a vertical continuation of deep color (the trim on the jacket, slacks and shoes) to create the longest silhouette possible. The open jacket reveals a good-looking camisole and great accessories. The pointy toe (even though flat) shoe is flattering, too.

Dressy

This dress is simple and sexy and does not overpower her petite stature. The surplice neckline is open and fresh. The outfit keeps the embellishment to a minimum, in the form of coordinated scarf, belt, jewelry and shoes.

CHAPTER 12

Babe's Dirty Dozen

REALITY CHECK
AND HOW TO COPE

"I base my fashion sense on what doesn't itch."
~Gilda Radner

What do sliding shorts, posture bras, wide bra straps, moleskin, opaque tights, roll-on deodorant, wide panty liners, stain removal, chamois, shoe orders, layering and skorts have in common? They are the "dirty dozen" items that take the edge off some of the realities of being a plus size woman and must be considered when looking to dress and feel sexy, sensational and successful.

1. Chafing
Chafing has become a microcosm of sorts for me when I contemplate the world of fashion for plus size women. Figuratively, chafing represents my feelings toward the fashion industry when they exhibit insensitivity to the needs of plus size consumers. Literally, I'm referring to the rashes and welts that form between the upper thighs as they rub together as we move around through the day. This is often the reason plus size women do not wear skirts and dresses.

Skirts and dresses are an important antidote to visual weight. Jeans and slacks have a tendency to make you look heavier, because the fabric extends and there is the presumption that the body fills up the fabric. Not so with skirts and dresses. The clean line of the fabric stopping around the knees shows skin and is therefore very pretty and fresh.

Bring skirts and dresses back into your wardrobe with a shaper resembling a pair of "sliding shorts" or "biker's shorts." This lightweight, stretch shaper or girdle is comfortable to wear and creates a barrier between the thighs, allowing them to rub together with no painful outcome.

2. Posture

Plus size women may get more fatigued throughout the day than some other people. The reality is that with every movement we are carrying substantially more weight. It is important to focus on posture for appearance, comfort and energy.

Posture bras are a breakthrough in the undergarment market. A posture bra is essentially a longline bra that closes in the front and is constructed more like a sleeveless shirt than a traditional bra with straps. Often, the material is firm but stretchy and is fairly comfortable. However, the bra may be built with boning (a plastic insertion to maintain the integrity and line of the bra). Boning can add some discomfort, so you may need to try a couple of brands to find one that fits comfortably. In the world of longline bras, the length of the bra is an important factor in determining comfort. Specifically, you will learn that if you are short-waisted, certain lines will be cut better for you. In addition, if you are long-waisted, you will have to find your length of comfort, otherwise the bra will "ride up" on you through the day, compounding your discomfort in addition to revealing excess skin. Here is the fix: Have an additional inch of the bra band fabric sewn to the bottom of the bra. The entire placket of hooks will need to be replaced for a smooth look. This repair will cost about forty dollars, but it is worth every penny.

This bra "encourages" the wearer to keep her shoulders rolled back, thereby enhancing her posture and appearance. This adjustment helps you breathe easier throughout the day, resulting in more energy or at least the appearance of such.

The posture bra certainly creates a win-win situation for many plus size women; it trims the tummy, creates a waist, erases back fat and enhances posture.

3. Bra Straps

For the plus size woman who has large, heavy breasts, the indentation of bra straps on the shoulders can be painful. There is a threefold solution short of breast reduction surgery. First, a well-fitted bra is foundational. This allows the bra itself to do the work of supporting your breasts as opposed to letting the straps do all the work. Second, if you don't want to wear a longline or posture bra every day, use a bra with at least four hooks in the back. Third, choose a bra that has three-inch wide padded straps specifically designed for comfort when supporting large breasts.

4. Foot, Leg and Back Pain

We put considerable weight on our feet each day and often wear shoes ill-suited for the task. Have your foot measured and choose a casual shoe with a built-in arch. Clogs can be a great option because of the firmness of the construction. Moreover, do not wear the same pair of shoes throughout the day. Keep extra pairs of shoes in your desk at work, in your car and at home and change your shoes regularly. The reason is that different pairs of shoes will offer different or additional support to your feet. Shoes get wet from perspiration. When shoes are wet, they change the way they support your feet, often causing discomfort. Also, if the shoes tend to become uncomfortable in any place, a different pair of shoes will give you some relief in that particular spot causing you trouble.

Moleskin is a great Band-Aid of sorts. It is a thick, wooly patch with adhesive on the back that you can cut and apply to an area that seems to gets friction from a shoe. It may add some bulk, but it offers great relief, especially if a blister has already started to form. One suggestion is to cut it big enough so that as you move through the day, if the patch happens to move a bit, it won't move off of the area you are trying to protect.

If you find yourself sedentary for a good portion of the day, try to stand up and walk around every fifteen minutes or so. I have found that when I sit for long periods of time and then stand up, it causes greater discomfort to my feet, especially my instep. Additionally, walking around tends to shift weight and that is a good thing for your back. Stand up and stretch frequently.

5. Veins
In terms of fashion, I suggest spider and varicose veins be dealt with three ways. The first is to wear slacks.

The second option is to wear Just My Size opaque tights. They cost about five dollars a pair and last forever (as long as you don't wash them with anything that could transfer lint). They are lightweight, very comfortable and offer significant opacity (the opposite of sheerness). Feel free to wear this product with a dressy skirt or dress as well as a casual skirt or skort. The sight of veins on your legs will be a thing of the past.

A third option, especially for summertime, is an artificial tanning product. Personally, I use Mystic Tan, which is a brand that involves going into a tanning booth and allowing a spray to coat your body. It takes a couple of minutes but last several days, almost through the week. It has definitely reduced the appearance of my spider veins.

As a woman who unsuccessfully tried sclerotherapy (a saline solution injected into the spider vein, purportedly causing it to fade), I recommend the options mentioned. I found the sclerotherapy process to be very painful, expensive (about $300 per session and I went six times) and ineffective.

6. Perspiration
If you find that underarm perspiration is noticeable, here is a low-tech, tried-and-true solution. Use a generous amount of an unscented roll-on deodorant, such as Ban Roll-On. Cover a wide area. While it is still damp apply powder. Choose a powder from the line of fragrance you use or something as simple and fresh as Shower to Shower (my personal choice). After it sets and dries, it will keep you dry enough and release the fragrance of your choosing throughout the day.

7. Dry-Cleaning

To begin, dry-clean your clothes as infrequently as possible as long as they are still looking fresh. The chemicals used in the dry-cleaning process will compromise the integrity of the fabric and garment over time, resulting in shininess or discoloration, especially yellowing of whites. If you go from dry-cleaning an item once a week to dry-cleaning it every two to three weeks, the garment will last two to three times as long and wind up costing you a lot less money. Here are a few ways to still look fresh while dry-cleaning less:

1. Take your clothes off as soon as you get home and hang them up in an area that allows some ventilation (not your closet) overnight. Hang dresses and tops up carefully so that the shoulders are placed precisely on the hanger, allowing the garment to drape as it is intended. For jeans and slacks, fold them so that the center crease is apparent. Hang them upside down (waist down) on a hanger with clips so that the greater weight of the garment (the upper half) is causing the crease of the legs to reset. For sweaters or knits, lay them on a dry, clean towel and drape them over your shower curtain rod overnight.

2. Spot clean a garment with a thin damp washcloth. Be sure the washcloth has minimal or no lint. Use club soda or cool water. Blot; do not rub harshly.

3. Use a lint roll brush to catch lint and pet hair.

4. Use panty liners. Recently, a larger (not thicker) panty liner was placed on the market (Kotex Lightdays Extra Coverage). It covers a wider area and is therefore more comfortable for some plus size women. This alone should save numerous trips to the cleaners for jeans and slacks.

5. Bring items to the dry-cleaner to be pressed only.

8. Laundry

When it comes to washing clothing in the washing machine, take advantage of the delicate cycle. Always wash with similar colors. I'm a big fan of Shout and OxiClean used together—they have saved me (and our baseball-playing son) many times. Minimize the drying cycle whenever you can. Shout makes a gel product and a spray product for stain treatment. Use the gel for small areas and rub it in with the brush inserted in the cap of the bottle. Use the spray for large areas and saturate. With both applications, let it sit for a few minutes before starting the wash cycle. Palmolive is also good for getting out grease stains.

A word from a big sister: Plus size women, because of how we are built, get more food spots on the chest area than smaller-busted women. It is critical either to get the spot out, use the alternative we'll discuss next or to throw away the stained garment if it can't be saved. It is an image killer for a plus size woman to walk around with a stain; it compromises all we are trying to achieve. If a plus size woman walks around with a stain on her blouse, it reinforces negative and harsh stereotypes about plus size women that we can't afford. Get rid of a stained article of clothing.

If you're attached to a particular article of clothing that is stained, consider this option. After the garment has been cleaned, cover the stain spot with an appliqué or a small cluster of them. Appliqués are designs made by stitching or gluing one fabric on another. This is sort of a funky idea, but I have been known to use it successfully a few times. If the stain and the appliqué can be joined, go for it. Just be sure to use this cover-up sparingly.

In terms of general care, dry clothes in a delicate cycle for fifteen minutes to fluff and remove some wrinkles and then hang them up for the rest of the drying process (even if this takes a couple of days).

Use the fluff cycle of the dryer whenever possible and hang the garments carefully, even if it takes a couple of days for them to dry completely. The best part of this is that you will never need to iron again. After being fluffed in the dryer, garments are less wrinkled. Coupled with the slow drying process, the few wrinkles that remain seem to smooth out.

There is another reason this tip is important: it reduces the shrinkage in a garment. Many times I have washed and dried a top after the first wearing and it has shrunk, resulting in the top being either unflattering or not wearable. What a waste of money.

9. Hard on Clothes and Shoes

Okay, so plus size women are hard on clothing and shoes. It's a no-brainer that additional weight will cause the appearance of additional wear. Here's my suggestion: When you come home, put on your play clothes and shoes. Get comfortable around your house, with yourself and with those you love. Hang your work and dressy clothing up right away.

With regard to shoes, wipe them off with a damp cloth or chamois (pronounced and also spelled shammy). A chamois is a cloth (often yellow) sold to clean cars. It is a great dry cloth option to wipe shoes and handbags. When you wipe the items, look to see if any repairs are needed. Is all of the hardware on the handbag working and in good repair? Do the lifts of the shoes need to be replaced? Do suede shoes or hand bags need to be professionally cleaned? Can you clean them yourself? Yes! Purchase a suede cleaning brush and use after each wearing. This great little item, which costs about five dollars, has two brushes built-in: a rigid one to scrape off debris and a smoother one to keep the nap soft and in the same direction.

10. Hard to Find Shoes and Sizes

"Fashion Law: If the shoe fits, it's ugly" (author unknown). Hey, that's not really true anymore. It is imperative that you have good shoes that fit well. There are many shoe stores popping up that sell comfortable shoes in a wide range of sizes. Seek them out. In addition, Nordstrom carries a wide variety of shoes, styles and sizes. But most importantly, ask the salesperson to bring in a particular size or style you are looking for. Ask the store to bring in the style and size you are looking to try on and do not pay for the shoes in advance or the shipping charges.

Recently, I wanted to support a new shoe store that caters to the "hard-to-fit." I was purchasing a pair of Dansko clogs and asked them to order some Munro shoes for me to try in a size nine and a half double wide. When I signed the credit card slip, I noticed that they had charged me for both pairs of shoes, which the salesman hadn't made clear to me that he would do. I expressed my dissatisfaction, got a refund for both pairs of shoes and then purchased the Dansko clogs at Nordstom. This is an example of the difference between being a sophisticated shopper and a desperate buyer. Believe me, I have trouble with my feet and I'm willing to pay for good shoes.

11. Feeling Too Warm

Often, the temperature of a plus size woman seems to register higher than her thinner counterpart. I'm not sure why this is, but I know there are a few things you can do about it. The first is to wear clothing constructed from natural fibers. Natural fibers breathe. They allow for air to move through the garment, keeping the wearer much more comfortable. Synthetics, on the other hand, tend to keep moisture inside, exacerbating perspiration and that clammy feeling. A small percentage of Lycra or spandex notwithstanding, substitute cotton and lightweight or tropical weight wools for synthetics wherever you can.

A second strategy is to wear outfits that are comprised of layered pieces. Be sure the bottom piece, though, is one you are comfortable being seen in if you choose to remove the outer layer. For example, often I will wear a sleeveless style tank top or shell under a blazer. However, because I am uncomfortable showing the upper half of my arms, I won't remove the blazer. If I think the weather will be warm, I may choose a short sleeve top for the underpinning so that the option to remove my jacket is with me through the day.

A third tip is to wear a top with three-quarter sleeves with a vest instead of a blazer or jacket on top. This allows for ease of movement, still gives good coverage and is cooler in terms of temperature.

A fourth hint applies when you are wearing a dress. Wear a full-length slip. Instead of providing additional warmth, it actually absorbs perspiration and therefore keeps you cooler through the day.

Finally, minimize accessories that may feel burdensome if you anticipate feeling excessively warm. For example, a scarf, a necklace, a bracelet or a heavy handbag may make you uncomfortable just when you need to feel light and unencumbered. All of this implies that it is a good idea to check the weather the night before.

12. Playtime Options—Open Up!

For summer, put together outfits that leave some bareness on both arms and legs. Look for necklines with a scoop or a V shape. The goal is to show skin. There is a message that is created when soft, smooth, tanned skin shows: "I'm ready to celebrate summer or recreational time and have some fun."

Choose simple lines and embellishments and loose but lean garments that skim and drape the body. This is where the skort reigns supreme. This simple pencil style skirt with a built-in pair of shorts underneath rocks! You get the best of both worlds: the graceful coverage of a skirt and the comfort of shorts. Create a fun color scheme with a top, sandals or mules and other accessories and go play.

T-shirt or polo style dresses, knee-length and with an A-line silhouette, also work well. You may want to add a (short) full-length slip underneath, again for the best drape and to absorb moisture.

When the weather gets a bit chillier, keep the same goals in mind. Simple, lean clothing with flattering drapes work best. The same skort you wear in warm weather works for cooler weather with a pair of Just My Size tights underneath. Choose a cotton sweater with a scoop or V neckline. Still try to show skin and consider three-quarter sleeves. Just a few inches of skin on the forearms and an open neckline makes a big difference. Open up!

CHAPTER 13

Bring Light to the Face

SPOTLIGHT
YOU

"Of all the things you wear, your expression is the most important."
~Janet Lane

Your most important feature is your face. Your face is the point that others' views will settle on and tune into. But, perhaps more importantly, it is the reflection of your inner self. If you feel good about your face, when you walk into a room or when you are conversing with others, a confidence and energy will emanate that will boost your image exponentially. Therefore, bringing out the beauty in your face is first and foremost. Said another way, the main objective is to bring light to your face. There are four components involved in this process: makeup, hair, jewelry and eyewear. In most books, you will see discussion of the latter two, jewelry and eyewear, confined to a less significant chapter, often relegated to accessories. For plus size women it is fundamental that your face is pretty, expressive and infused with vitality. Jewelry and eyewear are a direct means to that end.

Skin Care
For all women, regardless of weight or size, skin care is paramount. Skin is the largest organ a human being possesses. It is among the most

important benchmarks by which a person is judged in terms of lifestyle, socioeconomic status and age. Why? Because it telegraphs to the world whether you are in control of your circumstances or they are in control of you. It is important to take care of your skin and be mindful that it is an expressive caption about you and the state of your affairs.

Skin care strategies and products know no size. They afford equal opportunity to all women. But for the plus size woman they are perhaps even more critical. Why is this so? Here's a statement that only a big sister can make. Many people in the world view plus size women as lethargic, lazy and unkempt. Pound for pound, dollar for dollar, nothing can reverse this attitude as quickly as fresh, clear, dewy, even-toned, healthy looking skin. While I specifically address face and neck areas in this chapter, it is important also to care for the skin on the rest of the body.

There are four steps to good skin care that must become part of your routine, and you only need four products to accomplish it. There is no need to buy $300 moisturizing creams or a dozen products. In fact, I recommend against that. Find products that are compatible with your skin type, reflect current research and are pleasing to your sensibilities. Here are the four steps:

1. Cleanse
2. Exfoliate
3. Moisturize (day and night)
4. Protect

The steps and products you probably don't need are astringent, eye cream and youth serums

Cleanse

A cleanser should clean your skin and remove makeup with a single product and little effort. In addition, it may contain a toner, which closes pores and resets the proper balance of bio-chemicals found in healthy skin. Suffice it to say, the best cleansers are simple and do not leave your face feeling dry. I do not recommend "soap bar" products, because they tend to be drying.

If your skin is dry, cleanse with a cream or oil-based product that provides moisture as it cleans. If your skin is oily, choose a water-based cleanser with oil-retarding ingredients.

Cleansing should be like one-stop shopping: remove makeup (including mascara), clean the face without a lot of fragrance or extra ingredients and leave skin feeling supple and soft.

Exfoliate

In order for skin to be fresh, dewy and glowing, it is necessary to remove dead skin cells. Dead skin cells clog pores and can even accumulate and create spots. In order to prevent this, it is necessary to use an exfoliation product on a weekly basis. Pick one weekend morning and commit to it. It doesn't take long, maybe an additional five minutes. When you remove the cream, lotion, gel or mask from your face, your skin will seem refreshed, glowing and more youthful.

Moisturize

Moisturizer is a very important and personal choice. In this area, I'm convinced that more expensive is not necessarily better. Be wary of marketing programs that make you think you are buying into the fountain of youth. My uncle was a cosmetic chemist. My grandmother and my uncle's wife were identical twin sisters and both had terrific complexions. Every evening of their lives, they removed makeup with a cold cream product my uncle made for them. Then they bathed their faces in about a quarter of an inch of that same cold cream product (no exaggeration) and slept in it. My grandmother died at the age of ninety without a wrinkle in her face. My aunt still looks great; her complexion is remarkable. Genetics? Probably. But the key was not buying or using more products than needed.

The best thing about purchasing creams and cosmetics at upscale department store counters is that you get to try a product before purchasing it and receive advice from a trained expert (but be wary of the *sales* expert). In fact, many of the cosmetic lines will give you a sample to use at home that will last for a few days. The bad thing is that the products are expensive and more often than not, you can find a drugstore brand that will be just as effective. The good thing, though, is that if you keep your receipt, you can return the product if you are not satisfied and receive a refund in the manner in which you paid for the item. A few drugstore chains are following suit on this return policy, so it may be worth doing research before purchasing to afford yourself this cushion.

Moisturizer is the key to fresh looking skin and it offers the perfect base for foundation. For normal skin, use a lightweight moisturizing lotion or cream. For skin that feels dry or sensitive, use a rich hydrating cream or balm. For oily skin, choose an oil-free formula that hydrates and helps control oil production.

Oily skin is often misunderstood. If you have oily skin, choose an oil-free moisturizer. Even oily skin needs to be moisturized. In addition, use a foaming face wash that is designed for oily skin. Do not use an astringent, alcohol-based or otherwise. Do not strip your skin or its natural oils; just try to control the excess. In fact, oily skin may age better than dry or combination skin. Don't cheat yourself of this asset. A better way to control oil through the day may be blotting tissues, which you can purchase in the drugstore at a low cost. You simply pull one out, like a small tissue, and press down on an obviously oily area of your face once or twice and throw it out. Sometimes you may decide to follow up with a small application of loose powder and other times that won't even be necessary.

For a day moisturizer, find a lotion or cream that is suited to your skin type, consistency and fragrance preferences. Although every skin care line will try to sell you an additional product for your eye area, I use my moisturizer around the delicate skin around my eyes. I do, however, often use an additional product. About two years ago, I realized I had "dry eye" syndrome, not uncommon for women as they get older. The result was not only on the inside of my eye, but also on my eyelids and the outer corners of my eyes. As a result of this, I often take the smallest bit of 1 percent hydrocortisone ointment, run it between my fingers to warm it and gently pat it on my eyelids and around my eye area. When I do this, usually in the evening, I do not apply my nighttime moisturizer to my eye area.

Protect

A daytime moisturizer must have a sun protection factor (SPF) of at least fifteen to be considered acceptable. It is vital that you protect your skin from the sun on a daily basis, even if it does not appear that the sun is strong on a particular day. The sun is strong and damaging every day. Sun exposure is the single most important catalyst of pre-mature aging, wrinkles and dark spots and, more importantly, of skin cancer. No excuses; please wear an SPF of at least fifteen every day. The one I use, Super Defense by Clinique, has an SPF of twenty-five.

Makeup

I firmly believe that the best makeup application is one that looks the most natural. In fact, makeup should be used to create the illusion that you have a flawless face, a face that illuminates lovely, pretty or striking features. What should stand out are your features, not your makeup. The goal is to strive for the application of invisible makeup.

The specific challenge for a plus size woman is to minimize areas of puffiness, fatty deposits, dark circles and age spots to let sparkling, pretty features shine through. How can you accomplish this? You must use light and shadow to balance the face. You should seek products with sheer textures and lightly pigmented colors for a subtle, refined look. The fun part is achieving a huge improvement, a natural and youthful look, while using minimal makeup.

I favor this approach, because it helps pare down and simplify the daily application of makeup. Putting on makeup should take between five and ten minutes each morning. Purchasing a lot of products requires the undertaking of a complicated process that you may not be willing to follow each day.

Lip Conditioning

Begin your makeup routine by conditioning your lips. I use Vaseline, but there are many pleasant lip balms to use. At the end of applying my makeup, I take a damp washcloth and rub my lips clean of the Vaseline, thereby exfoliating them every day. Then I add pink lip gloss over the lip balm that remains. I love the soft, supple feel and coloration of lip gloss and this allows my eyes to be my more dominant feature.

However, if you prefer a different look, still simple and subtle, prepare your lips with a lip balm. Next, with a dry finger, pat your blush cake a few times and then press the powder into your lower lip. Start in the center and work out to the corners. Take a clean finger and do the same on your upper lip. When you're finished, you can dab a bit of lip balm or lip gloss to the center of your bottom lip for a perfect, sexy pout.

If you have a very thin upper lip, you may want to use lipstick that has more pigment. If you have thin lips, choose light to medium shades of lip color and avoid dark shades, which have a minimizing effect, as you are seeking a fuller look to achieve overall balance among your facial features. If you love the look and feel of lipstick, remember to keep it moist. I encourage you to stay away from a matte finish, which looks dry and uninviting. If you want a more defined lip, after you apply the lip color, line your lips with a soft neutral color that blends with the color applied to your lips. Using an obvious, dark lip liner is no longer fashionable and will date you, making you look older.

Use the natural coloring of your lips as a guide when choosing a lipstick shade. The most flattering shade will either match or be slightly richer than your lips. This is similar to the tip of using your blush to double as your lipstick shade. Both tips are based on enhancing your natural coloring.

Here's a money-saving and convenient tip. Go to a beauty supply store that is open to the public and test their lipstick or lip gloss products. You may find one you love. Then buy four of the same one. They usually cost less than five dollars. Tuck one in your makeup kit in the bathroom, one in your car, one in your desk drawer if you work outside your home and finally one in your handbag. Now, for the same or less money as one department store lipstick, you have the lipstick you want wherever you go. Lipstick or lip gloss is probably the one makeup product you will need to reapply throughout the day. Having multiples makes reapplying very easy to do, which, in turn, makes it more likely that you will do it. The one I wear is amazingly similar to a designer product I see in the stores in terms of color, consistency and quality.

Twenty years ago and maybe even ten years ago, it was important for me to show off a status lipstick, a designer whose packaging identified it as a coveted brand. I no longer feel that way. In fact, it's very becoming to pull out a no-name lipstick that gets the job done at a fraction of the price. That action is embedded with confidence that transcends status symbol packaging.

Moisturizer and Foundation

Every woman should wear moisturizer and foundation. Choose a daytime moisturizer based on your skin care routine. Moisturizer should be the first thing you apply to your face. Next, apply foundation. This achieves a perfect, glowing complexion in about forty-five seconds.

How do you determine if the foundation shade is right for you? Apply a swipe of foundation to your jaw line. Does it blend in easily? If you can see it, it is not the right shade. Keep looking. When you find the right shade, it will disappear. It is very important to match the shade perfectly.

Choosing what type of foundation you should use is a very personal decision. Fortunately, makeup counters will give you numerous samples. Each lasts several days, so you can try many different ones before committing to one in particular. Some women love a mousse, others heavier creams; some, like myself, use a liquid product dispensed through a pump. Some products are oil-free, others are water based and still others are rich with emollients. In addition, choose a foundation with a sun protection factor (SPF) of at least ten and enjoy additional sun protection beyond what your moisturizer affords.

The one thing I must recommend, though, is to avoid a matte finish. It looks dull and lifeless, regardless of the current trends. Look for a dewy finish; it looks youthful and supple every time. I can't emphasize this enough, because this is the antidote to falling into the stereotype of lethargy and laziness associated with being a large woman. A moist, radiant glow looks energetic and young or, in the alternative, young at heart, which is pretty good, too.

When you find a great match to your skin, use a damp triangle makeup sponge to blend the foundation and cover your skin. Use motions that go up and out to the hairline to blend seamlessly. Use the product sparingly. When the sponge is damp, the product will cover your face using a small quantity.

A great product these days is a tinted moisturizer (all-in-one). It offers a sheer, casual alternative to foundation and moisturizer. It feels very lightweight and still evens out skin for a soft, perfected look.

While you may enjoy the advice and samples that a high-end makeup representative may give you, the day will come when you can read the package in a drugstore, select a product that costs about one quarter of the department store brand and be just as happy. I use a foundation that costs about ten dollars and lasts for more than half the year. In the summer when I am tan, I buy the same product in a more golden shade.

Eyebrows

I can't say enough about the importance of strong, well-arched and perfectly cared for eyebrows for the plus size woman. They serve as architecture: well-defined angles to what otherwise may be a puffy, full face.

There are many eyebrow kits on the market that can help women shape flattering eyebrows. There are also products to fill in eyebrows with powder and even set eyebrows with gels that can be likened to colorless mascara.

However, I recommend getting your eyebrows waxed at a salon. The aesthetician will achieve perfect brows every time. All you need to do is to fill in with some powder or pencil what is "drawn" for you. Use your pencil or brush and work upwards in short, careful movements. The cost for an eyebrow wax will vary from location to location, but in general, it costs around fifteen dollars, a small investment to add flattering shape and angles to your face.

If you've never had your eyebrows waxed, here's what you can expect. You lie down on the aesthetician's table and she applies hot wax with a tongue depressor to the hairs she intends to remove. A few seconds after it begins to dry, she takes a piece of cotton fabric, presses down on the wax and then strips the fabric off, pulling the hairs with it. It may hurt for a few seconds and she may have to do the process once or twice more. Each subsequent pull hurts less, because there are fewer hairs left each time. After the aesthetician is done, she will apply some lotion to soothe your eyebrow area, but the area will be red for a while. The process is not a big deal at all and takes about five minutes. Depending on how quickly your eyebrows grow in, you should estimate getting waxed about once every few weeks to a month.

Mustache

If you have a dark mustache above your upper lip, you may want to have it waxed when you have your eyebrows done. It is unattractive for a woman to have facial hair or a dark shadow. If you have a light colored mustache, you may choose to leave it alone or have it waxed off. Although I'm blonde, I choose to have mine waxed, because I strive for a perfected complexion. In my opinion, a mustache gets in the way of this, because the hairs can catch the sunlight and look more pronounced. Interestingly, for me, the eyebrow and upper lip wax made the hair grow back lighter and less frequently. The mustache waxing process is similar to the eyebrow wax and it costs about ten dollars.

Concealer

Select a concealer that is a shade lighter than your foundation and has a yellow base. Like foundation, you will know when you have selected the right color of concealer when it disappears and blends seamlessly into your skin. Some people prefer a foam rubber wand in a mascara-type case; others prefer a cream with more density and apply it with a makeup brush.

This is the key: The light color of the concealer will make dark shadows, indentations or imperfections fade, which is the goal. Therefore, only apply concealer to shadows or spots. Do not use a rubbing or swiping motion to blend it in. Simply take a dry finger and pat the spot so the dab of concealer becomes less apparent. The concealer is almost worked into the skin, but still does the job of covering the dark area. Be judicious in how much concealer you use. Use too much and you can get a raccoon look—not good.

To lighten particularly dark circles, apply concealer under the eye to the lash line and on the innermost corner of the eye. Smooth and blend using your fingers and a tapping motion until the product has blended in.

Some areas to consider using concealer for on a heavier face include: the lines between the base of the nose and the mouth, shadows under the nose, the inside corner of the eyes, near the bone in your nose and the outside corner or your eyes. Further, to add an angular quality to your face, dab some concealer down the bridge of your nose and blend. This creates the illusion of a slimmer, angular nose.

Here's a good tip from the Bobbi Brown makeup counter: Apply concealer on the spot next to the inner corner of the eye and it will open up your eyes and give you a fresh, bright-eyed look. One of my tips for concealer is to put the tiniest amount of concealer on your eyelid, just about the center, and dab it in until it is subtle to achieve a fresh, open-eyed, energetic look.

Contouring Face Powder

The plus size woman may have a double chin and fatty deposits that detract from her prettier features. To counter this, choose a soft, light brown blush, one with very little pigment. Dab a full, round brush into the blush a few times then blow off the excess on the brush. Dust the blush under the face in motions going upwards and dab the blush across fatty deposits along the jaw line. Use the same brush and blush to contour just under the cheekbones. If they are not apparent, press in with your fingers and locate each cheekbone and then fill in the hollow or where the hollow would be. Use soft, light strokes, nothing obvious, to add just a hint of well-placed deeper pigment. To keep balance, lightly dab the same color blush around the hairline of the face.

If you feel you want some color in your loose powder, choose a pale yellow color. However, if your skin feels dry, dust the powder only around the nose and forehead.

Blush

Less pigment is better here, too. Find a powder blush in a color most like your own skin tone when you blush naturally. When you are considering different shades, pinch your cheek and match the shade it turns. When applying, make sure to blow off excess powder from your brush first. To apply blush, smile and brush soft, circular strokes on the upper half of the fullness of your cheeks that emerge when you smile (also called the "apples"). You can always apply more if you want, but it is messy to try to remove blush after it is applied.

Take the same blush and brush and feather it into the crease of your eyes, the sides of your forehead and on your chin as well. This affords a healthy but subtle glow and balance as well.

Eye Shadow, Eyeliner and Mascara

I love a light, matte color as eye shadow for the eyelids. The goal is to open up the eyes and appear fresh and alert. Use a color that complements your skin tone, such as warm ivory, light pink or peach. Dust a light eye shadow color from the lash line to the brow bone using an eye shadow brush.

The crease above your eyelid should be filled in with a soft, deep, natural color; an earth tone, if you will. If you have baggy skin above the creases of your eyes, do not draw attention to it with color. Either help it "recede" by applying a muted brown tone or leave it alone. By placing a light color on your eyelids, you will "raise" the lid areas and create contrast that will be most attractive.

If you choose to wear eyeliner, select either black or brown. Women who have dark or olive skin can choose black eyeliner; however, women who have lighter complexions should choose brown eyeliner. Apply it just above your eyelash lines, narrow at the inside corners of your eyes and gradually widening as you move to the outside corners of your eyes. This will make your eyelashes appear fuller. Another method is to begin the line at the eyelash lines just above the pupils of your eyes and draw the lines out to the outer corners of your eyes. Keep the line soft, smooth and rather thin. However, if you are looking for a bit more drama, perhaps for evening, draw the line thicker and a tad longer.

Mascara is the best bang for your makeup buck. If I had to run out of the house quickly and only had time to apply two makeup products, my choices would be brown-black mascara and pink lip gloss.

Mascara opens up and gives expression to your most important facial feature: your eyes. There are a variety of mascaras on the market. Look for one that lengthens, thickens and can be washed off with water. (Waterproof mascaras are a sure way to pull out your tender eyelashes.) I use a drugstore brand, L'Oreal Voluminous Original Formula. It costs about seven dollars and lasts about three months. (Three months is the maximum period you should keep "moist" makeup, as it becomes a breeding ground for bacteria after that.) I've tried many of the expensive department store brands, but I don't think they are any better than this product.

Similar to the discussion of eyeliner color, if you are dark skinned or have dark hair, you can choose black mascara; otherwise, choose a brown-black color.

If you choose to curl your lashes, do this before applying mascara or you will get a clumpy look and cause breakage to your precious lashes.

Loose Powder

When you are finished applying makeup, take a large, generous brush and dip it in transparent powder. Blow off the excess and dust your face to set your makeup. Focus, albeit lightly, under the eyes, from nose up through forehead, upper lip and then all over and under your face. If your skin feels dry, dust the powder only around the nose and forehead.

Touch-Ups

Keep a lipstick or lip gloss with you and reapply throughout the day as desired. Keeping your lips moist and with a little color goes a long way. If your skin is oily, keep some oil blotting tissues with you and touch up as needed through the day. Loose powder is also a great tool to keep you looking fresh throughout the day. A few brands, L'Oreal in particular, make an all-in-one product. A smaller size version of a loose powder container comes with a built in loose powder brush, which can be very effective especially if you tend to perspire a bit through the day.

Out For the Evening

If you are going out for the evening, you have two choices and they will be influenced by the available time you have. My absolute preference is to wash everything off from the morning application and apply makeup again from scratch. The difference is significant. For the plus size woman especially, let your beautiful face do your bidding. However, if time is not on your side, try these three steps:

1. Dust loose powder all over your face, lightly. Try to take care of oily spots.
2. Reapply all powders with a slightly heavier hand. Reapply eyeliner with a slightly heavier hand too. Reapply lip gloss or lipstick. Do not reapply mascara, because it will get cakey.
3. Dust with a loose powder again.

Many of the upscale lines of skin care products and makeup offer free makeovers. Make an appointment (or several with representatives of different lines), tell them your goal and further explain that you may not be ready to buy, but that you are trying to determine which products suit you best. This is important, because you should walk around for several hours after your makeover is completed to see how it feels. Are the products comfortable on your skin? Do they itch? Are you having an allergic reaction of any sort to the new products? Does the fragrance bother you in any way? Have you checked and rechecked how you look in a variety of lights, especially natural light? Did the quality and quantity of the products used seem like something you would be willing to handle on a daily basis?

Much of my basic makeup routine can be purchased from the Lauren Hutton line of makeup, which boasts a singular face disc (or case) containing the shadows and lightly pigmented colors needed to achieve the natural but refined look I recommend. In addition, the necessary brushes and an instructional video come with the purchase at no additional charge. This product was developed for the maturing woman, but I must say that the use of light and shadow for raising and receding parts of the face and for the illusion of balance works for the plus size woman too. The great thing about this product is that it is almost all-in-one.

Another line, which can be purchased in department stores and that I can personally recommend, is Trish McEvoy. This line offers a makeup planner that looks like a leather appointment book with a zipper around it and contains a magnetic page for all of your powder products and pockets for brushes and other items, like mascara and lipstick. This allows you to have everything you need in one organized place and you can rely on a trained makeup artist for your selections. When you purchase the planner, it will be filled with exactly what you need and choose.

A third line of makeup that may be particularly beneficial for a plus size woman is Bobbi Brown. This line is simple, straightforward and "brings a pretty face into focus," thereby camouflaging puffiness and other distracting features.

Hair

Your hairstyle frames your persona. In effect, it is your crown. The first thing people notice about you is your expression, which is your attitude as conveyed by your face. Therefore it is very important to get it right. Which hairstyle will promote the aura you intend to send and present you in your most attractive light?

Are hairstyle, image, cut and color different for a plus size woman than for her smaller counterpart? Yes and no. All women should get the most out of their attributes. Determining the best hairstyle for every woman begins with an understanding of the shape of her face. But plus size women may be more limited in the clothing and styles they select to wear and therefore should exploit other features, namely their hairstyles, to make their fashion statements. Simply put, a flattering hairstyle can create the image you seek. A great hairstyle can be manufactured.

Begin with what you have: a desire to enhance your image, the shape of your face and the texture of your hair. Image making often comes from intelligent observation and imitation coupled with discriminating reflection. Peruse magazines to find appealing pictures that you can liken yourself to and that you can relate to—think attitude, lifestyle and maintenance. Your pictures should reflect an understanding of the shape of your face and the texture and color of your hair. Collect them in your portfolio and mull.

Next, observe real-life women in your community who wear the styles you admire. Don't be intimidated to go up to a woman and ask who styles her hair. When speaking to her, get the name and location of her stylist. She'll be flattered and you will have taken an important step. When you are ready, call the recommended salon for an appointment and make sure to bring your cutout pictures with you to show the stylist.

Don't be afraid to dream. Forget for a moment that magazine photo sessions use all kinds of techniques to enhance looks that are not available in real-life: lighting, controlled air circulation, last minute touch-ups, fantasy and about six cans of hairspray per shoot. Think "outside the box"; don't censure yourself before you begin. There will be plenty of opportunity for a reality check later on.

Earlier, I told you that about ten years ago I took a hard look at myself and made a change. I alluded to what has become my star-quality signature feature: my hair. When I was about nineteen years old, my hair started to thin. I wore it slicked back in a chignon to cover the thin spots. It was chic, attractive and back then I had more of an oval shape face that lent itself to the style pretty well. However, after my son was born, my hair thinned a bit more, but I couldn't think of a solution to hide the problem. Interestingly, the very style I had wedded myself to was unhealthy and exacerbated the situation. Out of desperation, I visited a wig shop, behaved like a kid in a candy store, left a blonde bombshell and have never looked back.

Wearing a wig is not an option for everyone. But for me, it not only created my best feature, it also transformed my persona. Change is hard.

That moment of venturing "outside the box" by reframing the situation and the options at hand took courage. It was, however, the flashpoint of real change and, I dare say, a real improvement.

Face Shape

The shape of your face will determine the hairstyle that is most flattering and balance is at the center of a good choice. It is the point where all fantasy and exploration begins. Balancing your features, face and body is an overarching goal in finding flattering fashion and never more so than in determining hairstyle.

Plus size women need to avoid the pitfall of their heads looking small in proportion to the rest of their bodies. To maintain proportion, observe these key guidelines:

- Choose hairstyles that are soft and feminine with supple layering for overall balance.
- Create full-bodied hair, which will helps to balance the overall look. (There is a product on the market called Bumpits. They are plastic inserts or barrettes that are placed firmly into a hairstyle and create instant volume.)
- Be careful with bangs: they tend to add a horizontal line across your face, just when you may be striving to elongate the visual illusion of your face.

Here's a great technique for identifying your particular face shape. Pull all of your hair off your face with a shower cap or hair band and stand in front of your bathroom mirror. Then use a washable marker to trace your face shape onto the mirror. Note what shape it is: round, heart, square, pear, oblong, diamond or oval. Take a picture of the outline if possible. The shape of your face will be central to every subsequent decision you make regarding a new hairstyle.

Round Shape Face

This shape has the widest part of the face at the cheeks. The goal for women with round shape faces is to lengthen both the upper and lower portions of the face. This can be achieved by building height on the top of your head. You should avoid shorter, slicked-back styles.

Heart Shape Face

A heart shape face is triangular: wider at the forehead and narrowing to the chin. Layered styles angled toward your face will "widen" your chin, creating balance. Stick to shorter lengths that stop at the middle of your neck.

Square Shape Face

An angular jaw line and a square brow are the distinguishing features of a square shape face. Women with square shape faces should aim to soften sharp angles. This can be done by directing hair to the face, perhaps even covering the brow. Shorter hair lengths that extend just below the chin will further help to soften a square jaw.

Pear Shape Face

Pear shape faces are defined by a wide chin and a narrow forehead. Women with pear shape faces need to find hairstyles that widen their foreheads while minimizing attention to their chins. Keep hair fuller at the top and directed away from the face to achieve the illusion of balance. Avoid styles that are wider at the chin in order to soften a square jaw line.

Oblong Shape Face

This shape tends to be long and narrow. Do not add height in a hairstyle if your face shape is oblong. Keep your hair mid-length and add lots of layers on the sides to create width and volume.

Diamond Shape Face

Wide at the cheeks and narrow at the forehead and jaw line are the distinguishing features of this face shape. Keep hair chin-length or longer to create balance and fullness, and avoid height on the top of your head, which will emphasize the diamond shape.

Oval Shape Face
Minimal illusion is required for oval shape faces. Hair pulled back or swept up displays an oval shape face well. Long styles or shorter hair with some curl is great looking, too.

Neck Length
To pick an appropriate hair length, you need to determine the length of your neck. To do this, stand in front of the bathroom mirror, remove your shirt and use a washable marker to draw the line of your neck through the top of your shoulders on the mirror. If your neck is short, avoid longer hairstyles. If your neck is mid-length or longer, you have more options in terms of length.

Hair that is too long compromises overall style: It can age your face and detract from the image you seek to create. Women who wear long hair may seem dragged down, out of style and matronly. I have a client who, for too long, refused to cut her Farrah Fawcett–style, long golden tresses. Her hair looked great, but she didn't. In fact, when viewed from behind, one expected a twenty-something woman, but when she turned around, one saw a fifty-something looking woman. The surprise in age difference was counterproductive, which, eventually, she acknowledged.

Plus size women need to avoid the pitfall of their heads looking small in proportion to the rest of their bodies, but long hair may not be the best means to that end. Both my client and myself discovered that the combination of balance, proportion and age-appropriate styles is always most flattering.

Hair Color
You need to create your best hair color for plus size impact, but getting your hair color right can feel like rocket science. Here's the hard part: identifying colors that complement your skin tone, settling on allover color, highlights or lowlights and deciding if you're going to pay someone else to color your hair or do it yourself. Be careful not to

go overboard. Beautiful and fresh is best, so please leave the over-the-top looks to the rock stars.

You'll look best in a hair color that complements your natural skin tone rather than a color you like. Tone is used to describe the warmth or coolness of a color. In general, warm colors have yellow, peach or red undertones and cool colors have pink, violet or blue undertones. The two categories of skin tone are dark or olive complexions (cool) and fair to light complexions (warm). Here's an easy way to help determine which tones complement your complexion. Place a warm-colored garment next to your face. If blemishes and under-eye circles are minimized, your skin has a warm undertone. Now do the same thing with a cool-colored garment. Which coloration was more flattering? Which one minimized imperfections? That is the coloration to choose.

If you are cool, choose ash blondes, ash browns and black hair colors. If you are warm, choose hair colors with yellow, golden or amber tones. So how do you know if you got it right? One Web site called Stellure gives you a virtual facsimile of your selection. Very cool concept!

Color Tips
Here are answers to common questions women have when choosing a new hair color.
- *Who can be a blonde?* Anyone who at some point in her childhood was somewhat blonde can become blonde again.
- *Who should have allover color?* Women with short hair may choose to confine themselves to a single hair color.
- *What are the different types of highlights?* The four types of highlights are basic foil highlights (up to five different colors), baliage or hair painting, chunking or piecing and lowlights. All highlight techniques can range from natural looking to dramatic. Highlights around the face can be very flattering and youthful.
- *Can I do color my hair myself?* Yes, home kits are much easier to use than they were a few years ago. But limit your undertaking to

changing only two shades from your natural color and stick with a semi-permanent hair color, which washes out in about six washings.

- *When should I use permanent hair color?* Permanent hair color needs to grow out (it will not wash out). Use it when you want to cover gray hair or if you intend to go more than two shades lighter or darker than your natural color.
- *How important is it to hide gray hair?* VERY!
- *What color will require minimal upkeep?* Brown hair color is easy maintenance and also camouflages broken and abused hair better than other colors. Striking brunette coloration tends to be very dark or rather light. If your hair color is a medium tone, it tends to be non-descript—not a good thing.
- *What products can you recommend for home use?* L'Oreal Natural Match Hair Color and Clairol Nice and Easy are two dependable and inexpensive products.
- *What if I feel uncertain about selecting a color or with any part of the process?* By all means go to a professional colorist. Single process hair dyeing is not very expensive (probably around fifty dollars, depending on where you live and the length of your hair) and it will give you great insight, information and instant impact.
- *Is there anything to do to keep the color vivid?* Yes, there are color-enhancing shampoos and conditioners that can be used once a week. These products tend to be a bit pricey. Salons and beauty supply stores carry these products and the stylists can also give advice on how to use them.
- *What if you don't like the color?* There are all sorts of ways to fix color that is not to your liking. If you used a semi-permanent product, look for a shampoo with ammonium laurel sulfate to wash the color away quicker. If you used a permanent product, a knowledgeable colorist can make all the difference in the world with minimal damage to your hair. If you went to a professional colorist, she should correct it without charge.

If you ever wanted to decorate a room on a tight budget of time and money, you know that the impact of painting a room a new color can be phenomenal. Hair color can be likened to this type of makeover. The best part is that you take the transformation with you everywhere you go!

Jewelry

I like to think of jewelry as the first cousin of attitude. Therefore, our attitudes, as reflected in our jewelry, must be commensurate with large, important assets. When we enter a room, eyes often turn to us; therefore, we must make that first impression an excellent one. It is important to love your jewelry. It should help you to feel important, sensational and sexy.

Earlier, we discussed how to consider your personal style: luxurious, preppy, artistic or ethnic. All are good. Now what we must do is integrate the styles in all aspects of how we present ourselves. Whatever style you settle on, jewelry in that style must bring light to your face. It must make you sparkle and light up your best facial features. Interestingly, beautiful jewelry will focus attention on your best facial features. Here's why jewelry is important to plus size women's overall styles:

- We need big impact jewelry. Layering jewelry provides big impact and deep interest with abundant light and movement.
- We often wear dark neutral clothing or monochromatic palettes, which are perfect backgrounds for big impact jewelry pieces or an overall set of jewelry.
- We may not have a lot of time to dress in the mornings, so ready-to-go sets of fantastic jewelry is a very welcome resource.
- Consciously or unconsciously, we may avoid big impact or trendy clothing, but we can more than make up for it with "wow" jewelry and other accessories.
- We need to provide a bit of coverage for skin that is not firm and taut as we get older.

Jewelry should be used to achieve balance. The jewelry plus size women wear must be proportionate to them as whole persons. We may take up more space than our smaller counterparts, but this is not a bad thing. Frankly, it presents the opportunity to be spectacular. It also presents the opportunity to look out of proportion, small head and large body, if you wear tiny pieces of jewelry.

Large women cannot afford small, unimportant jewelry. It is lost on us. It is useless, because it doesn't direct enough light to the face. Plus size women need to become comfortable in plus-impact jewelry. I do not mean jewelry that is outlandish and huge. It looks ridiculous on us as we go about our everyday lives. Further, it is uncomfortable to wear. If we're uncomfortable, even in our jewelry, that will show on our faces and then it will directly squash what we are trying to achieve: beautiful, confident light from within.

Important, well-selected pieces offer drama, whimsy, style and richness in ways that are impossible to measure. When we feel beautiful and stunning, we look the part. The reciprocal is true as well. Jewelry, real or faux, has the authority to boost our images. What may not be obvious is that the glow actually comes from within. There is great joy in wearing beautiful jewelry.

Rethinking real versus faux jewelry opens up spectacular options. Eighteen or fourteen karat gold jewelry and precious and semiprecious stones have traditionally been categorized as "real" jewelry. This thinking is limited, outdated and counterproductive, especially for plus size women. It would cost a fortune to have enough eighteen or fourteen karat gold jewelry to make the type of impact needed every day. Reframe your thinking to this: Real jewelry is pieces that will endure in terms of style and quality and is worthy to be passed down from generation to generation. Jewelry constructed of .925 silver can be categorized as an heirloom as easily as jewelry made of fourteen karat gold.

Personally, I am a fan of Silpada jewelry. It is made of the finest silver along with natural stones and other natural materials. I feel the quality is commensurate with that of high-end designer jewelry at a fraction of the price. The woman from whom I buy my jewelry has taught me to layer pieces for maximal impact. Often, a set of jewelry, maybe seven or eight pieces, will be the same cost of one designer piece.

Further, fourteen karat gold jewelry can be mixed with fine silver jewelry. If you can't afford fourteen karat gold or .925 silver jewelry, don't worry; it is not that important. What you must seek, however, is beauty, deep interest and focusing light to the face. You do not need real jewelry, gold or silver, to get that done. Choose sets of jewelry that complement your skin tone. Most women will benefit from gold tone, silver tone or gold and silver tone mixed as well as coral and turquoise sets of jewelry.

If you have a lot of real jewelry, revel in it. As long as it is significant enough to catch light and add sparkle to your face, wear it all the time. Jewelry that brings light to the face includes shiny metals, light toned manmade materials, light colored stones that radiate fire and sparkle, light colored pearls and enamels and, of course, diamonds. If your collection needs some help, add faux pieces to your jewelry wardrobe. Pieces that are sentimental should be worn with love and pride. I will discuss ways to redo and maximize fourteen karat gold jewelry and sentimental jewelry that may not offer the impact needed later in this chapter.

Earrings

The most important piece of jewelry is earrings. This is because earrings gather the light and direct it to the face. If your best feature is your eyes, smile, skin or hair, earrings will spotlight that feature. When it comes to jewelry, earrings can be high impact for little money. They cost less than a necklace and can be your statement piece. Additionally, earrings help to focus attention on your face as a whole and, therefore, what you are saying. Earrings give you credibility.

It is crucial to make a good selection. The only "small" earring I can abide is a large diamond, at least one carat, real or faux, or a ten millimeter or greater pearl stud. However, in terms of proportion to our overall size, I believe we can do better.

A general guide is not too small and not too large. Just as an earring should not be too small and dainty, neither should it weigh you down. If an earring stretches the earlobe, it is the wrong choice. Anything that doesn't fit well or looks like it doesn't fit well is counter-productive. Earrings that are too long will shorten the neck. Earrings that are chunky and lack grace will transfer that inference to you.

In general, look for earrings that elongate, as plus size women should be seeking in all aspects of their wardrobes. Usually a half-inch to a one-inch drop is best. Hoop earrings in current style proportions and finishes always work well. Earrings that sport an overall oval shape are usually flattering.

I like jewelry that has a three dimensional and bold quality. Stones that have depth, metal that has texture and shine and beads that have richness seem to be commensurate with a large woman's stature.

If you use the phone a lot, earrings must be comfortable for that function. Often, a clip or long post will not work well. Wires and hoops or omega backings (a shorter post that goes through a ring that holds the earring in place against the earlobe) will work better.

The most important quality of earrings is focusing light on the face. Dark stones may not do this well. Recently, I had a lovely pair of twenty carat hematite, a gray/black stone, emerald-cut stones reset. I found that as beautiful and rich as they were, I never wore them. They sat in my jewelry bag for years. My jeweler added a round half-inch mother-of-pearl circular disk to each earring. The result was spectacular: enormous contrast and interest. Why did this work so well? There are three reasons. The first is that the disk elongated the drop of the earring. The second is that the white mother-of-pearl stone created great contrast to the black hematite stone. The third and most important is simply that the earring was too dark before adding the white disk. It was the addition of mother-of-pearl that brought light to my face.

Pins

Next to earrings, pins are a great jewelry choice for plus size women. Pins can be large and important without sacrificing comfort or spending a lot of money. If you want to uplift your image in about thirty seconds, affix a brooch, be it traditional or trendy, to the shoulder of the garment you are wearing. Flea markets are fun resources to develop a collection of pins, which usually cost between twelve and twenty dollars.

A pin brings light to the face and doesn't compromise the vertical line we are after with a horizontal line, as does a necklace. The magic of a pin is that it can create the extraordinary out of the ordinary. It doesn't need to be made of real materials; faux will work just as well. It does, however, need to be significant. If the pin is not large, cluster two or three together that share a unifying influence (e.g. theme, coloration or texture).

The placement of the pin is important. Recall the goal of light to the face. Place the pin on your shoulder, off center and high, closer to your face. If you want to emphasize your cleavage, you can wear the pin on your lapel. If you want to draw more attention to your cleavage, place a pin just above the "V" of a V-neck sweater.

Pins can be placed strategically for other effects too. For example, I have a very plain raincoat with a hidden placket of buttons, so there is essentially no embellishment on the coat. Therefore, I affixed, semi-permanently, a beautiful two-inch enamel butterfly pin encrusted with cabochon stones in the colors I usually wear. Pins offer a kind of transportable elegance and emphasis. They can be placed wherever you want to draw attention.

Necklaces

Often, a necklace can be the most significant piece of jewelry that a woman wears. However, it is not always the best choice for a large woman. As plus size women, we seek a continuous, elongated vertical line as we present ourselves. A necklace is a horizontal line just under the face, actually corrupting the sleek vertical quality we are after. If your jaw or neckline is full or fatty, you must carefully select a necklace or not choose one at all.

If you want to wear a necklace, one way to choose wisely is to select a flattering length in a necklace. There are three options. This first is a well-fitted choker. The second is a necklace or pendant (the charm on the chain) that falls between the bottom of the neck and the top of the cleavage area. The third is a very long string of chains or beads that hangs to the waist.

However, here is what we must be careful of: We do not want to achieve light to the face by sacrificing attention to unflattering areas. If our neck is not our best feature, why would we focus attention there? If our bust is very large, we don't want the necklace to protrude out as it lies against the bosom before it flows down. Neither do we want the necklace to fall on the fullest part of the bust. If the necklace draws attention to an area we are choosing to deemphasize, we have defeated the purpose we set out to accomplish.

Comfort is the sister of style. If you find yourself adjusting the necklace over and over, it doesn't suit you. If a choker is too tight, it can't be attractive. If a long chain gets in your way as you move through your day, it is burdensome and unattractive.

There are a few necklace choices that will flatter plus size women most of the time. A gold or silver chain about eighteen inches and at least a quarter of an inch thick is flattering, because it actually falls in a "U" shape on your chest. A string of graduated pearls falls similarly. Every woman looks great in a string of pearls; they are instant refinement and light to the face. Faux pearls, in a class by themselves, look great every time. The other reason pearls are flattering is because there is a bit of openness between the pearls where the silk thread is double-knotted. This openness lifts and eases the visual weight of the look. Currently, I love strands of stones made of several different sizes, shapes and colors. Designers have taken this look one step further by creating open links and connections in a necklace; the wearer enjoys a more graceful quality. This is critical for the plus size woman.

Some necklaces can be adjusted with a built-in extender. This is great for identifying the most flattering length for you as well as providing the foundation for enhancing layering options. A layering style can bring necklaces back into your wardrobe easily.

Bracelets

Bracelets, unlike the other items in your jewelry box, do not bring light to the face. But they are a great way to emphasize beautiful hands. Fit is key. If a bracelet is too tight, it detracts from, rather than adds to, your total look. Layering bracelets is a rich, interesting option too. I tend to like bracelets that are bold and simple; bangles work well. In fact, I wear the same set of interlocking silver bangles every day. It has become a sig nature for me. Charm bracelets have an attractive dangle against a larger hand and can be chosen proportionate to a larger woman's stature. Also, charm bracelets can help boost a theme and they're sexy.

A cuff bracelet is a bold and beautiful option, but the plus size woman needs to be very careful. I would love to have a matching pair of cuff bracelets but have never found the look to be flattering on me, not to mention that I find them uncomfortable. However, if you are a plus size woman with slender arms and hands, this may be a great option for you.

Watches

For some people, women and men, a watch is a microcosm of the world to which they aspire. Whether the watch is made of real or faux materials, often a person gravitates to a style of a watch that is more important to them than just providing the time. The style of a watch aligns them to a lifestyle. For many, it is still considered a status symbol.

The watch, similar to the other pieces of jewelry we have discussed, should be large and significant enough to keep with the plus size woman's overall proportion. The design of the watch, traditional or trendy, should be bold and clean. Plus, the added benefit of a larger watch is that the face is easier to read.

One way to boost your image with your watch is to change watchbands. First, it is important for a watch to fit well. Second, when a watch boasts a rich skin band (alligator or crocodile), it looks like it costs ten times what you may have paid for it. Watches that have a stretch band can be uncomfortable for a plus size woman if it fits only when being stretched a bit; this will pinch and need adjustment throughout the day.

The dress watch can be a difficult choice for the plus size woman dressed in formal or semiformal attire. Often slight and delicate, the traditional dress watch may have proportion that is not attractive. There are several alternatives for plus size women, though. Dress watches made of marcasite tend to be bolder. Watches with pearl bands seem more significant too. There is always the option of a pocket watch, which can easily be slipped inside your evening purse on a black velvet ribbon.

Rings

For many women, myself included, their wedding rings are among their most treasured possessions. If your ring is dainty and seems small for your overall size, there is always the option of having it reset in a bolder mounting. Other women are proud of the rings their husbands gave them and wouldn't consider changing a thing. That's fine too. However, just make sure the ring is fitted well, meaning that if your hand has gotten larger or tends to swell, have the shank (the band of the ring) enlarged to fit comfortably and attractively. It is unattractive when flesh seems to bulge around the ring, making it seem too small. It makes hands look short and stubby, too.

If you want to wear a larger, cocktail style ring, fantastic options abound. My recommendation, though, is that you do not wear more than two or three rings at a time, both hands included. Too many rings make a cluttered appearance. The attractive, well-dressed plus size woman sports a bold but clean look.

If you wear rings, of course you are drawing attention to your hands. Therefore, have your hands in manicured condition at all times, even if that means an at-home manicure.

Something Old into Something New

We've discussed the importance of bold, significant jewelry. What about slight, dainty, heirloom, sentimental or other small but still good-looking pieces? I am fortunate to have a very fine jeweler nearby. His is one of the most impressive jewelry stores in which I have been. There is a respect my jeweler has given me over the twenty years I have been his customer that you can seek with the right jeweler in your hometown. He uses pieces I already have and turns them into spectacular pieces for a fraction of what they would cost to buy. I will add that while my jeweler's shop is very upscale and chic, he has never made me feel unimportant with my redesign requests, many of which have been on the modest side.

In order to acquire redesigned jewelry you love, two things must be in place. First, you must have a clear idea of what you are trying to achieve. Identify pieces that you want to reuse. Cut out pictures from magazines of jewelry you would love to own. File the pictures in your Pretty Party Portfolio. Observe how the pieces you seek could be developed from the pieces you own. Second, the pieces you want to work with must be worthy of investment. The pieces must be made of at least ten karat gold; fourteen karat gold is preferable. Here are three redesign suggestions.

The first idea is resetting dark earrings on a brighter background. Earlier, I described the redesign my jeweler did on my hematite earrings. He reset the dark stones on mother-of-pearl disks. They went from a pair of earrings never worn to one of my favorites, because they echo white and black, a color combination I frequently wear, and the earrings are now flattering and comfortable.

A second option is developing a charm bracelet. Often, there are smaller pieces of jewelry you can assemble that signify a theme. I have nicknamed one of my charm bracelets "the men in my life bracelet." It is filled with things that represent my dad, husband and son, which either they gave me or I bought to finish the bracelet. For example, my dad often wore a black onyx ring with a small diamond in it. After he died, I cherished it, but had no way to wear it. Additionally, he wore a pendant with a prayer inscribed on it on a gold chain. Those two items are on the bracelet. My husband's logo is the life preserver, so I asked my jeweler to make him a life preserver gold lapel pin. He also made one for me, which I put on my charm bracelet. Our son is a baseball player, so once as the team mom I was given a gold baseball charm. This is on the bracelet, too.

A third redesign is similar to the charm bracelet and will create a pin of grand importance. Purchase a gold or silver safety pin and have items similar to what I described for the charm bracelet put on gold or silver rings so they dangle from the pin. Be sure the whole pin is executed in either gold or silver tone. This has become a wonderful and interesting piece of jewelry for me, quite a conversation piece, because it is easy for people to see and comment on. Because the point of the pin is somewhat thick, I usually wear it on loosely woven sweaters. It has a three dimensional quality that is so becoming to knits.

Eyewear

Eyewear for vision correction or protection from the sun needs to be part of the conversation of bringing light to the face. Perhaps even more than jewelry, glasses are similar to an appendage to those of us who wear them daily. Therefore, the importance of the eyewear you choose is paramount.

There are four decisive factors in choosing eyeglasses well. The first involves the material or textile from which the frames are constructed. Will the material catch light and focus it on the face as would a well-selected piece of jewelry? The second factor is the coloration of the frames. The third factor is the shape of the frames. Finally, the fourth factor involves the characteristics of the lenses selected.

Material

For those of us who are seeking to boost our styles, the materials that we seek in selecting eyeglasses frames will be on the more expensive side of the price continuum. This is because the materials selected by many designers tend to be of higher quality but do a good job of focusing light and beauty on the face. The consistency and integrity of the frames are more substantial. Even in softer colors, the quality of the plastic, metal or titanium alloy from which the frames are constructed allows for rich pigmentation and detail.

Often a frame manufacturer will pair up with a designer or brand name. There are three excellent manufacturers of frames: Marchon, Luxottica and Signature. Each makes several lines reflecting particular styles or brand associations. For example, Marchon makes an upscale Calvin

Klein line. Signature makes Bebe, Hummer and Cadillac lines. Luxottica makes Armani and Versace lines. The choice of manufacturer is yours.

Coloration

The criteria to determine one's best colors are based on skin tone, eyes and hair color, in that order. The reason skin tone takes priority is that there is more skin showing when compared to eyes and hair. Further, there are subtle distinctions in eye colors (blue eyes or brown eyes) that range from warm to cool. Finally, hair color can be altered.

To help you figure out the best color palette for selecting eyeglasses frames, consider this: All people have either a warm (yellow-based) or cool (blue-based) coloring (recall the same process for selecting hair color). Next, everyone looks best in her own color base. If you have selected correctly, minor imperfections (moles, age spots and small scars) on your skin will fade. If you have selected unwisely, imperfections will seem more prominent. Eyewear should compliment personal coloring and, therefore, be a seamless transition to your clothing, which should also reflect your coloration.

Skin tone, then, is the prime element in determining coloring. All complexions fall into one of two color bases: yellow (warm) or blue (cool). A warm complexion has a "peaches and cream" or yellow cast. A cool complexion has blue or pink undertones. Olive skin is considered cool, because it is a mixture of blue and yellow. In the United States, cool, blue-based complexions are more common than warm, yellow-based complexions. Approximately 60 percent of the population has cool complexions.

Eye color is usually a secondary element in determining coloring because of the wide range of eye colors. For example, blue eyes can range from a cool, almost violet, shade to a pale blue-gray, which is warm. Brown eyes can vary from a light cider shade, which is warm, through a medium-brown to a cool almost black.

Hair color is also considered warm or cool. Warm hair colors include golden blond, flat black, brown-gold, "carrot" and "dirty" gray. Strawberry blond, platinum, blue-black, white, salt-and-pepper and "dishwater" brown are cool.

Once you have determined if you are warm or cool then you can evaluate the eyeglasses frames that will be most flattering. Some examples of frame colors best for warm coloring are camel, khaki, gold, copper, peach, orange, coral, off-white, fire engine red, warm blue and blond tortoise. For cool coloring, the best frames colors are hues that are black, rose-brown, blue-gray, plum, magenta, pink, jade, blue and demi-amber (darker) tortoise.

The Vision Council of America (VCA) suggests eyewear should repeat your personal best feature, such as a blue frame to match blue eyes. I do not necessarily agree with that. An important objective in selecting a frame is to bring light to the face, which is what will accentuate your best feature, especially if it is your eyes. Weak shades of blue for glasses frames will do little to that end; in fact they can be a rather dull choice.

Shape
According to the VCA and consistent with the principles in this book, it is important to use the elements of scale and contrast to achieve balance and beauty.

Therefore, frames' shape should contrast with face shape and the frames' size should be in scale with the face size. The tricky part is that most faces are a combination of shapes and angles. There are seven basic face shapes: round, oval, oblong, pear, heart, diamond and square.

A round face has curvilinear lines with the width and length in the same proportion and no angles. To make the face appear thinner and longer, try angular, narrow frames. A clear, distinct bridge (the bar between the eyes) widens the eyes and frames that are wider than they are deep, such as a rectangular shape, also lengthen the face.

The oval face is considered to be the ideal shape because of its balanced proportions. To keep the oval's natural balance, look for eyeglasses frames that are as wide as or wider than the broadest part of the face or walnut-shaped frames that are not too deep or too narrow.

The oblong face is longer than it is wide, has a long straight cheek line and sometimes a longish nose. To make the face appear shorter and more balanced, try frames that have a top-to-bottom depth or frames with decorative or contrasting color temples (the stems that fit along the side of the head to the ears) that add width to the face. Frames with a low bridge will shorten the nose.

The pear face has a narrow forehead that widens at the cheek and chin areas. To add width and emphasize the narrow upper third of the face, try frames that are heavily accented with color and detailing on the top half or frames that are cat eye shapes.

The heart face has a very wide top third and smaller bottom third. To minimize the width of the top of the face, try frames that are wider at the bottom, very light colors and materials and rimless frame styles, which have a light, airy effect, because the lenses are simply held in place to the temples by a few screws.

Diamond shape faces are narrow at the eye line and jaw line with cheekbones that are often high and dramatic. This is the rarest shape face. To highlight the eyes and bring out the cheekbones, try frames that have detailing or distinctive brow lines, rimless frames or oval or cat eye shape frames.

A square face has a strong jaw line and a broad forehead, plus the width and length are in the same proportions. To make the square face look longer and soften the angles, try narrow frame styles, frames that have more width than depth and frames that are narrow ovals.

Lenses

Lenses are important to consider also. The goal is for the lenses to look sharp and fresh and, of course, for you to see as well as possible. There are several choices.

If you choose rimless frames you will be limited to polycarbonate lenses. This is the material out of which the tops of patio furniture are made. It is durable, shatter-resistant and won't chip. These lenses cost about thirty dollars more than plastic lenses. Value added is that they are a little thinner and lighter than plastic lenses.

A refined variety of plastic lenses is called mid-index or high-index. This is directed to creating a thinner pair of lenses, which is definitely desirable. The thinnest are high-index lenses. They cost about one hundred dollars to $150 more than plastic lenses. Often, you can purchase a one-year anti-scratch warranty. However, they do tend to scratch and that is not a good look.

The nicest product on the market today, in my opinion, is an anti-reflective treatment. The top of the line is Crizal Alizé and Teflon, which are two anti-reflective brands. The process hardens the lenses a bit, which makes it a little harder to scratch them. This will add another one hundred dollars to the cost of your glasses but will yield an immeasurable benefit, added clarity and crispness to your vision. Beware of cheaper anti-reflective coatings. This, too, is not an area to try to save money. There may be products developed in the future that are even better—ask for the best!

Glass lenses are becoming obsolete. They are heavy, but they do not scratch much. Depending on your prescription, this is probably not a great choice and of course, there is a safety issue.

Transition lenses, which go from clear to tinted on exposure to ultraviolet (UV) rays, are a convenient option. Here's the downside: if you are driving in your car, they won't get very dark, even if you find the sunlight to be very bright. This is because since 1975, the windows in cars have a UV protection; therefore, not enough UV rays shine through to make the lenses dark enough. If, however, you are outside a lot, they could be a terrific option.

Tinting lenses is also a possibility. If you are trying to hide under-eye circles, choose a soft, neutral brown and rose mix, about 4 percent. This treatment is on the lenses permanently, you can't remove it, so be sure before you select this addition. The cost for tinting is nominal, about fifteen dollars per pair of lenses.

CHAPTER 14

Create Your Best Feature

ONLY SHE
KNOWS FOR SURE

"She wore a short skirt and a tight sweater and her figure described a set of parabolas that could cause cardiac arrest in a yak."
~Woody Allen, *Getting Even*

Every woman is born with a best feature. Some spotlight it well and others can't seem to find it with a magnifying glass. This chapter has three objectives: first, finding and refining your best feature(s) and drawing attention to the area(s); second, manufacturing great features where nature may have shortchanged you; third, creating a signature feature or style.

Think about a pretty woman you know. What pops out at you? What is her best feature? Is it her eyes, skin, hair, height, personality or style? If it was one of the first four, then she was born with it but probably works it pretty well, meaning, if it stands out to you, it is intentional on her part. How does she do that? If it's her eyes, she has her makeup just right, maybe wears contact lenses or maybe has a "wow" pair of eyeglasses that frame her eyes perfectly. If it's her hair, she probably has a favorite hair stylist who knows her hair well and sets her up for success with each visit.

Another option is to manufacture a great feature. I turned one of my unattractive features into a star quality, so this twist is another choice. As I mentioned, my thick, curly brown hair started to thin when I was young. After wearing my hair pulled back in a chignon in order to hide the bald spots, I decided to visit a wig shop, became a blonde bombshell and never looked back. That's not the end of the story. Today, I've made it into more of a signature feature. I choose a light, two tone blended blond color with dark roots showing. I love the contrast and the depth provided by the dark hair. Very striking and pretty.

Is there some trade-off? I guess a little. Yes, there are times when my son is pitching in an early springtime baseball game, the wind is blowing ferociously, my hairdo is wrapped in a Hermes style scarf and I'm wearing bold black sunglasses trying to affect a movie star look. At times like these I'm worrying more about whether my *lid* will blow off than if my son strikes out the next batter. But I can cope; blonde bombshells can, you know.

White Teeth

What do Julia Roberts, Tyra Banks and Brad Pitt have in common? Great smiles. Big smiles. White teeth. And one more thing: they love to smile. There is an openness about their smiles that conveys they know "they can turn the world on with a smile," as aptly captured in the opening song of the Mary Tyler Moore television show of the 1970s.

Teeth whiteners have become an obsession of both men and women and rightly so. When a woman feels her teeth are white and beautiful, she opens up her smile and correspondingly, the options in her life seem to widen as well. People respond to a smiling person differently, with greater warmth and interest. It seems that people with open smiles garner more of their share of likeability and credibility than those who do not smile.

The taglines for teeth whitening products and services may seem cliché, but I think they're right. With a poor, discolored smile, you may avoid social situations, be afraid to meet new people and become moody. A great smile does increase confidence, makes you and the people around you happier, draws attention to you and can give you the motivation to change aspects of your life.

This may be particularly important for plus size women (and men). Often, large women exhibit a self-deprecating quality, often couched in shyness or a false bravado. Interestingly, these two affects, seemingly opposite, are two sides of the same coin: insecurity. An open and genuine smile, perhaps more so than the traditional notion of eyes, may in fact be the window to the soul or at least a window to self-confidence and a joie de vivre, "joy of life/living."

Women seeking dazzling white teeth, such as those of the celebrities mentioned, can turn to a vast array of pastes, gels and strips that promise to give you a movie star smile and that work at home or in the dentist's chair. Polishers and hydrogen peroxide seem to be among the basic tools of the trade and, in and of themselves, not too intimidating to use.

Whether the culprit is diet, age or other, those who have inquired about teeth whiteners at their dentist or drugstore know that there are a mystifying number of products available. But many of them work the same way: by removing surface stains as opposed to actually changing the hue of the teeth, which is possible as well.

Teeth Whitening Products

There is a dizzying amount of teeth whitening come-ons and products on the market these days, but what works and at what expense in terms of discomfort and cost?

A few home teeth whiteners are rather impressive in terms of effectiveness, speed of results, ease of use and price. Also, these products are all completely safe and made in the United States. Try Crest Whitestrips Premium and the follow-up, Crest Whitestrips Renewal. The cost is about thirty-five and forty dollars, respectively.

There are other options as well. I tried the custom whitening trays made for me by my dentist and used at home. It was pricey, about $400 for each tray, upper and lower. The results were quite good, but I did experience sensitivity and while it was only for a few seconds and only a few times, I remember it well!

Teeth whitening is a pretty easy way to create your best feature. A great and open smile is inviting and does invoke a joie de vivre, something I hope more big sisters will flaunt. Until that time, a great, white, open smile helps us "fake it 'til we make it."

Manicure and Pedicure

"Act as if…" This is a powerful and helpful phrase. Act as if you live the lifestyle of which you dream. Act as if you feel your beauty and worth deep in your soul. Sound lofty? It is, because it can propel you to a higher place.

There are folks who tell you that they can read you like a book by looking at your hands. What do your hands say? Are you nervous and rushed or leisurely and calm? Your hands, especially your cuticles, tell the story.

If you want to create a signature that can be implemented for about ten to twenty dollars each week, treat yourself to a manicure. A French manicure, where the tips are polished white, is a beautiful way to elongate and freshen your hands. Keep the white tips thin; it's more current. A manicure does wonders for your hands, your image and your head. The same is true for a pedicure, no matter the season.

If a manicure and/or pedicure doesn't fit your budget, that's okay too. You can do some maintenance yourself to keep your hands looking great. The key is to keep all nails the same length (just covering the tips of your fingers is the easiest to maintain and probably looks the best). Use a cuticle cream to push your cuticles back. File the ends lightly, reflecting the shape of your nail bed, either square or more rounded. Then use a cuticle and nail oil, like Sally Hansen Vitamin E Oil, which costs about five dollars. Follow with a rich hand cream, like Sally Hansen Radiant Hands Nails & Cuticles Crème, about six dollars per tube. Wash your hands and dry thoroughly. Finish with a sheer, nude polish and a clear topcoat. This signature says chic and well-dressed.

The whole process shouldn't take more than ten minutes once a week.

Very long nails, chipped polish and loud adornments like rhine-stones and designs in bright colors work against sexy and successful and make a counterproductive signature statement.

Skin

You can create beautiful skin! It is well worth the extra effort. A simple, inexpensive two-process treatment is all you need. To begin, find a body mask made mostly made of sugar (sucrose). This can be found in a beauty supply store, drugstore or upscale cosmetic counter in a depart-ment store. All brands seem to work similarly. The body mask I use is called Cleansing Sugar Glow made for Marianna Industries, Inc., which costs about six dollars.

Squeeze a quarter-size amount of the sugary-crystallized substance from the tube onto your hand and rub it into all areas of the skin on your body, especially callused areas like elbows and feet. Then rinse with warm water in the shower. Do it as often as you like; it can't hurt your skin.

After turning off the shower water, follow-up with Johnson's Baby Oil. Rub it all over your body and then dry off with a towel. The combi-nation will create fresh, glowing, soft, supple skin. Similar products in the department store cost a great deal more. I prefer products without fragrance, but you can choose fragrances to your liking.

Fragrance

The olfactory sense is among the most powerful of the human senses. A great signature can be your fragrance. A word of caution: experiment, but use good judgment. Be thoughtful of others; too much fragrance is memorable for the wrong reasons. A plus size woman wearing a big fragrance can be overwhelming.

A fragrance has three levels: The top note is the primary fragrance burst upon application, usually fruity or floral. Next, the heart or mid-dle notes that make up the core of the perfume as it rests on the skin are usually floral. The last level is the base note, which determines how long the fragrance will last, and is often comprised of sandalwood, musk, amber or vanilla. Try a spritz of a lighthearted, fresh fragrance with a citrus or light floral top note. Because each of the notes is made up of smells, simple and lighthearted may be best. While the language of fragrance is subliminal, plus size women do not need to carry the additional bulk of a weighty fragrance around all day.

I love my husband's cologne, Lanvin L'Homme, and recently adopted it as my own. Who said we need to limit ourselves to traditional women's fragrances?

Tanning

Think how good people look when they have a tan! The look can be created in a matter of minutes. There are some terrific benefits of having a tan: looking slimmer, richer and healthier.

Another benefit is that a tan makes the appearance of spider veins fade considerably. In fact, for many people, tan legs opens up the possibilities of wearing shorts, skorts (my personal favorite), skirts and capris in warmer weather.

Spray tanning and magnetic tanning utilize no UV rays and offer rich tans that few can cultivate by sun alone. It's not cheap in terms of dollars, but it is very cheap in terms of time and discomfort. (Often, a set of tanning sessions can be purchased at one time saving 50 percent.) These are two products that give great results.

For a spray tan, literally you are sprayed with a golden mist. Magnetic tanning consists of a fine mist that has a positive charge; the plate you stand on has a negative charge. Opposites attract. The mist is attracted to your body, not sprayed on to you as in the first example. The result for both applications is a very smooth, even, golden color. You can select the intensity of the color. The results last for several days (not quite a week).

Here's how to get the most out of your spray or magnetic tanning session:

- Shower and exfoliate beforehand.

- Remove all makeup and jewelry. Wear the garments that will give you the tan lines you seek—or none at all.
- Cover your hair with a shower cap (usually provided and then discarded).
- Cover your feet with booties or a thick layer of barrier cream.
- Apply a thick layer of cream to hands, especially cuticles.
- Stand with your feet, legs and arms apart; bend slightly at the knees.
- Keep eyes closed.
- Breathe when the spray is at your feet.
- Dry yourself vigorously as if you just got out of the shower.
- Don't shower or bathe for four to six hours.

Here's a rather inexpensive option: Jergens Natural Glow Daily Moisturizer (Nivea makes a similar product). This product, used as your daily body moisturizer after showering, will give you a summer glow or tan. It is easy to use: smooth it on all areas you want to appear tan, wash your hands right away, wait a few minutes before dressing and a subtle development of color will appear in a few days. This can be purchased at the drugstore or grocery store in the cosmetics section. It costs about five dollars.

Jewelry

If you are going to create a best feature, a signature, jewelry is a great way to go. Select a piece of jewelry or a style of jewelry that is bold and memorable. Make sure it enhances YOU. Choose jewelry that is comfortable and flattering so that you will wear it all the time.

Does it have to be real? No. Does it have to be big? No, but it has to be significant enough to be proportionate to you and notable in a positive way. Can it be a set of jewelry or a style of jewelry? Yes. This is actually what I recommend. I admire women who lavish jewelry on themselves, layering pieces that share a unifying quality—metal, stone or material—for impact. In fact, I think of it as a composition displayed against a clean, monochromatic background of soft, neutral colored clothing. There is a particular set of interlocking silver bangles that I wear often that has become my signature. I'm crazy about it for a few reasons: One, it's comfortable and flattering; two, it goes with just about everything; three, it has a unique rhythm, sound and fluidity that moves with me through the day.

Let the clothing create a "svelte" look and the jewelry explode— that too is a signature! Have jewelry that is well thought-out and ready to go!

CHAPTER 15

Yikes, My Closet's Naked!

TWENTY-ONE
GUN SALUTE

"I like my money right where I can see it...hanging in my closet."
~Sarah Jessica Parker

T he pretty party plan is based on the concept "fade and focus": camouflage the negative and accentuate the positive, not unlike the photographer's lens that seeks to achieve perfect balance in a beautiful photograph. Plus size women need to think of fade and focus in daily dressing and that will be facilitated by what's in their closets.

Fade

The six principles of design and how they can be reframed for the plus size woman were introduced at the beginning of the book. Recall that the first goal is to camouflage the negative and reduce the appearance of the areas of the body that seem too large or disproportionate—this is the fade element. The following list represents some of the best items and products I have found to do just that. While I mention the brands I use, by no means are these the only brands that will work. However, if you don't know where to start when shopping for an item, I suggest you try the brand I list to create a point of reference and then purchase items that are more comfortable for you to buy, either in terms of cut, appearance or price point.

The items fall into three groupings. The first five items are essential undergarments that you may not have or of which you may not realize the importance. The next twelve items are black garments, usually made of soft, stretchy, jersey or knit fabrics that, when worn on top and on bottom, will create an inner, linear column that slenderizes and achieves a camouflaging black line. These items open up some exciting options for jackets, vests, dusters or other garments rich with color or interesting details. The last four items are of complete monochromatic outfits and accessories. Put on a monochromatic outfit, add some exciting and colorful accessories, especially near the face, and walk out the door.

1. Black sliding or bike shorts—shaper/girdle (SPANX, Rago)
2. Black posture bra (Cortland)
3. Black corset top (Fredericks of Hollywood)
4. Black full length slip (Shadow Line)
5. Pants liner (SPANX)
6. Black silk or satin camisole (Lane Bryant)
7. Black opaque tights (Just My Size)
8. Black knit shell (Misook, Lane Bryant, Dana Buchman, Elisabeth, Jones New York, Talbots, Michael Kors, Caslon, Eileen Fisher)
9. Black knit cardigan or shrug (Misook, Lane Bryant, Dana Buchman, Elisabeth, Jones New York, Talbots, Michael Kors, Caslon, Eileen Fisher)
10. Black cashmere mock turtleneck sweater (Lands' End)
11. Black short sleeve turtleneck (Sutton Studio of Bloomingdales)
12. Black surplice T-shirt or with three-quarter sleeves (INC, Caslon, Eddie Bauer)
13. Black knit skirt (Misook, Lane Bryant, Dana Buchman, Elisabeth, Jones New York, Talbots, Michael Kors, Caslon, Eileen Fisher)
14. Black slacks (Caslon, Semantiks, INC)
15. Black jeans (NYDJ, Ralph Lauren, Lane Bryant)
16. Black skirt, pencil or A-line (Michael Kors, Talbots, Marina Rinaldi)
17. Black skort (Elisabeth)

18. Monochromatic warm-up suit (Soft Surroundings)
19. Monochromatic suit: jacket, skirt and pants (Lafayette 148, Talbots)
20. Black microfiber ankle boots or pumps (Stuart Weitzman)
21. Sunglasses (Jackie O or aviator style)

Focus

A lot of women who read the fade list might be understandably turned off and therefore think, *Black again. Great, that's original.* But I ask you to keep your mind open just a little longer. Recall the goal was to fade or establish a svelte core with the previous list of items. The focus list seeks to accentuate the positive, to bring focus to your assets with color and interesting classic pieces that will work beautifully with the group of fade items. The first ten items of the list represent complete Go-To outfits with color. The next six items of the list include great outerwear pieces that boost your image immediately and exponentially. The last five items of the list are shoes and accessories that bring clout via timeless elegance. (There's nothing wrong with achieving focus through trendy items, as long as they're not too expensive, because season to season they represent fun, not an investment.) Furthermore, you can build additional outfits by substituting a couple of tops, but the core of the plan stays the same.

1. A-line (jersey) dress with a pattern (think Pucci; buy Tatiana or Ulla Popken)
2. Surplice style or faux wrap (knit) dress (think Diane Von Furstenberg; buy Talbots)
3. Monochromatic suit: jacket, skirt and slacks (Jones New York, Lafayette 148)
4. White jeans (Ralph Lauren, Lane Bryant)
5. Dark blue jeans (NYDJ, Ralph Lauren, Lane Bryant Seven)
6. Patterned skort (Lands' End)
7. Tweed skirt, pencil or A-line (Lafayette 148, Talbots, Semantiks)
8. Tweed blazer or jacket (Lafayette 148, Talbots, Semantiks)
9. Colorful twinset (Joan Vass, Soft Surroundings)
10. Matching satin camisole for the twinset (Soft Surroundings)

11. Colorful topper/duster (Ralph Lauren, Ellen Tracy)
12. Safari style jacket (Soft Surroundings, Talbots)
13. Denim or leather jacket (Tibor Leather, Talbots, Casual Living USA)
14. Trench-style raincoat, probably beltless (Ralph Lauren (men's), Cinzia Rocca)
15. Metallic or trendy car coat (Michael Kors, Ellen Tracy)
16. Vest (Ralph Lauren, In Suede, Eddie Bauer)
17. Black or brown boots to the knee (Silhouette)
18. Nude, metallic or animal print pumps with coordinating bag
19. Coordinated set (in terms of color): scarf, shell or camisole, shoes and bag
20. Clogs/mules with polyurethane sole and fun coloration (Dansko, Aerosoles)
21. One complete set of jewelry: couple of necklaces to layer, watch, bracelet, ring and earrings (Silpada.com)

Before You Walk Out the Door, Ask Yourself…
- Have I camouflaged a negative (fade)?
- Have I drawn attention to a positive (focus)?
- Does this outfit project the longest unbroken vertical line possible (through color, design and construction)?
- Does this outfit have at least one fitted or narrow aspect?
- Is some skin showing (leg, forearm or neck/chest)?
- Am I wearing undergarments that smooth and firm?
- Is everything clean and in good repair?
- Do my accessories boost my image?
- Have the garments been altered to show me at my best?
- Am I comfortable with this outfit physically and emotionally?

Pear Shape Diamond Winners
Dresses
- A wrap dress that closes at the natural waist is great for the pear shape diamond, because the outline of the dress— a fitted top and a wrap

skirt that falls in an A-line—matches the outline of your figure. Keep the length just below the knee for balance. Look for a substantial weight jersey fabric; it will drape beautifully.

- The empire waist dress is also a winner for the pear shape diamond. This style draws attention to the bust or upper half of the body, because the embellishment and focus tends to be at the neckline, just where you want it. Choose detail at the neckline, such as cut (e.g. V or boat neck), trim (e.g. buttons), patterns or piping.
- A "dress look" made of separates allows the pear shape diamond the opportunity to pick a top in a smaller size and a skirt in a larger size, reflecting her proportions.
- The trumpet dress, with a flare starting at the knee, is a flirty, flouncy option, too.

Skirts
- The A-line skirt parallels your lower half and so variations on this theme are the way to go for you. Look for fabrics that are substantial but drape well. Tropical weight wools work well and can be used for three seasons of wear.
- The gored skirt is a great option, too. It is made of panels or sections and flares at the hem. Look for one with relatively wide panels (six inches or so), because you don't want to create a horizontal line with all of the stitching going across too many panels. In fact, it is the stitching going top to bottom that subtly suggests a vertical line, which is, of course, most desirable.
- A straight skirt can be a good option if you follow specific guidelines. This style skirt is slim without any fullness. The key is to buy one that is truly large enough for your largest area and then alter it accordingly to fit in other areas. Choose a skirt that has a bit of gathering at the waist and some stretch in the fabric. The straight skirt is a reminder that less fabric is sometimes best, especially because it will taper at the knee thereby fabricating an hourglass shape.

Slacks and Jeans

- A full, straight leg is best. It lengthens your line and skims your hips. A defined waist at the navel or your natural waist is the best choice. Do not go for a high waist; it will exacerbate the difference in your upper and lower halves by making your upper half look shorter.
- A dark coloration is a good choice. When you are purchasing jeans, avoid trendy or unconventional washes and faded styles. A simple style is best and a dark blue or black will be most slenderizing.
- A style with little or no waistband is the best choice. Look for a clean finish and a flat front (no pleats).
- A gentle flare at the hem is another option that provides balance to your hips and has a current feel as well.

Jackets

- Don't try to find a long blazer that will cover your hips or backside. It tends to pull and draw attention to that area. Don't hide in large, unshaped garments; they actually provide more focus than fade.
- Look for a rich cropped jacket that falls at your high hip. Cropped jackets have straight cuts, straight sleeves and are often collarless. This style elongates and offers a smooth transition line to a gently draping bottom piece.
- Find bolero and toreador jackets that are waist-length jackets that balance a larger bottom with a lot of character.
- Choose styles that have interest at the neck, lapel or shoulders. The goal is to broaden shoulders to provide balance to your larger lower half.
- Try an Eton style jacket, which has a straight cut with wide lapels and balances out your lower half too.
- Choose a jacket with a mid-level stance (where the jacket closes and creates shape) and wear it over a light or bright colored camisole to focus attention to the face and bust.
- Wear jackets and coats that are fitted at the top but gently flare at the bottom with a straight pair of slacks or a skirt. A single-breasted topper or duster also works well.

Tops

- Necklines that draw the focus upward are what you should choose. Use buttons, pockets, trim and embroidery at the neckline and upper portion of a garment as the focus for all outfits. Keep the bright colors on the top.
- Contrasting colors between your top and bottom will emphasize your smaller waist.
- Scooped necklines and V-shaped necklines as long as they are fitted.
- Epaulet shirts, with detail on the shoulders and patch pockets, keep the interest and focus high up on your frame.
- Body shirts can be a neat option, because with its fitted side shaping seams, it shows your sleekness through the torso.
- Dress shirts are traditional button-down blouses and sleek but offer some balance to your lower half as well.
- Small shoulder pads broaden your shoulders to balance your hip. Don't wear shoulder pads that add bulk. Choose a thin, straight-edged pad often called a Dolman shape.
- Wrap tops, similar to the thinking behind wrap dresses, can be very pretty as long as they emphasize your waist and end at your high hip.

Round Shape Diamond Winners

Dresses

- A shift with princess seaming or diagonal darts nicely follows your hourglass proportions. Finding one with three-quarter-length sleeves may be optimal but tricky. Select sleeveless dresses and consider a fitted cardigan or shrug (a combination of a sweater and shawl) to coordinate with them.
- A classic coat style dress has closure from neck to hem down the front, but choose only single-breasted styles for a good choice. Choose garments that are lean with simple details.
- A wrap dress works if you have a defined waist. Use appropriate undergarments to smooth you out and always wear a full-length slip underneath.

- A dress with an empire waist, surplice wrap at the bodice (the upper area of the dress) and a gentle jersey bottom looks good.
- A peplum style dress, which I love, is fitted at the waistline with a ruffle of fabric below. A one or two-piece version emphasizes the waistline and covers the tummy. This style is great for other diamonds as well. Newer styles combine two fabrics or two colors, but are actually a one-piece dress, which helps with fade and focus.
- The sheath and chemise style dresses are straightforward options too. Both styles have straight cuts, but the sheathe dress has darts to make it fitted while the chemise dress does not. They work well in dark, neutral colors with an interesting shrug or jacket.
- A sweater dress, knitted and styled similar to a sweater, is a great fall wardrobe addition.

Skirts
- A pencil skirt, straight and tapering at the knee, is a knockout, because it draws attention to your great legs. Choose fabrics with some stretch, especially lightweight wools.
- A straight skirt that has a small waistband with slight gathering works too. It is essentially the same as a pencil skirt but without the tapering at the knee. A significant weight jersey fabric or even leather, suede or ultra-suede work well.
- The bias cut skirt is cut on the diagonal of the fabric and is very sexy. It grazes your curvy hips with movement and grace. Look for fabrics and patterns that have fluidity built in.
- The gored skirt works as well. Keep the skirt knee-length and be sure to pair with fitted tops with great open necklines.
- The kilt, a Scottish wraparound skirt, is a plaid skirt with a lot of personality. When paired with a dark, neutral top, it is a great look.
- The sarong, a wrapped skirt, is a sexy option that hides some tummy.
- The trumpet skirt, similar to the trumpet dress with straight lines and a large circular flounce at the hem, is a great option to shown off sexy legs.

Slacks and Jeans

- The straight-legged, flat front pair of slacks is a go-to item for you. Choose slacks that sit at your natural waist or navel and select front or side closures. Use elastic in the waist only if needed. Elastic tends to create more fullness through fabric, which is a negative; however, it also reduces any pulling or discomfort, which is a positive. Pick lightweight stretch wools or similar synthetics. Own several pairs.
- A boot cut hem, which widens subtly at the hem, worn with a heel is a great, sleek look for you and it helps balance hips.
- The boot cut leg is an especially good choice in jeans. Just be sure to choose jeans that are dark and clean (forget the ornamentation with details and washes).
- The capri or cropped slacks, both in varying lengths above the ankles, work for you, because you tend to have pretty ankles. Look for a firm fabric (not a stiff one). Choose patterns that are simple and tonal. Avoid loud Hawaiian prints.
- The gaucho works well, too. It drapes like a longer skirt, but offers the comfort of slacks.

Jackets

- An English riding coat/jacket is my favorite. This is a longish blazer with a seamed fit and flare built into the jacket. It can be especially flattering on round shape diamonds who have some height.
- A denim or leather jacket that has princess seeming built in and long enough to sit on the hipbone will work well, too.
- A cardigan jacket is slimming with its straight lines and collarless look. You have different choices that you can match to your height: hip-length, mid-length or knee-length. Keep the lines, fabric and pattern vertical. If you purchase a great dress for evening that is sleeveless, you can find a cardigan style jacket in a rich fabric such as satin, brocade or a knit with sequins to pair with it for great impact. Keep the dress simple if the cardigan is particularly well-embellished.

- A single-breasted jacket with some shape (and even some stretch in the fabric) that echoes your shape is flattering too. This is the style that will be easiest to find. Wear it open with a simple, pretty camisole underneath for a light, feminine look. The openness will create a vertical line.
- A bolero is a great way to cover arms when choosing a sheath or chemise dress.
- A knit shrug, black, white or a color, can bring sleeveless dresses back into your wardrobe.

Tops
- Choose tops with great open necklines: V, boat neck (opening wide toward the shoulders), asymmetric (different on either side of the center) or a deep scoop and that fall to your high hip or below your tummy, depending on your needs. Remember, where the top ends is the place where the eye is drawn. Match the length of the top to your most flattering point.
- Choose fitted tops that meet the edge of your shoulders with some definition but without pull. Avoid big loose arms if you can.
- Select sleeves that are large enough and have no pull, but are shaped. You want some definition between your torso and you arms; otherwise you can to look very horizontal and wide.
- Pick fabrics that drape, like matte (not shiny) jerseys, merino knits (made of high quality wool yarn) and silks or similar synthetics.
- Wear tailored shirts with vertical seams open or closed, which is very fresh and pretty. You can't beat a white tailored shirt.

Heart Shape Diamond Winners
Dresses
- A drop waist dress has a waistline below the natural waist and skims the line of your body through the hip. This style smoothes you out through the torso and adds interest with a soft flare at the knee.
- A shift or straight style dress with darts for shape at the top skims over your mid-section and tapers at the knee where your legs are

probably very pretty. A great look is to wear a black shift dress with an interesting cardigan over it, providing the best of worlds: fade and focus.

- A T-shirt or tank dress with an A line looks great. Three quarter sleeves are best in a mid-weight cotton fabric.
- The sweater dress is a great option, especially when two pieces are selected in the sizes you require for the top and bottom for a singular look
- The trumpet dress is a great way to balance a larger torso and smaller bottom with a pretty, flirty flounce at the hem.
- The wedge dress should be a go-to style for you. This style dress is cut full, tapering to the hemline in a wedge shape.

Skirts

- A pencil skirt—you have the legs for it! Choose a style with a minimal waistband. Match this with a long, torso-grazing top.
- A straight skirt in a fabric that drapes, like lightweight stretch wool or matte jersey, looks good. Side slits can be very pretty and feminine, too.
- A bias cut or gentle A-line skirt is flattering. It provides some balance to your larger top half. Keep the fabrics soft and graceful.

Slacks and Jeans

- A skimming, narrow leg is great for you and will probably be your go-to item. Choose a straight, slim pair of slacks without a waistband or with a small waistband. If you need some elastic in the waistband, that is okay.
- The cigarette style leg, which is slim and slightly shorter, can be very sexy for you. Worn with a top that provides the coverage you need to feel comfortable, you can still show off your slender legs.
- A boot cut leg pair of jeans with a contoured waist. The boot cut is the straight leg you need with a flare at the hem to provide balance for your larger upper half.
- The gaucho style pant is an option.

- A pair of cargo pants is trendy and fun. They have large pockets in the back and front and provide a nice balance to the larger top portion of your frame.
- A pair of pants in another fabric, such as denim, firm silks and stretch cottons, are great in addition to the stretch lightweight wools and matte jerseys previously recommended.

Jackets
- A collarless, skimming A-line jacket is a good choice for you. Keep the fabric soft and the lines vertical. Pockets should be limited to the high hip area.
- A blazer worn open over a similarly colored camisole or tank is a good choice. Keep the blazer straight-cut and single-breasted. The shoulder of the jacket should pair up with your natural shoulder; you don't want a droopy line at the shoulder. In general, keep the jacket close to the body, fitted and skimming.
- A three button jacket, fitted and closed, with three-quarter-length sleeves is very flattering too.
- A cardigan offers a draped shape and can be selected based on the most flattering length for you. Pair this with straight skirts and slacks.
- A blouson jacket has a bunched effect at the waist or below and is a good choice to soften a broad shoulder line.
- A knit shrug, black, white or a color, offers the opportunity to wear more sleeveless dresses.

Tops
- A tunic style top: There is no end to varying this style with different necklines, sleeve lengths, fabrics, trim and color. Tunic tops are great with a slim, straight skirt or slacks; this should be your go-to combination.
- A tailored shirt, fitted through the torso, also works well. Look for straight, skimming cuts infused with Lycra or Spandex.
- A knit top in firm silk or matte jersey for flattering fabrics.
- The darker or deeper color should be kept on the top.

Marquise Shape Diamond Winners

Dresses

- Empire waist dresses bring eyes upward and away from your tummy. Choose fabric that has enough body to drape well but not hug your tummy.
- Chevron patterns of inverted Vs disguise tummies well.
- Cocoon style dresses resemble your own shape and therefore are good matches. Be sure that balance exists by not tapering too much at the knee. A gentle curve is best.
- Sweater dresses can do a great job of fade and focus for you. Choose colors and knits that are vertical and camouflage your tummy while drawing attention to your neckline and knees.
- Trumpet dresses are a way to detract from your tummy and draw attention to your legs with a flounce hemline.
- Chemise styles are straight, imbedded with simplicity and elegance and can take you from daytime to nighttime activities seamlessly.

Skirts

- A straight skirt is the best option. Often, a pattern or embellishment will fool the eye and detract from your tummy.
- The skirt needs to be long enough to balance your upper half. The appearance of longer legs will balance a larger tummy.
- The pencil skirt will work well for you too, because you have great legs. Just be sure that the top you choose does the job of covering your tummy and provides balance for the whole outfit. A top with some length will work best with the pencil skirt.
- The bias cut skirt is very sexy. It grazes your curvy hips with movement and grace. Look for fabrics and patterns that have fluidity built-in.
- A kilt, with a beautiful plaid, will enhance your shapely legs, making it a good choice.
- A sarong is a great way to hide one's tummy and show off shapely hips and legs.
- A trumpet skirt, with a flounce at the hem, also shows off great legs.

Slacks and Jeans

- The slacks or jeans you choose should have a bit of volume to balance your tummy. Don't choose cigarette style pants "because you can." Although they may show off your legs nicely, they will yield an over-all disproportionate look for you.
- A boot cut pair of slacks is ideal, because it provides some balance for your tummy.
- A tailored jean's (more like a denim pair of slacks) drape is more flattering to you; fabrics such as Tencel work great.
- A mid-rise (at your navel or slightly below) pair of slacks or jeans gives you your longest leg line.
- A pair of slacks or jeans that have front creases for a strong vertical line are flattering. Permanently stitched-in creases are available, too.
- The cargo pant style will emphasize your slender legs beautifully.
- A pair of leggings are a great option under a long tunic. Leggings are tight pants to the ankles made of thin Lycra or other spandex knit fabrics.

Jackets

- A structured jacket does two things well: This creates an illusion of firmness and balance and it does wonders to hide a tummy.
- A structured shirt, made of silk stretch shantung, works just as well and provides a lighter look.
- A duster or topper with three-quarter-length sleeves is a real winner. Pair a duster with vivid coloration over a dark neutral top and bottom for instant svelte.
- A blouson jacket is a good way to disguise a tummy too.
- A jacket with a silk or nylon lining to enhance the drape is a good choice.
- A jacket worn open creates an additional vertical quality to the outfit.
- A jacket that is the correct length will make a difference. Remember, where the jacket ends is where the eye will be drawn. This concept can be used to disguise a large tummy.

Tops

- A blouson top, somewhat full and banding below the tummy, in a dark color works well, especially over slacks with some color.
- A weskit falling longer than your tummy is a great option. This is a jacket style garment made of fabric traditionally used for a blouse and are sometimes difficult to find.
- A great way to camouflage a tummy is to cut the body in half in terms of the top and the bottom of the outfit, right over the tummy, using fabric and coloration.
- A white blouse with significant vertical seaming falling below the tummy is a good choice.
- A blouse in stiffer, stretchy material holds shape better and is more flattering.
- A blouse that has ruching or other effects takes the eye away from a larger tummy as well.

Emerald Shape Diamond Winners

Dresses

- A straight dress that offers the appearance of contour through seaming, ruching, necklines and patterns is flattering.
- An outfit of separates looks better, because it is easier to suggest more shape with two pieces—a top and a bottom.
- A sheath or chemise dress are straightforward and simple options that invite pairing with interesting, coordinated jackets and cardigans.
- A sweater dress is a great way to build shape and contour, so don't overlook it.
- A trumpet dress gives you great coverage throughout the torso, but ends with flounce and curve at the hem.
- A coatdress is a good choice as well.
- A Mondrian style dress is a color-blocked sheath that can give you the style and coverage you seek.

Skirts
- A skirt that is just below knee-length balances a larger top.
- A straight skirt with curved or angled seams built-in.
- A dark or deep-colored top paired with a lighter, textured or embellished skirt creates contour and a waistline.
- A skirt with a handkerchief hem or asymmetric hem, both uneven, provides softness and break in the width of the fabric. Recall the concept of visual weight.
- A skirt made of fabric that is firm enough to drape well, but is not be stiff. Choose silks, matte jerseys and tropical weight wools infused with Lycra or Spandex.

Slacks and jeans
- If you are petite, choose a straight leg (not a boot cut) pair of slacks or jeans.
- If you are tall, choose a boot-cut leg that flares a bit at the hem.
- Wear a wider leg pant to balance the body. In fact, a wide leg pair of slacks in a mid-weight fabric is a good go-to garment for you. Choose dark, deep neutral shades.
- Choose flat front slacks over pleats.

Jackets
- A jacket with deep V necklines provides shape and contour.
- A jacket that has gentle, pretty seaming provides the appearance of contour. Often, a single button jacket with a mid-level stances provides a V, which gives shape, contour and a break in visual weight.
- A shorter jacket, one that comes to the high hip, provides the appearance of longer legs.
- A pair of small shoulder pads helps balance a large lower body.
- A cropped jacket, even if it is a little boxy, is flattering when it has texture that is neutral in coloration.
- A longer blouson jacket is a good way to inject contour and softness into an outfit.

Tops
- Blouses with vertical seaming and infused with Lycra or Spandex are smart choices.
- Soft camisoles and shells are great under jackets and provide balance in terms of a heavier jacket and a softer underpinning.
- Sweaters that fit well look great. More fabric is not necessarily better, but be sure the garment isn't pulling anywhere.
- Tops with great open necklines: V, boat, asymmetric or a deep scoop. A boat neck style creates a wider neckline, which balances a bigger bottom. An open V-neck achieves the same thing.
- Blouses or sweaters with patterns that keep the focus upwards. When paired with a dark bottom, this is a go-to look.
- Tops that are soft, pretty and feminine.

Bad Advice for Plus Size Women
There are many experts in the world of fashion. However, many don't understand the specific needs of the plus size woman. Meaning no harm, they give bad advice.

Let me emphasize some of the good advice for a plus size advantage.

Good, but be careful…
- Bangs
- Lower lid eye makeup
- Fragrance
- Loud hair, nail or lip color

While the core items in every woman's wardrobe will be similar, each body diamond shape needs different cuts and lines to achieve fade and focus. Choose clothing pieces that are relevant to your body diamond and make sure every outfit you put together does the best job of making you look great.

Instead of choosing…	Choose…
"ready-to-wear"	alterations
the waist the garment provides	to alter to your natural waist
magazines to inform your purchases	catalogs
a trendy, must-have item	a purchase that fits into a cluster
a statement necklace	a statement brooch or earrings
a cuff	a bangle
brown shoes	nude shoes
black shoes	metallic shoes
to spend money on clothing or handbags	to spend money on shoes
a thin, high heel (stiletto)	a stacked heel
sweatpants	jeans
slacks	skirts
jeans	a casual dress
shorts	skorts
foundations that hold you in	foundations that smooth you out
a minimizer bra	a posture bra
no shoulder pads	dolman style shoulder pads
bare legs	to wear hosiery (if it enhances your legs)
expensive support or designer hosiery	inexpensive hosiery with some Lycra
support pantyhose	a shaper
a half slip	a full slip
all black	strategic black
white foundations	nude foundations
big	fitted
unstructured	structured
shiny clothing	matte clothing
matte makeup	dewy makeup
stiff, bulky fabrics	fabrics that drape and stretch

Instead of choosing…	Choose…
additional pieces	a layered look achieved through illusion
to have a lot of clothing	to have less in your closet
the same old, same old	risk-taking
to save or hoard	to wear the stuff you love

CHAPTER 16

Body Language

GOT TWENTY
SECONDS?

"What a man enjoys about a woman's clothes are his fantasies of how she
would look without them." ~Brendan Francis

Plus size women often exhibit shame, discomfort or disappointment
because of the way they feel about their bodies and convey these
sentiments every chance they get, verbally and non-verbally, through
humor, self-deprecation, conversation, gestures and even through the
way they carry themselves. The intent of this chapter is for you to
become aware of that projected self-effacing and the message we give to
the world in order to become beautiful and confident women.

There is a saying often heard that may be helpful here as well:
"Fake it till you make it." The thinking is that a person is more likely to
adopt a certain confidence, trait or lifestyle if she fakes the behaviors of
that quality until the behaviors become integral to one's personality.
Sounds simple and it is. But it's not easy and it requires a lot of practice.

The demeanor and attitudes we have displayed for years as plus
size women, perhaps almost a lifetime, are deeply imbedded. They may
be as natural as breathing. We have cultivated them to be liked, to be
funny, to be non-threatening and "to pass with a push." They are our
defense mechanisms. And you know what—they work! The rest of the

world is only too happy to have us place ourselves in this defensive posture. It implies they are superior, because they are thin. Because we are plus size, we are inferior. But it doesn't have to be that way. To paraphrase something I said earlier, change is possible; the impossible just takes a little longer. When it comes right down to it, it's how people read you. It is the text of your affect we may be seeking to change.

The success of any meeting begins the moment someone sees you. You create the message and you are responsible for what it says. In fact, you start talking before you open your mouth. Some people call it your aura.

Improving your aura or charm doesn't cost a dime and yet it's worth a fortune, because it can enhance your people skills, attractiveness and general mood. It can pay off big time and may well be worth investing energy in. To paraphrase my father-in-law, "Charm is something that if you have it, you don't need anything else. And if you don't have it, it doesn't matter what else you have."

Think of a woman you consider sexy, assured and comfortable. That woman may be well-known or a colleague, relative or friend. These are real people, sexy and assured, from whom we can learn. If there is not one person who comes to mind, try to make a composite of a few individuals whom you admire. Think of someone you really have had the opportunity to observe and interact with several times, someone you've seen under pressure or someone you've admired and maybe even tried to imitate. Try to focus on a woman who is real. When you look at the outer package, the woman may or may not be beautiful. There is the very real chance that she would not make it to the cover of a fashion magazine, yet this is the person who comes to mind when you conjure up "sexy and assured." Most women wouldn't mind being thought of in this way.

Take this process a bit further and try to isolate the characteristics and qualities you admire. Some of the characteristics may be sincerity, confidence, intelligence, attractiveness, physical comfort, interest, approval, energy, enthusiasm, calmness, graciousness, astuteness and quick-wittedness.

With body language that is conscious, you can be this woman. Do you know why? Because "sexy and assured" is as much about aura as anything else and body language is your means to "walk the walk."

People communicate with each other on multiple levels. Experts say that non-verbal communication may have more sway than spoken words. Studies have found that body language makes up 55 percent and paralanguage (sighs, pauses and intonation) accounts for 38 percent, leaving the actual words spoken accounting for only 7 percent of what people interpret you to be saying by your communication.

Have you ever seen someone sitting or standing with her head slumped forwards, looking down, spine curved, shoulders slumped inwards? Your reaction was probably pity or disinterest, because the person looked depressed, off-putting or disconnected from her surroundings. The message the person was giving, intentionally or not, regardless of her clothing, accoutrements or environment, was, "stay away" or "I'm not worthy of your interest." The body language at work, then, compromises anything else intended to be positive—words, dress or environment.

The opposite is true as well. Have you ever been walking toward someone and as she approached, you noticed that she was walking straight, head up, shoulders back, looking around and soaking in the environment? You probably concluded she felt well and was infused with energy and purpose. You can do that too. If you sit or stand with your back straight, shoulders back, tummy in, chest out and head upright, you're ready to take on the world. This is one way to fabricate confidence, energy and enthusiasm. The previous slumped posture drains you of those qualities.

Further, if you want to communicate interest and respect for another, turn your body toward the person when they are speaking to you. This says you are interested in hearing what she has to say. It is an act of friendliness and respect and often the other person will reciprocate it back.

Do you want to be trusted? If so, after you have established an initial level of comfort with another person, you can begin to open up. Uncross those arms and legs and remove any barrier between you and the person with whom your speaking, such as your handbag, a briefcase or a grocery bag. Keeping an item in front of you communicates that you feel you need to be guarded.

Moreover, if you want to establish a rapport with another person, you may want to copy the other person's movements. This is called modeling.

Often, the other person feels comfortable and open to your message without realizing that you may be copying her movements, such as uncrossing arms or legs or turning the body this way or that way.

Small movements can go a long way, too. Recall those qualities that you admire in others, qualities that are synonymous with sexy and assured: sincerity, confidence, intelligence, attractiveness, physical comfort, interest, approval, energy, enthusiasm, calmness, graciousness, astuteness and quick-wittedness.

Visualization
Practice in front of a mirror at first. Visualize how you would stand and sit to feel assured, calm and friendly. Remember "fake it till you make it"? Don't eschew the idea. It has worked for thousands of people and it is a useful way to learn something new. In addition, acting a certain way lends itself to feeling that way. If you smile a bit more, you will find that you feel a bit happier. If you sit straight you will feel more energetic and in control. It you slow down, move with softness and project confidence, you will feel calmer. Your feelings will actually reinforce your new behaviors and the artificial or forced quality will fade.

Eye Contact
Eye contact is a great way to be sure people are listening to you. It communicates that you are looking closely to see where the conversation is going. It puts you in a position of power.

Take Up Some Space
Taking up some space while sitting or standing by separating your legs about a foot or so conveys self-confidence and comfort with your body.

Relax Your Shoulders
Your shoulders tense up when you're uptight and the more your shoulders are tense, the more uptight you feel. Make an effort to shake your

shoulders and loosen them up. Try rolling your shoulder in three circles frontward and then backward; it will calm you down.

Nod While People Are Talking To You

While you don't want to look like one of those cute puppy dogs in the rear window of a car, an occasional nod does signify that you are listening, approve of what is being said and, of course, are interested.

Lean In

If you want to show that you are interested in what someone is saying, lean toward the person talking. If you want to seem confident and relaxed, lean back a bit. Both are good in moderation.

Smile and Laugh

People are a lot more inclined to listen to you if you seem to be a positive person. Try not to be the first one to laugh at your own jokes, though, it makes you seem nervous and needy. Smile when you are first introduced to someone, but then let the smile fade or you'll seem insincere.

Keep Your Head Up

Don't keep your eyes on the ground; it makes you seem nervous. Keep your head straight and your eyes toward the other person's eyes.

Slow Down a Bit

Walking slower makes you seem more secure and confident and it will also make you feel less stressed. If someone calls you, don't snap your neck in her direction; turn it a bit more slowly instead.

Use Your Hands Confidently

Use your hands to describe something or give emphasis to a point you are trying to make. Fold them with your thumbs up to convey a positive approach, or press your extended fingers together, almost in a prayerful pose, to communicate confidence. But don't use them too much or you will seem distracted and unnerved.

Lower Your Beverage
Don't hold the glass with your drink in front of your chest. In fact, don't hold anything in front of your chest; it will make you seem guarded and distant. Lower the object and hold it to the side.

Keep Your Spine Straight
Keep your whole spine straight and aligned for better posture. It's just a more attractive, confident and energized posture.

Keep a Good Attitude
Stay open, relaxed and optimistic. This will be what you convey through your communication and it will likely be what you get in return.

What to Avoid
The following behaviors are ones to avoid when communicating with someone and trying to project an open and confident image.

- **Don't cross your arms and legs.** It makes you seem guarded and unapproachable.
- **Don't stare.** It makes people uncomfortable and your goal is to put people at ease.
- **Don't touch your face, hair or necklace or fidget.** It makes you seem nervous and distracted.
- **Don't stand too close.** We all need our space. As you get more comfortable or intimate with another person, you can decrease the distance between you.
- **Don't stand with your hands on your hips.** It suggests you are suspicious and expect the worst.

Affirmation

Many people and organizations use affirmations to uplift and instill self-belief. The following affirmation I've adapted for plus size women's use from the "Just for Today Reading of NA" page of the NA Works Web site, part of NA World Services, Inc. Try this affirmation to feel an aura of confidence, calmness and graciousness. You may want to copy it onto one of your index cards, slip it into a plastic sleeve and keep it in your handbag to refer to through the day or when needed:

Just for today,
I will expect the best of everything;
I will not revisit yesterday nor contemplate tomorrow;
I will celebrate this day and rejoice in all that is good and
beautiful in my life;
I will walk with my head up, calmly, confidently and soak up all
that surrounds me;
I will acknowledge and be grateful for my importance
in God's plan;
I will walk hand in hand with God and I will fear nothing.

As the common saying goes, shoot for the moon. Even if you miss it you will land among the stars. One more thing: never, ever discuss dieting. It's boring and nobody cares! Furthermore, you regress to that self-deprecating posture that the substance of this chapter seeks to obliterate.

Filing, Styling and Smiling

"The lamb began to follow the wolf in sheep's clothing."
~Aesop

Filing

Acceptance is a great gift. Self-love is better. The refinement of one's heart is best. The day is dawning when plus size women will embrace the pretty party encounter because it reflects all three of those things. Vanity must exist within a context of good taste and reality. In fact, for the plus size woman, it must coexist within the realm of available clothing and, especially, footwear that is insensitive to her needs and seemingly indifferent to her pocketbook. *Pretty Plus* changes all that. The pretty party experience enhances the way you present yourself each day and in every occasion of your lifestyle. Through the usage of a few tools and the implementation of some powerful information, you are empowered. The result: self-confidence, refinement and independence.

The Tools

The tools work together to develop a wardrobe within the context of your lifestyle and not vice versa. The days of declining invitations because of having "nothing to wear" are over. The well-dressed plus size woman knows the type of events she participates in and has two go-to outfits for each occasion at the ready. The Pretty Party Portfolio, the Essential Inventory Card and the Go-To Guide ensure that.

If however, that excuse ("nothing to wear") has excused or exonerated you from attending functions that made you uncomfortable for deeper reasons, you may want to explore and understand the reasons and excuses that have allowed you to hide. Remember, I say it so bluntly because I've been there and done that. If I've enjoyed some evolution in this area, I attribute it to the self-confidence I have earned, in part, based on looking so damn good!

The Pretty Party Portfolio
The Pretty Party Portfolio is about gathering and reaching for beautiful things. File items in your Portfolio that inspire. Target things that will make you smile. The importance of the Portfolio is not in identifying the actual pieces that you will head to the stores to buy, but rather to inform your purchases. The Portfolio should be packed with items that engender the image you seek for yourself. Nothing less. You must release your creative, aesthetic, sensual sensibilities and give them a voice for once in your life. Shake yourself free of the repressive sound bites that have crippled your take on fashion: "I can't wear that!" "I'll be laughed at." "I'll look ridiculous in that." "That's only for thin women" "I can't spend that much money." "I don't deserve it anyway!" Oh yes, you do deserve it. And you will have it. But you will access it with good judgment and with an eye for proportion. There is plenty of time to edit with a reality check later on. In fact, what you may actually purchase may only contain similar elements, colors, lines, proportions or embellishments as the items filed in your portfolio. But they will nevertheless articulate the image you seek. They may just say it in a dialect of sorts.

The Essential Inventory Card
The Essential Inventory Card is about organizing and discerning what will work for you given your lifestyle. This is where your dreams meet reality and you control your shopping experience rather than the availability of what fits controlling you. The Essential Inventory Card

contains a detailed plan for the go-to outfit (or cluster) that is good enough to represent the image you seek and is at the same time appropriate and flattering to you. Think of it as an insurance policy: if you adhere to the stipulations on the card, you're covered. If you deviate from the parameters set forth, you are in violation of your policy and may not be covered for unplanned contingencies.

To be fair, I too have bought items that weren't indicated on my Essential Inventory Card and stuffed them into my closet, because I worried that I might not find something comparable that would fit and flatter at a later point. Leave the tags on the garment until you've developed the whole outfit. If you can't put the whole outfit together inside a month, return the original item.

The Go-To Guide
The Go-To Guide is about simplifying the task of dressing and empowering a woman as she dresses each day. The power of what's in your closet is in its workability. It doesn't matter if you have a thousand items or ten items. It doesn't matter if the worth of your clothing is six figures or three figures. What matters is that you have a working picture (and I recommend literally not figuratively) of what goes together to make a go-to outfit. All of the pieces must be ready and in good repair. All you have to do is "gather and go!" The result: freedom and self-confidence.

This concept, less is more, is very hard for many plus size women to accept. For many of us, stuffing our closets may be akin to overeating, anesthetizing the pain of "not fitting in" with a gulp of instant gratification. This is where body language and channeling the power of affirmations are important. With their aid, the pull for more material things will lessen and self-confidence will rise.

Why affirmations? Author Ralph Marston put it well: "There is a thought in your mind right now. The longer you hold on to it, the more you dwell upon it, the more life you give to that thought. Give it enough life, and it will become real. So make sure the thought is indeed a great one."

People who are successful program their minds with affirmations, images and visualizations then back these up with action, persistence and gratitude. By using affirmations, images and words either consciously or subconsciously, you can create a comfort zone in the areas of fashion, shopping and, in general, having enough resources.

Until that takes hold, *fake it till you make it.* You'd be surprised how much falls into place when you act the part.

Styling

"The goal I seek is to have people refine their style through my clothing without having them become victims of fashion." ~Giorgio Armani

Remember the four simple principles to incorporate as the cornerstones of your pretty party style: First, fade: Camouflage the negative. Second, focus: Accentuate the positive. Third, erect: Build from the bottom up. Fourth, fashion: Create a signature statement that spells you.

I selected the metaphor of diamonds for body figures not only because it is effective but also because it is intended to get you to appreciate the value of your "real estate." You may have originally thought that your size was a liability. But as you reflect on your new tools and information, I hope you will see that your very size becomes your asset, because you can set the four cornerstones in place. You have more "area" to implement the principles of fade, focus, erect and fashion.

The metaphor of the diamond provides a visual and accessible perspective with which to work. Choose items that will fade or make your disproportionately larger areas recede. At the same time keep the focus on your most attractive areas. Erect your outfits starting with footwear then anchor pieces. You and the outfit are symbiotic. If you look uncomfortable the outfit will look out of sorts too. Apply your aesthetic and creative insights to the remainder of the outfit, working within the framework of Go-To Clusters. The Go-To Clusters are an efficient and cost-effective way to build a pretty party wardrobe. Invest in the big picture and you will reap the dividends every time you open your closet door. It's important to infuse each outfit with fashion:

something you love; something notable enough to be dubbed your signature; something of significance that others associate with you and recall favorably. Don't save and hoard your favorite pieces for some time in the future; that time may never come.

The important goal is to capture your longest, streamlined, shapeliest figure using the principles of design to emphasize and erase, drawing attention to your attractive features and drawing attention away from what you consider to be less attractive. Diamond in the rough? Not if you accept the asset of your size and seize the opportunity to make the art of *trompe l'oeil* your own.

Smiling

"While clothes may not make the woman, they certainly have a strong effect on her self-confidence—which, I believe, does make the woman." ~Mary Kay Ashe

How will you know when you have internalized the claim of *Pretty Plus*? First of all, you'll be smiling a lot more. Secondly, the time will come when you share the message with other big sisters. I implore you to tell other curvy women to "Take courage;" it is the flashpoint of real change for both of you. To quote author and diarist Anais Nin, "Life shrinks or expands in proportion to one's courage." There is always a choice. Choose to take courage—because you can.

When you ask other big sisters to "take courage," you are asking them to take a big risk, to move off center from a powerful gravitational pull, a place of familiarity—if not a place of comfort or beauty. It is only by your own example that you can communicate that the opportunity to dress sexy, sensational and successful is within reach. You'll find that the better you look, the more comfortable you will seem, the more you will smile and the more credibility you will have. Frankly, the more clout you'll have too—in all aspects of your life. Your world will expand.

Never discuss dieting; it's boring and nobody cares. Discussing dieting is about buying time and an excuse for not being thin. It screams inferiority. It's like saying, "I, too, will be good enough one day, when the scale says so." That load of self-deprecation just doesn't fit in the *Pretty Plus* paradigm.

Is there anything wrong with healthy dieting? Obviously not. What is wrong, however, is putting your life and self-esteem on hold until you lose weight. How much weight? When will you be good enough? Big sister, you're never going to be a waif of a woman. And a waif of a woman will never have the grounding or the transformative power you have culled via the *Pretty Plus* journey. You pick. There is always a choice.

I hope you find this quote by T.E. Lawrence as inspirational as I did: "All men dream but not equally. Those who dream by night in the dusty recesses of their minds wake in the day to find that it was vanity; but the dreamers of the day are dangerous men, for they may act their dream with open eyes to make it possible." Big sisters, being plus size and dressing sexy, sensational and successful is indeed possible.

Turn the pity party into a pretty party and never look back. There is always a choice. Choose acceptance and self-love and silence the angst in your heart. Look the best you can look now and enjoy it.

APPENDIX A

Sleek and Cheap

"I did not have three thousand pairs of shoes. I had one thousand and sixty."
~Imelda Marcos

Here is a list of items I recommend that will expand your wardrobe and save you money that you can spend elsewhere.

Footwear
- Munro shoes
- Just My Size black tights
- Kiwi Select Express Shine Sponge
- moleskin
- rubber wedge/platform sandal with metallic straps (flip-flops)

Undergarments
- Bra hook patch
- Carol Wright Gifts camisole bra
- Spanx
- Nylon knee socks
- Just My Size black tights

Accessories
- Foster Grant Sunglasses, aviator style
- Dressy satin clutch
- Hermes-style oblong scarf
- Synthetic or leather replica of the current trendy bag
- Straw bag

Coats
- Rain coat shell from the Ralph Lauren outlet
- Slicker
- Denim jacket from Casual Living USA
- Vest from Ralph Lauren

Sportswear
- Camisole bra from Carol Wright Gifts for under a V-neck T-shirt
- Mules in white or khaki from either Alfani or Keds

Beach Wear
- Matching set of beach accessories from Target
- Havaianas sandals
- T-shirt dress in black or a bold bright color

Wardrobe Building Supplies
- Accordion portfolio
- Index cards (five by eight inches) and plastic sleeve
- Three-ring notebook and plastic photograph inserts (four by six inches)
- Bi-level hooks
- Matching set of hangers with rubber insets
- Peel-off labels and shoe boxes

Alterations
- One yard of white cotton with 3 to 5 percent Lycra fabric
- One yard black sheer organza

- Black bias tape, two inches wide
- Shoulder pads in a dolman style
- Appliqués

Beauty Supplies
Face
- Crest Whitestrips
- Sugar wash(Cleansing Sugar Glow)
- Jergens Natural Glow moisturizer
- Nivea Glow self-tanner
- Vaseline lip balm

Hands
- Johnson Baby Oil
- Sally Hansen Vitamin Cuticle Oil
- Sally Hansen Radiant Hands Cuticle Crème
- OPI Designer Series Nail Polish

Makeup
- four lip glosses of the same color
- L'Oreal Original Voluminous mascara
- L'Oreal Bare Naturale loose powder
- Covergirl Advanced Radiance foundation in a pump bottle
- Oil blotting tissues

Hair
- L'Oreal Natural Match Hair Color
- Clairol Nice & Easy

Jewelry
- Bangles
- Brooches
- Faux Baroque pearls
- Necklace extender

Sample Go-To Clusters

"Your imagination is your preview of life's coming attractions."
~Albert Einstein

Casual

Select three color schemes and build three sets of tops and jewelry that will work together, interchangeably, with a variety of anchor pieces. The anchor piece could be a jacket, dress, skirt or slacks. It is the item that the rest of the outfit is built around. When you feel insecure with other items in your wardrobe, this is the piece that won't let you down.

* color set one (example: coral and brown)

** color set two (example: turquoise and silver)

*** color set three (example: red, black and camel)

@ for all daytime dressing needs

Anchor	Top	Footwear	Accessories
blue jeans hemmed for 2" heel	sweater*	mule 2" heel	slicker jewelry* handbag@
blue jeans hemmed for flats	significant tops***	metallic flats	jewelry***
skort/skirt**	vest or blazer**	mule 2" heel	jewelry**
black jeans hemmed for 2.5" heel	eather or denim jacket shell**	ankle boot 2.5" heel	jewelry**
white jeans hemmed for 2.5" heel	duster*** camisole***	ankle boot 2.5" heel	jewelry***

Work

@Use the same handbag and trench-style coat for each outfit. Metallic (or nude toned) coloration for the handbag will work for black, brown, navy, nude or metallic colored footwear and clothing.

Anchor	Top	Footwear	Accessories
soft neutral suit (skirt or slacks)	shell*	mule 2" heel	slicker jewelry* handbag@
print dress**		nude tone pumps	jewelry**
brown slacks hemmed for 2" heel	tunic*	nude tone pumps	jewelry*
pinstripe slacks hemmed for 1" heel	vest**	mule 1" heel	jewelry**
black slacks hemmed for 2" heel	twin-set**	nude tone pumps	jewelry**
tweed skirt	jacket***	knee high boots	jewelry***
black skirt	sweater***	knee high boots	jewelry***
denim skirt	twin-set**	mule 1" heel	jewelry**
solid dress*		mule 1" heel	jewelry*

Dressy
@@The same trench-style coat and evening handbag should work for each outfit.

Anchor	Top	Footwear	Accessories
black dress bias cut		metallic pumps 2-3" stacked heel	jewelry*** trench-style coat@@ evening bag@@
black suit (skirt or slacks hemmed for 1.5" heel)	camisole**	black pumps 1.5" kitten heel	jewelry**
embellished skirt	tunic*	metallic pumps	jewelry*
grey slacks hemmed for 2.5" heel	twin-set**	black pumps 2.5" heel	jewelry**
grey slacks	duster***	metallic pumps 2.5" heel	jewelry***

APPENDIX C

You'll Need

"Women usually love what they buy, yet hate two-thirds of what is in their closets." ~Mignon McLaughlin, *The Neurotic's Notebook*

Casual
- Two pairs of blue jeans (hemmed for different shoes)
- One pair black jeans or slacks
- One pair white jeans or slacks
- Two jackets or vests
- Five significant tops
- Two skorts
- Two T-shirt dresses

Work
- Three pairs of slacks
- Three skirts
- Three blazers, jackets, vests or dusters
- Three twinsets or significant sweaters
- Five significant tops or blouses
- Two dresses

Dressy
- One suit (slacks or skirt)
- One dress – bias cut
- One embellished skirt
- One pair dark, neutral slacks
- Two structured dressy tops (jacket, shantung blouse)
- One metallic-shot twinset or duster
- Heels and evening bag

Must Haves
- Go-to dress
- Black blazer or jacket
- Black turtleneck (short sleeve and long sleeve)
- Cashmere sweater (long and skimming)
- Denim jacket or leather jacket (black or brown—match to boots)
- Duster/topper
- Twinset
- Structured blazer, jacket or shantung shirt
- Vest
- Raincoat
- Black slacks or jeans
- White slacks or jeans
- Skort
- Metallic pumps or sandals
- Knee high boots (black or brown)
- Sunglasses

APPENDIX D

Resources for Plus Size Clothing

"Today, fashion is really about sensuality—how a woman feels on the inside. In the '80s women used suits with exaggerated shoulders and waists to make a strong impression. Women are now more comfortable with themselves and their bodies—they no longer feel the need to hide behind their clothes." ~Donna Karan

I had the good fortune to chat with the proprietor of Chezelle, the best plus size clothing store I know, about the resources that exist and how she selects her stock. The merchandise is very chic and represents the cutting edge of what the industry offers. Her clients tend to be well-to-do and discerning. I recall the conversation because of her vantage point, which is a segment of clothing that we all aspire to whether or not we can afford the exact items. My goal is for plus size shoppers to use the best and the brightest offered by the industry to inform their tastes and selections, even if their budgets are limited.

There are only about ten stores like Chezelle throughout the country. One reason that these stores can be powerful allies to the plus size market is that they are small and have identifiable ownership that can provide feedback to manufacturers. The kind of information I am referring to is size, cut, fabrics, price point and, generally, the items that sell quickly. Further, they can provide feedback as to the types of interpretations of missy size items that will work well for larger women. Chezelle and its kind can provide trunk shows (with items that can be customized according to fabric, fit and length), marvelous anchor pieces and accessories that truly provide one-stop shopping for the sophisticated plus size woman.

These small specialty shops are more responsive to the needs of the consumer in a direct way: Their profit depends on listening to and meeting her needs. For many department stores, there seems to be a disconnect as to what the consumer needs and will buy and the merchandise on the floor. I attribute this to buyers who just don't "get it," either because they are not plus size, they are not in tune with the consumer or both. The following listed designers are good not only for the specific items they produce but also because they can inform our tastes and raise our expectations in terms of the merchandise we are able to buy.

The Best of the Best
This section offers the plus size shopper information on designers with which to reference all purchases. I recommend becoming familiar with these designers not only as a source for purchasing but also for learning, as a means of building a Pretty Party wardrobe. As I mentioned earlier, often I buy an item that is a relative bargain and dub it my designer name piece, because it exudes the embellishment and stylistic details that I deem comparable to an item created by that particular designer. It's fun, it keeps me in the designer landscape and it works!

For each designer I address four things:

- **Important and relevant to the plus size woman**: addresses the question, "How does this brand, specifically, help you look sexy, sensational and successful no matter what you weigh?"
- **Insights that define the market:** provides the history of the brand, which may create a more knowledgeable and discriminating wardrobe-building experience.

Casual Clothing	Work Clothing	Dressy Clothing
AK Anne Klein	Basler	Michael Kors
Carolyn Taylor	Caslon (Nordstrom brand)	Marina Rinaldi
Caslon (Nordstrom brand)	Ellen Tracy	Ellen Tracy
Eileen Fisher	INC.	Carmen Marc Valvo
Elena Miro	Jones New York	Ming Wang
Kenar	Layfayette 148	Tadashi
Maritime Cloth	Maritime Cloth	Talbots
Michael Kors	Michael Kors	Bloomingdales.com
Lands' End	Misook	Neiman-Marcus.com
ONYX Nite	Ralph Lauren	Saksfifthavenue.com
Ralph Lauren	Talbots	Encore at Nordstrom
Talbots	Tilbor leathers	Amanda Uprichard
Tilbor leathers	Ming Wang	Anna Scholz

- **Quality:** The continuum of terms is outstanding, excellent, very good and acceptable.
- **Price point:** The continuum of terms is very expensive, expensive and moderate.

Alfani

Important and relevant to the plus size woman: This brand and concept fascinate me, because it represents a growing trend in the plus size fashion industry. The women's collection by Alfani consists of

European-inspired career separates for plus size women, offering jacket alternatives and knitwear layering pieces.

Insights that define the market: Federated Department Stores carry Alfani as a private label brand, clothing exclusive to a specific store, chain or mail order company. In recent years, women's private label sales have increased, surpassing the sales of national brand and designer clothing, according to Cotton Incorporated's article *What's So Private*. Carrying private label clothing in stores allows the retailer to have control over the development and marketing of the labels as well as cost advantages, which can be shared with consumers. Stores can tailor their private brands to target their specific demographic of shoppers.

Each of Federated's private labels targets specific consumers in certain age ranges: Charter Club, non-working or suburban women ages thirty-five to sixty; I.N.C, single, active women over the age of twenty-eight; Style & Co., employed women, usually married, ages twenty-five to fifty-five. Each of these "brands" make terrific plus size clothing.

Quality: Good
Price point: Moderate

Amanda Uprichard

Important and relevant to the plus size woman: Amanda Uprichard brings chic, sexy clothing onto the plus size shopper's radar. The line offers simple, classic and feminine pieces in bold and bright silks.

Insights that define the market: Known for sexy yet romantic designs, Amanda Uprichard's magic is overstated charm.

Quality: Excellent
Price point: Very Expensive

Anna Scholz

Important and relevant to the plus size woman: Excellent tailoring, detailing and color palettes define her clothing designs. Incorporating bold features keeps her clothing proportionate to plus size women's statures. Her collection is available from size eight to size twenty-six.

Insights that define the market: Anna Scholz is a model turned designer, because she was frustrated by not finding clothing that fit her well. As a student at Central Saint Martin's she concentrated on designing for large sizes and focused her thesis on what she called "The Tyranny of Thinness." For Scholz, fashion is about the end of marginalizing the plus size woman. She is a designer with a political as well as aesthetic mission.

Quality: Excellent

Price Point: Very Expensive

Basler

Important and relevant to the plus size woman: Basler offers modern styles that appeal internationally. The style is cut for European women meaning if you're slimmer in the hips and legs than on top (heart shape), you will enjoy the fit of this brand. The unique style of Basler embraces high quality fabrics and construction that translates into investment pieces. The look is sophisticated and continental.

Insights that define the market: Basler continues to update and develop their collection and styles. The European style of the Basler collection, made in Germany, is becoming a modern classic.

Quality: Excellent

Price Point: Very expensive

Carmen Marc Valvo

Important and relevant to the plus size woman: Carmen Marc Valvo makes clothing that is proportionate to a plus size woman's stature. The clothing is rich, sophisticated and showcases great detail and embellishment. If you want to feel like a queen, wear Carmen Marc Valvo.

Insights that define the market: Carmen Marc Valvo began as a designer for Nina Ricci and then Christian Dior. In 1989 he launched his own label, becoming a success through his sportswear and especially his eveningwear. He has since gone on to create the well-known labels Carmen Marc Valvo Couture and CMV. His collections and designs now include, in addition to sportswear and eveningwear, swimwear, eyewear, lingerie, home décor and evening bags.

Through his many collections, Valvo has honed his skills in cutting and draping fabric to enhance the female figure. He is known for excellent tailoring, a deep comprehension of fit and extraordinary detailing.

Quality: Excellent

Price Point: Very Expensive

Eileen Fisher

Important and relevant to the plus size woman: Eileen Fisher clothing is based on comfort and style. The fabrication tends to be organic and eco-friendly in reality and in appearance. Her approach to fashion is based on achieving beauty that is simpler for you and better for the environment.

Insights that define the market: Eileen Fisher worked as an interior designer and then as a graphic artist before founding her clothing company in 1984. She seeks to create pieces of clothing that build on one another and allow women to express themselves, move and play.

Quality: Very good

Price Point: Expensive

Elena Miro

Important and relevant to the plus size woman: Miro designs trendy plus size clothing for curvy women who are well-informed and seek the current fashion styles.

Insights that define the market: Elena Miro was introduced in the 1970s as a class plus size brand. It has since evolved to a ready-to-wear plus size clothing brand that uses plus size models.

Quality: Excellent

Price Point: Expensive

Ellen Tracy

Important and relevant to the plus size woman: Ellen Tracy uses top-quality fabrics and clean lines to create a complete wardrobe for the working woman. When building a professional wardrobe, the plus size shopper, alongside the missy shopper, can think Ellen Tracy.

Insights that define the market: In 1949, Herbert Gallen began his clothing business, inventing the name Ellen Tracy. Linda Allard was hired in 1962, expanded the line and has been the driving force behind Ellen Tracy ever since. Ellen Tracy focuses on investment clothing, with some fashion at the request of its customers. Consistent design and quality have increased sales, and more women continue to discover the line's stylish and comfortable professional clothing.

Quality: Excellent

Price Point: Very expensive

Emme

Important and relevant to the plus size woman: Emme designs clothing that work with women as well as their lives and their budgets. Her most recent collection, me by Emme, consists of luxurious, easy-care, fashionable separates and activewear for plus size women. The balance femininity and ease in Emme's designs give women confidence.

Insights that define the market: Emme has been a model, television host, author, lecturer and clothing designer. She was the first full-figured model to secure a cosmetics contract.

As a model, she spoke before a congressional subcommittee to increase awareness about eating and body image disorders.

Quality: Good

Price Point: Moderate

Lafayette 148

Important and relevant to the plus size woman: This line gets big praise from me precisely because of the confidence it inspires. Lafayette 148 pieces will become your go-to anchors and take the trepidation out of dressing for important occasions. Best known for separates, novelty embellishments, leathers and knitwear, Lafayette 148 has chic designs coupled with excellent craftsmanship.

Insights that define the market: Lafayette 148 was founded in 1996 and is driven by designer Edward Wilkerson, whose elegant and wearable pieces are inspired by the women he meets. Wilkerson continues to

create collections based on his customers' needs and desires.
Quality: Outstanding
Price Point: Very expensive

Magaschoni's

Important and relevant to the plus size woman: Magaschoni designs a stylish line that is also functional and that includes separates and suiting. The collection pieces are designed to work with one another, but also versatile enough to work with shoppers' existing wardrobes.
Insights that define the market: Magaschoni was established in 1989 and continues to evolve to meet the lifestyle demands of modern women. Magaschoni is known for its attention to color, detailed embellishments and tailored lines.
Quality: Excellent
Price Point: Very Expensive

Marina Rinaldi

Important and relevant to the plus size woman: Marina Rinaldi clothing brings a sleek, Italian-cut of clothing to the plus size woman. There is nothing big, gauzy and flowing about this line. The line offers flattering silhouettes in vibrant fabrics to women sizes ten to twenty-two.
Insights that define the market: Marina Rinaldi has expanded to include ready-to-wear, sportswear, business attire, occasion dressing, outerwear, travel attire, luxury collections and a full range of accessories and shoes. This is a luxurious line of clothing and accessories that includes the plus size woman but is not limited to this market.
Quality: Excellent
Price Point: Very Expensive

Michael Kors

Important and relevant to the plus size woman: Kors's initial vision of chic, luxurious American sportswear remains the impetus to all clothing in his line. Fortunately for plus size shoppers, he has invited us to participate. More so than any other line, Michael Kors gives the plus size woman access and relevance to the world of the chic and famous.

Insights that define the market. Michael Kors formed his own label in 1981 after working for renowned boutique Lothar's. Since then, Kors has gone on to develop full clothing, handbag, shoes and accessories lines. The boldness and size of his accessories make them particularly well suited to the larger woman. The Michael Kors Collection is sold worldwide and is worn by many celebrities.

Quality: Very good
Price Point: Expensive

Ming Wang

Important and relevant to the plus size woman: Ming Wang is known for its knit separates, which provide excellent drape, contour and coverage for the plus size woman. The bold graphic styling offers good proportion for plus size women.

Insights that define the market: Ming Wang began making knitwear in 2000. Wang uses Amica yarn, so the garments are wrinkle-free and retain their shapes, perfect for travel. The pieces are well worth the investment.

Quality: Excellent
Price Point: Expensive

Misook

Important and relevant to the plus size woman: There is a sleek, flat quality to Misook knits that works amazingly well for the plus size woman providing excellent drape and contour creating the most flattering silhouettes imaginable for the larger woman. True confession: Misook is the backbone of my own wardrobe.

Insights that define the market: Misook clothing has a common element, often a lot or a little of the same black knit is infused into most of the garments produced. This allows mix and match opportunities to abound.

While the price point is quite expensive, often a new cardigan will create a completely "new" outfit.

Designer Misook Doolittle's knit collection offers styling that is classic and timeless. The combination of beauty, comfort and easy care makes Misook's knits truly special to own. The clothes don't wrinkle, can be washed at home as delicates and can be worn year-round by professionals and travelers.

Quality: Excellent
Price Point: Very expensive

Tadashi

Important and relevant to the plus size woman: Tadashi is perhaps the upscale go-to source for (plus size) women who have a special occasion in their lives. The line extends missy sizes to plus sizes seamlessly.
Insights that define the market: Luxury and elegance define Tadashi's designs, winning him a loyal following among celebrities. Think *red carpet* when you wear Tadashi.
Quality: Excellent
Price Point: Expensive

Talbots

Important and relevant to the plus size woman: Talbots presents modern classic styling for an everyday sophistication. This brand is "money in the bank" for the plus size shopper when you need to find something specific that will fit, for example, a pair of camel slacks or a glen plaid blazer. Talbot's missy and petite missy extend through size twenty. Talbot's woman and petite woman collections go up to size 3X. Importantly, the ability to wear a missy size can be a sleeker, more streamlined option for many plus size women and I applaud the ability to consider the choice. I can wear Talbot's missy size twenty and woman's sixteen. This is helpful, because sometimes I want less fabric, less bulk and sometimes I need more room for comfort. For example, I may choose a pair of slacks, tropical weight wool with spandex in size twenty, for a leaner look, but a silk blazer in a woman's size sixteen to afford me ease of motion as I move around.

Insights that define the market: Talbots was founded in 1947 and has created a legacy for trustworthy and versatile staple wardrobe items. Modern flair helps create timeless wardrobe pieces. Worn by First Lady Michelle Obama, Talbots clothing offers sophistication accessible to all women.
Quality: Very good
Price Point: Moderate/expensive

Online Plus Size Stores

Store Web site	Style	Sizes	Price Point
Alight.com	trendy meets lighthearted	to 30	moderate
Avenue.com	casual meets vivid	to 34	moderate
Bloomingdales.com	sophisticated meets updated; trendy meets refined; upscale meets accessible	to 3X	expensive
Casuallivingusa.com	updated meets feminine; sexy meets appropriate	to 3X (28W)	moderate
Catherines.com	comfortable meets pretty	to 34	moderate
Chadwicks.com	classic meets updated	to 26	moderate
Jcpenney.com	classic meets updated	to 24	moderate
Jessicalondon.com	classic meets updated	to 34	moderate
Junonia.com	casual clothing meets activewear and swimwear	14	moderate
Landsend.com	casual sportswear meets activewear; classic style meets durable function	to 3X	moderate
Lanebryant.com	cutting-edge meets accessible; updated meets classic; sexy meets appropriate	to 32	moderate
LordandTaylor.com	chic meets affordable; classic meets updated; work clothing meets sportswear	to 3X	moderate/ expensive
Macys.com	updated meets chic, work clothing meets sportswear	to 3X	moderate/ expensive

Store Web site	Style	Sizes	Price Point
Neiman-Marcus.com	chic meets sleek	to 3X	expensive
Nordstrom.com	pretty meets updated	to 3X	expensive
Onestopplus.com	classic meets trendy; affordable meets variety	to 44W	moderate
Pluswoman.com	attractive meets basic; natural fibers meet updated looks	to 10X	moderate
Roamans.com	basic clothing meets sexy and trendy	to 44W	moderate
Saksfifthavenue.com	chic meets classic; dressy meets work; work meets casual	to 3X	expensive
Silhouettes.com	basic clothing meets sexy and trendy; wide selection of footwear styles meets wide selection of sizes	12W +	moderate
Softsurroundings.com	very pretty meets updated; excellent cuts meet excellent fabrication	to 3X	expensive
Sowhatif.com	saucy attitude meets accessible	14W +	moderate
Talbots.com	classic meets updated; dressy meets work, work meets casual	Missy to 20; Missy petite to 20. Woman's to 3X; petites to 3X	moderate/expensive
Torrid.com	sexy meets a lot of fun	14W +	moderate
Ullapopken.com	earthy meets trendy; sportswear meets real women	12 +	moderate

GLOSSARY

"A little knowledge that acts is worth infinitely more than much knowledge that is idle." ~Kahlil Gibran

Activewear: Any garment designed to be worn for active sports comes under this category. This is, however, different from athletic uniforms worn by athletes.

A-line: The shape of the garment reflects the shape of the letter A: gradually widening from the top to the bottom or hem of the skirt or dress.

Anorak: A hooded, hip-length jacket that is waterproof by a Scotchguard finish on cotton, a synthetic material or sealskin. It has a zip-front and drawstring hem.

Appliqué: A surface pattern made by cutting out fabric or lace designs and attaching them to another fabric by means of stitching or gluing. Appliqués can have themes such as sports, flowers and emotion phrases.

Arch: The built-up portion of a shoe under the arch or center of your foot. It supports and distributes weight.

Arizona Sun Supply Inc: Makes sports fabrics that are weather resistant, which means they resist water and wind because of a tight weave. Some are breathable; others don't breathe as well. These sports fabrics are made from synthetics such as nylon, polyester or a cotton blend and have a high thread count. The fabrics are strong, vibrant and durable, designed to withstand tough outdoor use. In addition, high UV performance provides lasting color and protection from the sun in any athletic application.

Art to wear: The clothing in this category tends to be more fun-oriented and not for the business world. It represents a craftsmanship in fabric artistry to design clothes with originality and individuality.

Asymmetric hem: A hem that differs on either side of an imaginary line drawn down the center front of a garment. It is a great way to break up a wide horizontal line.

Audiere: A small, very luxurious evening bag.

Aviator: This style adapts the clothing and props of pilots, especially during the earlier part of the twentieth century, for modern wear. This style of eyewear is large and softly angular. Notice that the lens will be wider at the sides of the face and sloping toward the nose.

Balmacaan coat: A raglan-sleeved, loose-fitting style coat with a small turned-down collar that buttons from the neck down.

Baroque: Pearls that have irregular shapes, as opposed to round, smooth pearls. They may be simulated, cultured or genuine Oriental pearls. They are celebrated for their shape, color and luster. The color is often blue-gray or off-white.

Beach shift: Also called a beach dress, it is a simple cover-up designed to be worn over a bathing suit.

Beret: Fashionable in France between the 1820s and 1840s, it originally was a cap with a large flat halo crown and sported beautiful trim. Today it is a soft hat without a brim that is draped and tilted to the side of the head, usually made from a knit.

Better goods: In the world of consumer-based fashion, there are categories that represent price points. Better goods falls in the continuum between bridge (which is just under designer) and moderate goods (which is towards the low end).

Bias cut skirt: A skirt cut on the diagonal or the bias of the fabric. The bias cut was introduced by Madeleine Vionnet in the 1920s and was popular through the 1930s. Revived in the 1980s, it has remained a classic. The cut tends to drape or graze hips forgivingly.

Blazer or **jacket:** A single-breasted sport jacket first introduced in Great Britain in 1890. Originally it was crimson colored. Today the blazer can be double-breasted and made of a vast array of fabrics, colorations and details.

Blouson jacket: A jacket with a bunched or bloused effect at the waist or below. The fabric is gathered into a knitted waistband or pulled by a drawstring.

Blouson top: Can be characterized by fullness at the waist and is usually gathered into a band.

Bodice: Refers to the close fit of the upper part of a woman's dress. For a visual, think of the cross-laced feature in a peasant style dress.

Body shirt: Fitted through side shaping seams that fit closely to the body lines. The shirt was introduced in the 1960s and enjoyed great popularity. Sometimes the body shirt has a snap at the crotch.

Bolero: A waist-length jacket, usually collarless with a rounded front and no closures. Copied from the Spanish bullfighters' embroidered jackets and worn by women since the late nineteenth century.

Boot cut: A full-cut leg that subtly widens at the hem.

Bridge: Bridge is a consumer price level between designer or couture and better goods. Merchandise in this category tends to be more of an investment. Think about the concept of "cost per wearing." If you wear an item more often or if it represents the anchor piece in a cluster you are building, it has considerable value.

Brocade: A type of fabric traditionally woven on the Jacquard loom, giving a raised appearance to its design. Made with all types of rich yarns including gold, silver, rayon or cotton against a satin background.

Brooch: While the term shares the same denotation as pin, the connotation of brooch implies a pin with age and character, usually sizeable as well.

Camel hair: Refers to fibers from the crossbred Bactrian camel of Asia, which produces soft luxurious yarn that is resistant to heat and cold.

Camisole: A lingerie item that describes a waist-length straight-cut top with straps, trimmed with lace or embroidery.

Capri pants: Three-quarters in length and tend to be tight fitting with short slits on the outside legs. Worn in the 1950s, the name was inspired by the Italian resort Island of Capri, where the style first became popular.

Car coat: A sort of utility coat made hip to three-quarter length. It's particularly comfortable for driving a car and became popular with the station-wagon driving ladies in suburbia in the 1950s and 1960s. It has been a classic since. It is also called a stadium coat, toggle coat, ranch coat, benchwarmer and Mackinaw jacket.

Cardigan jacket: A straight box-type jacket with no collar. It is usually long-sleeved and may have trim or an interesting weave around the neck and down the front. It was named for the 7th Earl of Cardigan who needed an extra layer of warmth for his uniform during the Crimean War in 1854.

Cardigan: A collarless jacket or sweater made with a plain, round neckline and buttoned down the center front.

Cargo pants: Pants with large bellow pockets in back and two extra large pockets in front that have extended tops which form large tunnel loops for an optional belt.

Chemise: A straight-cut dress with a few darts and no waistline. Introduced in 1957 by French couturier Hubert de Givenchy, it can also be called a sack dress.

Chesterfield: A semi-fitted, straight-cut classic coat. It can be single or double-breasted, often with a velvet collar.

Chevron: A pattern made of straight lines that form inverted Vs.

Cigarette style leg: A slim, slightly shorter slack often in a thinner fabric; think Audrey Hepburn in *Sabrina*.

Cleavage: Traditionally refers to the separation between a woman's breasts, made more obvious with a low-cut neckline. The parallel holds true for shoes: toe cleavage is a peek at the sensuous area of the separation between the toes.

Clog: A shoe made with a thick sole of wood, cork or polyurethane. Usually the upper is made in a sandal style, sometimes with a closed toe and open heel. The style was very popular in the 1960s and has remained a classic since.

Cluster: Consists of many pieces of an outfit: footwear, anchor piece (often a bottom or dress) and a set of jewelry. A woman can substitute a new top, sweater or jacket and produce another outfit, extending the wear-ability and usage of the cluster of items.

Clutch: A that bag has no handle and is carried under the arm.

Coat dress: Boasts closure down the front from neck to hem, like a coat, and can be single or double-breasted, belted or unbelted. The dress has been a classic since the 1930s.

Cocoon style: Rounded and full from the shoulders through the middle of the garment but begins to narrow toward the knee.

Corset: A one-piece laced or hooked garment for shaping the figure, usually made of substantial materials and even boning for added shape.

Cropped jacket: A boxy, straight-cut jacket that is short in length, usually ending at the waist or high hip. It is often collarless and has straight sleeves.

Cropped pants: Cut in varying lengths between the knee and the ankle, they tend to be cut fuller than Capri pants.

Denier: This refers to an international textile and hosiery system used for numbering yarns. The low numbers represent greater sheerness and the high numbers represent more opacity. This is mostly relevant in fine hosiery. If you prefer to wear finer hosiery, this term will help you determine if the denier number is sufficient to cover imperfections on your skin.

Designer: The highest consumer price level.

Designer jeans: Designer jeans were especially popular in the 1970s and with good reason. They elevated the wear-ability of jeans and promoted jeans to evening wear. The same is true today, especially for plus size shoppers. While the designer jeans of the 1970s and designer jeans today (more branding than designing, per se) are very pricey, the cut can make all the difference. My suggestion for plus size women is to seek two or three brands that flatter you, even if they are pricey, and limit yourself to two or three pairs. I have found some great jeans in Marshalls and TJ Maxx for under twenty dollars that have excellent fabrication with stretch and are cut with a slight flare at the hem. They look fantastic and I don't worry about ruining them or wearing them out.

Dolman shoulder pad: A small, straight-edged shoulder pad inserted in a garment to define a straight edge of the shoulder.

Dolman sleeve: Gives the appearance of a cape in the back but a sleeve in the front.

Double-breasted: Refers to a closing where the garment is fastened with two parallel vertical rows of buttons on the center front.

Dress shirt: The traditional button-down-the-front shirt, emulating the men's oxford shirt. Choose shirts that are cotton but infused with stretch.

Dropped waistline: The waist of the garment falls below the natural waist of the wearer. It can be flattering for a woman with a larger waist who tends to narrow through the hips and legs.

Duster: A coat-jacket or cardigan that stops just above the knee.

Embellishment: Refers to any kind of detail or trim that heightens the interest and richness of the garment. Embellishments can include beading, piping, metallic trim, interesting buttons or other fasteners.

Empire dress: Has a high waistline just under the bust and is defined by an inserted piece of fabric or seam. The style was originated by Empress Josephine of France with the neckline low-cut in the front and back, small puffed sleeves, ankle-length straight skirt and a sash tied under the bust. Today the style refers to any dress with a high waistline and a straight or A-line skirt.

Empire waist: The waist of the garment is indented just below the bust.

Epaulets: Ornamental shoulder trim, often a flat band of fabric fastened with a button with a military inference.

Epaulet shirt: Has long sleeves with epaulets and buttons on the shoulders. This allows the wearer to roll the sleeves up and fold them under the straps with the buttons. Other features are a buttoned front, convertible collar and patch pockets. Each of those details tends to balance the lower half of a pear shape diamond's frame.

Eton jacket: Straight-cut with a collar and wide lapels. It can be worn unbuttoned or with only a top button closed. The jacket is essentially waist-length or just a little below. The style was adapted from Eton College in England.

Fabrics: The goal for a plus size shopper is to seek fabric that provides great drape without adding bulk. To do that, you must become aware of the surface quality of different fabrics. Weaves that add texture may add interest, but they also add unwanted bulk. Surfaces finished with shine may be pretty on the hanger but will add the appearance of additional volume to your figure. The best fabric for plus size women is a matte stretch fabric, usually jersey.

Avignon: A lightweight silk taffeta lining fabric made in France. It fosters flattering drape of a fabric from the inside. Less expensive versions that achieve the same objective are acceptable too.

Antique satin: A reversible fabric with a dull face and a satin back. It is very interesting and rich without offering additional bulk.

Austrian cloth: A fine woolen or worsted fabric woven from the highest grade of merino wool. Merino wool is among my personal favorites and I recommend it highly.

Cashmere: A very soft, luxurious knit fabric made from the hair of the cashmere goat native to India. It is a great fabric for plus size women because, depending on the ply (the thickness), it has great coverage and drape. It is very wonderful to the touch.

COOLMAX: Several manufacturers have their own trademarked version of a dry-weave fabric and are quite good. COOLMAX fabric transfers moisture from the skin through the fabric. Many associate performance apparel with extreme sports, but everyone can benefit from wearing this fabric for sporting or casual occasions. It has a seamless application to casual wear that is not sports performance related. COOLMAX is a registered trademark of INVISTA.

Crepe back satin: A lightweight fabric with a smooth, lustrous finish on the face and a dull crepe appearance on the back. Either side may be used for garments. Look for this fabric in dresses and blouses.

Damask fabric: Made in the Jacquard weave in white, colored floral or geometric designs, the pattern may be large or small and reverses on the other side. The print or design is woven into the fabric.

Double Dry Cotton: Developed by Champion, a division of Sara Lee Corporation, it is a cotton alternative to synthetic dry-weave fabrics. This fabric keeps skin dry while providing the comfort of cotton, a perfect combination for active and casual occasions.

Dupioni silk: Made from yarns reeled from double cocoons in which the silk is intertwined, making an uneven yarn that gives an interesting texture or finish to a garment. While the jacket is still queen of my world for its structure, drape and coverage, blouses cut like jackets in this fabric (also referred to as shantung) are terrific too. Synthetics that imitate this look are acceptable as well.

Gabardine: A durable, closely woven fabric with definite ridges caused by the warp-faced twill weave. Gabardine may be made of cotton or wool and, when infused with stretch, is a powerful ally in slacks and jackets.

Interlock: Refers to a knit made on a machine having alternate units of short and long needles. The result is a thicker product than plain knits, but in this case it is a good thing for plus size women, because the finished product offers good body and elasticity. Look for interlock knits in sportswear tops.

Jersey: A classification of knitted fabrics that are knitted in a soft, plain stitch. Originally, all jersey was made of wool, but now manmade yarns translate into jersey very well. When infused with additional stretch yarns, this is the go-to fabric in plus size women's wardrobes. This fabric is originally from the Isle of Jersey off the coast of England.

Metallic cloth: Any type of fabric made with metallic yarns. While I don't like fabrics that are completely shiny, I do like metallic yarns subtly sewn through a fabric, because they add richness and interest. Look for subtle metallic yarns in blouses, dresses and knitwear.

Raw silk: A nubby silk product. When infused with stretch it can have great drape and offers rich body. Without stretch, it can add bulk.

Rayon: A generic term for synthetics and manmade fibers derived from trees, cotton and woody plants. It was originally known as artificial silk, so that gives a good idea about its application. It works well with every type of garment.

Rib knit: A fabric that shows alternate lengthwise rows of rib and wale on both sides. It tends to be more elastic, heavier and durable than plain knitting and the vertical line we always seek is imbedded into the fabric, making this a win-win!

Shantung: Gives the appearance of raw silk; it is a tightly woven fabric that lends itself to a structured blouse rivaling a jacket in usage.

Supplex® Nylon: A heavier and durable shell fabric made of nylon that is breathable and water repellent. Great for athletic clothing as well as travel clothing and warm-up suits.

Tweed: A general term applied to rough-textured fabrics made of coarser wool in yarn-dyed effects. Look for jackets and skirts made of plain, twill or herringbone weave. The little bit of bulk on the surface is a reasonable tradeoff for the classic, rich appearance of the garment.

Taffeta: A crisp fabric with a fine, smooth surface usually made in a plain weave and sometimes with a small, crosswise rib. Seek the former in shirts or blouses finished like jackets and avoid the latter altogether, as it is imbedded with a subtle horizontal finish.

Tropical worsted: A lightweight fabric, often wool, made in an open weave to permit circulation of air. It is finished by singeing to give a clear finish. When combined with some stretch, it should be the backbone of your professional wardrobe.

Weighted silk: Has metallic particles added to it in the finishing process to give the fabric more body so that it drapes better. This fabric should be identified as such on garments' tags and is a great fabric.

Wool: An animal fiber from the fleece of sheep or lambs. It gives softness and warmth and takes dyes well. Look for merino wool; it is more flattering than Shetland, angora or cashmere varieties.

Fade: Camouflage the negative.

Faux: Refers to facsimiles of pure materials. Although it generally refers to false, counterfeit or imitations used in connection with gems, pearls and leathers, the quality reflected by faux items in today's market can be excellent and very worthwhile to pursue.

Fedora: Originally worn by men but now also styled for women with a turned-up back brim. It was popularized for men after Victorian Sardou's play *Fedora*, produced in 1882.

Focus: Accentuate the positive.

Gaucho: Calf-length or longer pants, traditionally made of leather. Copied from pants worn by the Spanish as part of an Andalusian riding suit and later adapted by South American cowboys, the garment today can be made of stretch jersey and other current fabrics.

Gored skirt: Fits through the waist and flares at the hem. It may be made of many panels or sections.

Hacked: A term meaning hemmed on an angle. The front of the hem sits on the toe of the shoe and the back of the hem is longer, covering a good portion of the heel of your shoe.

Hacked pockets: Pockets whose openings are cut on a diagonal, not a horizontal line.

Handkerchief hem: An uneven hem that has flounce and movement.

Havaianas: An upgraded flip-flop type of sandal of Latin origin.

Heel: The part of the shoe that elevates the foot. The inside edge of the heel is called the breast of the heel. The extra replaceable piece on the bottom is called the heel lift. Heels may be made of wood, plastic, Lucite or metal.

Hermes: Pronounced "air-mes," it refers to the house of Thierry Hermes, a French saddle and harness maker of the nineteenth century. Hermes couture began under Emile Hermes in 1920, originally producing mainly leather garments but expanded to include sweaters, capes and shoes as well as the famous, spectacular and opulent designs found on their quintessential silk scarves. The scarf designs include floral, graphic, equestrian and gold chain themes.

Hopsack: Refers to fabrics plain and loosely woven, often sporting coarse or uneven yarns.

Insole: The portion inside the shoe on which the sole of the foot rests. It can be covered by a sock, synthetic or leather lining. An insole made of a natural fiber will breathe better and absorb moisture.

Key fob: Based on the concept of the watch fob, it is a short chain, leather strap, ribbon or charm attached to a key. It is not uncommon to have one's initials engraved on the fob.

Kilt: A Scottish skirt made in a wraparound style. The center front is plain and I recommend keeping pleats sewn down. The hanging end can be fringed, which makes for a great vertical line and a large, decorative safety pin offers another vertical embellishment.

Kitten heel: A shapely, miniature heel, usually about an inch or inch and a half high.

Leggings: Essentially, very tight pants to the ankles made of thin Lycra or spandex knit fabrics. They come in dark, neutral or wonderful bright colors and are often sported by dancers.

Longline bra: A bra beginning at the bust or ribcage and extending to the waist or a bit below. Sometimes it is boned and wired to be worn without straps.

Maillot: Classic one-piece, fitted swimsuit, usually backless. It sometimes has a detachable strap tied around the neck or buttoned to the back of the suit.

Matte finish: A dull finish dubbed by the textile industry. It can also refer to makeup that has no shine.

Merino wool: A high quality wool yarn made from fleece of merino sheep, which is short, fine, strong, resilient and takes dyes well.

Mid-rise: A bottom whose waist sits at your navel or slightly below.

Minimizer bra: A bra with large cups made of a smooth fabric that tends to flatten and smooth the breasts.

Moderate goods: A consumer price level below bridge and better goods, toward the low end of price points.

Mondrian dress: Straight and unconstructed but achieves the look of contour with blocks of color and neutrals strategically banded with black. The dress was introduced by Yves Saint Laurent in the fall of 1965. The look was inspired by the modern linear paintings of Piet Mondrian.

Monochromatic: A singular color scheme.

Mule: Similar to the loafer, it is a moccasin type shoe that slips on with an open back. It is often trimmed with metal links or hardware over the instep. The heel is usually between one half and one inch high.

Natural waistline: The narrowest part of your midriff.

Necklines: An intriguing neckline is important for a plus size woman, because it draws attention upwards and to the face.

    Asymmetric neckline: A neckline that appears different on either side of the center front of the garment. Another variation is for the closure to be on one side of the shirt.

    Boat neck or **bateau neckline:** Has a "boat-shaped" opening at the neck extending toward the shoulders. It tends to sit high in the front and back. This neckline was popular in the 1930s and 1940s and was given new life in the 1980s. The wide opening tends to offer great balance for wide hips.

    Crew: A rounded and soft neckline usually finished with a knit ribbing.

    Drawstring: A neckline threaded with a cord and gathered through pretty casing. It can be adjusted high or low. It was inspired by the peasant style and introduced in the 1930s.

    Florentine: Wide and square-cut, extending toward the shoulders.

    Halter: Sleeveless and held by a strap around the neck, leaving the back and shoulders bare.

    Henley: Round and made with ribbing and a front placket opening. It was inspired by the crew racing shirts worn at Henley, England.

    Horseshoe: Scoops low in front in the shape of a horseshoe.

    Jewel: High and round, made with or without binding, as a simple background for jewelry.

    Keyhole: High and rounded with a wedge-shaped or keyhole piece cut out at the front center of the garment.

    Mandarin: A Chinese inspired, raised neckline.

    Nehru: Standing-based and similar to the mandarin neckline. It became popular in the 1960s.

    Sweetheart: Moderately low with a heart-shaped center point in front. Sides of the neckline slant toward the neck in front.

    Turtleneck: A high band collar, usually knitted, that fits very close to the neck and folds down snuggly. A mock turtleneck has a separate band stitched down to look like a turtleneck, but it doesn't fold down.

Overcoat or **topcoat:** Refers to a lightweight coat designed to wear over a suit jacket. It can be styled any way.

Pencil skirt: Narrow from the waist through the knee, tapering more at the knee.

Peplum dress: Either fitted or belted at the waistline with a short or medium length ruffle of fabric extending below. The style was popular in the 1930s and 1960s and revived in the 1980s.

Pick stitching: Hand stitching on the lapel of a jacket or dress.

Pintucking: A decorative hand stitching or a machine-produced facsimile.

Piping: A pretty seam achieved by sewing interesting fabric in a slightly raised quality into the seam for noteworthy contrast and distinctiveness.

Platform: The mid-sole of the shoe, often made of cork or polyurethane, raising the foot off the ground on a platform varying in height. The style was introduced in the 1940s, reintroduced by Roger Vivier in Paris in the 1960s and has been a staple on the shoe scene since.

Pleating: Refers to folds of fabric that are usually pressed flat. The size and details of the stitching creates varied looks.

Power suit: This is a term used in the late 1980s and 1990s for a man's or woman's tailored suit worn for business. It is sometimes worn with a top and bottom that don't match. A great jacket with a different pair of slacks or a skirt is undoubtedly a great option and gives great flexibility. However, for plus size women who seek the unbroken vertical line, a well-cut suit of a matching jacket and bottom can be a powerful go-to outfit or cluster anchor in your closet.

Princess seaming: Vertical panels shaped close to the body through the torso without a horizontal waistline.

Prints

Abstract: Resemble optical art and geometric designs.

African: Tend to be bold geometric designs frequently represented in browns, blacks and whites.

Allover: Covers the entire surface of the garment in a repeated design.

American Indian: Bold, stylized designs carried out in bright colors.

Animal: Designs imprinted on fabrics in imitation of the fur of leopards, giraffes, tigers and zebras. They are usually made in cotton, jersey or modacrylic fiber fabric to look like furs.

Art nouveau: Flowing prints of stylized leaves, flowers and vines inspired by the twentieth century French art movement.

Aztec: Designs based on Native Mexican geometric motifs.

Batik: Usually dark blue, rust, black or yellow designs copied from the Indonesian technique of painting with wax before dyeing.

Border: Designed so that one selvage forms a distinct border that is used at the hem of a dress or shirt.

Burnout: A print style made by weaving the design and background of two different types of fibers. Chemicals are applied to dissolve one fiber, leaving the design in high relief against a sheer background.

Calico: An allover print of tiny natural flowers on a colored background.

Fleur-de-lis: A styled lily design used in pageantry and part of the coat of arms of France's former royal family.

Floral: Usually a rich design using flowers in a natural or stylized manner.

Hand-painted: A pattern painted directly on the fabric.

Japanese: Usually a scenic print featuring pagodas, foliage and mountains in a repeat design.

Laura Ashley: A trademark design of a company by the same name, manufactured in England. The design represents provincial, small florals, is typically Victorian in inspiration and is often copied from antique designs printed on cottons.

Photographic: Tend to be large and cover the whole front of a garment, often expressed in black and white.

Pucci: Refers to the designs of Emilio Pucci, an Italian couturier, and tend to be highly original, rich and hard to imitate. The patterns are abstract and composed mainly of brilliant unusual color combinations outlined in black.

Raglan sleeve: A wide sleeve that extends to the neckline, avoiding the confinement of the traditional armhole.

Raincoats

Burberry: A trademark of Burberrys International, Ltd., London, and is the gold standard of rainwear. It represents an expensive unisex trench coat style raincoat. Made in lightweight polyester and cotton, it has a well-recognized black and tan plaid zip-out lining. A multitude of accessories are available as well: skirts, scarves and umbrellas, to match the plaid lining. Details include hand stitching on the collar, handmade buttonholes and D-rings on the belt for holding objects. These coats were first used by officers in 1914.

London Fog: The trademark for a company with the same name, a division of Interco, Inc., for men's and women's raincoats of classic styles.

Rain or shine coat: A fabric coat treated with a water-repellent finish so it can be worn as an all-purpose coat.

Raincoat shell: A lightweight fabric coat treated with a water-repellant finish so that it can be worn as an all-purpose coat. It is usually a simple Balmacaan style, loose-fitting and straight with a small turned-down collar.

Slicker: A bright yellow oilskin coat or similar coat of rubberized fabric in other colors and prints usually fastened with clips in the front. This coat was originally worn by sailors.

Reefer style: A takeoff on the British brass-buttoned Navy coat. It is usually double-breasted.

Retro: Refers to the return of a fashion look of an earlier period; it is an abbreviated use of the word retrospective.

Ruching: Trimming accomplished by pleating a strip of lace, ribbon or fabric so that it ruffles on both sides in a puckered effect. Currently, this is a popular trim on the front center placket of a button-down blouse.

Sarong: A wrapped skirt usually made of bold geometric or floral prints. The fabric is traditionally cotton but today look for fabrics infused with stretch. The style was popularized by the actress Dorothy Lamour in the film *Hurricane* in the late 1930s.

Sculpted or **sculptured heel:** A broad, medium high heel (made with a see-through center) introduced in the 1960s.

Shapers: Refers to a truly new generation of girdles. They are much less restrictive, made of friendly, soft, stretchy fabrics and come in many length and waist heights.

Sheath dress: Generally straight and fitted without a waistline. It is shaped to the body by vertical darts or with a set-in waistline. The ease of the skirt is enhanced by inverted pleats at the sides or center back. The style was popular in the 1950s and 1960s and made a comeback in 1986.

Shift: The mainstay of the 1960s. Basically, a straight-lined dress that drapes away from the body. The shift dress introduced a diagonal upward dart from the side seam, which improved the fit. If you come across the term A-line dress, it probably refers to this style as well.

Shirring: Involves three or more rows of gathers made by running small stitches in parallel lines. It produces fullness at the top of the stitched area for a pretty effect.

Shoulders. The shoulders of a garment are a very important style detail for plus size women, because the garment will usually begin its drape from that point. Another reason for their importance has to do with the fit. The fit must be unrestricted or it becomes a negative focal point. Also, pretty shoulder detail cuts a wide horizontal line across the shoulder.

> **Dropped:** Extends over the upper arm. The sleeve seam comes on the upper arm rather than at the natural armhole.

> **Natural:** Follows the body lines with a sleeve set in at the natural armhole without padding.

> **Padded:** Pads are sewn inside the garment to make the shoulder appear broader. This balances a wider lower half of the body frame.

> **Raglan:** Traditionally has no seam across the shoulder as the seam comes from under the arms directly to the neck in the front and back.

> **Saddle:** Has a small yoke at the shoulder made by not bringing the raglan sleeve to the neck in a point, but by widening it so that it is three to four inches in width at the neck. This is a very pretty look because the gathers soften the shoulder line and create a bit or interest and drape for the fabric.

Shoulder pad: A triangular (recommended) or a rounded pad filled with wool, cotton or synthetic fibers and fitted to the inside of the garment's shoulders to create the illusion of a broader or better defined shoulder. Introduced in the 1940s and rein vented in the 1980s, the shoulder pad can be used to balance a wider hip or create an angular drape off the shoulder of a garment.

Shrug: A shawl and sweater combined, fitted over the back like a shawl. Another version of the shrug is a short-sleeved sweater baring the midriff with a long V neckline and fastened with one hook under the bust.

Silhouette: The outline of an outfit and should be a reflection of the shape or contour of your body as expressed by the designer.

Skort: The term was originally a trademark for a mini-skirt with shorts underneath. The benefit is the appearance of a skirt with the protection from chafing of shorts. It became popular in the 1960s and styles and lengths have expanded since then. The term scooter skirt is sometimes used to mean the same thing. The prettiest style, in my opinion, and the backbone of my own sports wardrobe is the skort in a pencil skirt style made by Elisabeth.

Sole: The bottom portion of a shoe, under the foot, usually consisting of three parts: outsole, midsole and innersole.

SPANX: A trademark for support lingerie. It has become the gold standard among fashionable women and the term SPANX is often used to refer to a pants liner although many other manufacturers have followed suit and offer similar products.

Stacked heel: Built up of horizontal layers of leather or wood. The stacked heel is a medium high heel and is usually thicker and curved in shape.

Stance: Refers to where a jacket closes, thereby creating shape at that point.

Straight skirt: Any slim skirt without fullness.

Surplice: The top wraps rather than buttons for closure, producing a flattering ruched low V neckline. The term "surplice front" applies as well.

Sweater dress: A knitted dress styled similarly to a sweater with or without a waistline and introduced in the 1930s. A two-piece version can be a great resource for diamond shapes who want to select different sizes for the top and bottom, still achieving a uniform look.

Swing style: An exaggerated A-line; very full at the bottom of the garment.

Tailored shirt: Fitted, though not necessarily snuggly, through the torso and resembles a man's dress shirt.

Tankini: A bathing suit consisting of two pieces: an empire-waisted top without sleeves, falling in a gentle A-line and a bottom that can be fitted like a bikini bottom or have a skirt.

Tap pants: Panties styled like shorts with a flare at the hem. Usually made of satin or floral print and trimmed with lace. Often paired with a matching camisole.

Toe or **toe box:** The front portion of a shoe covering the toes.

Tone on tone: A singular color scheme that includes different values and shades of a particular color.

Toreador: A waist-length jacket with epaulet shoulder trimming frequently braided. The jacket is worn unfastened.

Tortoise shell: A substance made of a combination of yellow and brown coloration from horny back plates of sea turtles native to the Cayman Islands, Celebes and New Guinea. It is used to ornament buttons, combs, jewelry, buckles and eyewear.

Trapeze: An exaggerated A-line.

Trench coat: Originally made for British officers in World War I, the trench coat of World War II is the prototype for the classic we know today. It was an all-purpose coat made of water repellant fabric in a double-breasted style with a convertible collar, large lapels, epaulets, fabric belt, slotted pockets and a vent in the back. Over the shoulders it had an extra hanging yoke and an extra flap hung from the front right shoulder. In the 1940s women adopted the trench coat and it has been worn as a classic since. The house of Burberry has become most famous for this style with the addition of the notable black and tan plaid lining.

Tromp l'oeil: Pronounced "trump loy." It is generally applied to embroidery and painting, but can also be applied to dress and clothing. The idea is to create an illusion that "fools the eye."

Trumpet dress: Has a flared flounce starting at the knees. It was worn in the 1930s as a tight fitting dress to the knees (not for a pear shape diamond). It was reintroduced in the 1980s as a full-length evening gown with shift-like proportions and later edited to a day dress.

Trumpet skirt: A straight-lined skirt with one large circular flounce at the hem that flares like an inverted trumpet.

Trunk shows: Presentations of designer or brand lines to store personnel and/or customers that showcase a new line. These can be a source of great fun and anticipation. My hope is that the plus size fashion industry catches up with missy fashion lines and turns trunk shows into events for curvier women, too.

Tulip skirt: Gathered to a defined waistline with a gentle balloon effect through the hips and tapered at the hem.

Tunic: A straight, loose fitting, thigh-length top. With or without sleeves, it usually has a good bit of trim and embellishment.

Twinset: A matching shell and cardigan.

Unstructured: Refers to a boxy, unfitted style.

Upper: The term used by the shoe industry for all parts of the shoe above the sole. It includes the counter, quarter, vamp and lining.

Vamp or **throat:** The front part of the shoe covering the toes and instep.

Vest: A sleeveless jacket extending to the waist or below. Especially for plus size women, it is an excellent three season option as an outer garment to complete an outfit, as it is comfortable through the armhole and adds little bulk.

Vintage clothing: Can be clothing or styles from earlier eras that claim to be worth recalling. Basically, vintage is used clothing and accessories that are refurbished and sold again. Often, vintage designer fashion is considered trendy.

Visual weight: Refers to the illusion that the body is as large as the extension or expanse of the fabric. The goal is to minimize the appearance of visual weight in every outfit you put together.

Warm-up suit or **sport suit:** Clothing designed to support activity in a sport. The top and bottom match or are coordinated. Today, a jogging suit, warm-up suit, etc., is worn to do errands around town.

Wedge dress: Cut very full with large shoulders and dolman sleeves. The dress tapers to the hemline in a V or wedge shape.

Wedgies: Shoes with wedge-shaped heels completely joined to the soles under the arches. The variety of styles is wide and the heel heights vary too. The style was popular for women in the late 1940s, but women today who seek height with comfort should embrace this style.

Weskit: A jacket style made of fabric traditionally used for a blouse.

Whip stitches: Short and overcast stitches, usually rolled over the edges of an item, finished or raw.

Wrap coat: Usually made without (obvious) buttons or fasteners and is held closed with a long fabric sash. Sometimes called a clutch coat.

Wrap-dress: Can close in the front or to the back. It has an extra lap of fabric that is approximately equal to the width of the skirt.

Zigzag stitches: Give a saw tooth effect; they may be decorative or may functionally connect two pieces of fabric.

BIBLIOGRAPHY

Calasibetta, Charlotte Mankey and Phyliss Tortora. *The Fairchild Dictionary of Fashion*. New York: Fairchild Publishing, 2003.

Clancy, Deirdre. *Costume Since 1945: Couture, Street Style and Anti-Fashion*. New York: Drama Publishers, 1996.

Laird, Charlton and Editors of Webster's New World Dictionaries. *Webster's New World Dictionary and Thesaurus*. 2nd ed. Ohio: Wiley Publishing, Inc., 2002.

Mullaly, Bob. "Oppression: The focus of structural social work." In *The New Structural Social Work*. 3rd ed. Oxford: Oxford University Press, 2007.

Newman, Alex and Zakee Shariff. *Fashion A to Z: An Illustrated Dictionary*. London: Laurence King Publishers, 2009.

Pendergast, Sara and Tom Pendergast. *Modern World Part II, 1946-2003*. Vol. 5 of *Fashion, Costume, and Culture: Clothing, Headwear, Body Decorations, and Footwear Through the Ages*. Michigan: Thomson Gale, 2004.

ACKNOWLEDGMENTS

Personally...

Thank you to my Dad, who told me I was "utterly beautiful"—and made me believe it. They say it only takes one person in your life...he was that person in mine and I miss him more than I can say.

My love and gratitude to my Grandma Minnie, who rescued me more than once and nicknamed me "beauty-in-the-house"—she made me feel so darn good.

Thank you to my girlfriends, Deb and Lynn, who listened and made me think I had something worthwhile to say.

Loving thanks to my son for making my value on this earth one that transcends vanity. Mostly, my love and thanks to my maverick of a husband, Bruce, who dubbed me Babe—and helped me become one.

Professionally...

I want to thank Maryann Karinch, an extreme athlete, author and agent, for her willingness to consider that we may be "two sides of the same coin" —and run with this project. Shout out to April Dukes for her fantabulous illustrations and trusting her maiden voyage to me.

Many thanks to the folks at New Horizon Press, for their professionalism and insight. My good fortune was to land with a socially conscious publisher, who may well lighten the burden of plus size women everywhere.